Policy Making and Effective Leadership

A National Study
of Academic Management

J. Victor Baldridge,

David V. Curtis, George Ecker,

and Gary L. Riley

Policy Making and Effective Leadership

Jossey-Bass Publishers

San Francisco • Washington • London • 1978

POLICY MAKING AND EFFECTIVE LEADERSHIP
A National Study of Academic Management
by J. Victor Baldridge, David V. Curtis, George Ecker,
and Gary L. Riley

Copyright © 1978 by: Jossey-Bass, Inc., Publishers
433 California Street
San Francisco, California 94104
&
Jossey-Bass Limited
28 Banner Street
London EC1Y 8QE

Library of Congress Catalogue Card Number LC 77–82909

International Standard Book Number ISBN 0–87589–351–1

Manufactured in the United States of America

JACKET DESIGN BY WILLI BAUM

FIRST EDITION

Code 7752

The Jossey-Bass Series
in Higher Education

A Publication of the Higher
Education Research Institute
Alexander W. Astin, President

Preface

In 1970 under a grant from the National Institute of Education, the Stanford Center for Research and Development in Teaching began a major study of American colleges and universities: the Stanford Project on Academic Governance. Directed by J. Victor Baldridge, the project continued with funding until 1974, by which time its staff had produced half a dozen books, a score of articles, and about seventeen research memoranda. By the close of the funding period, most of the staff had left Stanford, but their joint writing efforts continued. In 1975, *Unions on Campus* (Kemerer and Baldridge, Jossey-Bass) and *Managing Change in Academic Organizations* (Baldridge and Deal, Eds., McCutchan) were published from project research. Writing continued at the Higher Education Research Institute in Los Angeles and at the University of California, Los Angeles, and in 1977 two more volumes were finished: *Governing Academic Organizations* (Riley and Baldridge, Eds., McCutchan) and this present book. With the publication of this volume, the project is formally completed. (A complete list of books and articles from the project is included on pp. xxiii–xxv.)

The project consisted of seven members, four of whom are the co-authors of this book: J. Victor Baldridge, David V. Curtis, George Ecker, and Gary L. Riley. Also included on the project were:

Frank R. Kemerer (Ph.D. in higher education, Stanford, 1974), assistant to the president at the State University of New York College of Arts and Science in Geneseo since 1973.

Sharon Renee Tolbert (Ph.D. in higher education, Stanford, 1975), a research scientist at the Institute for the Study of Educational Policy at Howard University, Washington, D.C.

Janet Wheeler, publications director for the project; a counseling psychologist, writer, and currently researcher with the American Institutes for Research in behavioral science, Palo Alto, California.

Research Methods

We wanted to use a variety of research techniques in this project. Although survey instruments were the project's backbone, we also analyzed historical documents, interviewed college presidents, analyzed case studies, and extensively reviewed literature on organization theory and higher education administration.

Second, we were dedicated to the concept of *comparative analysis*. Many studies in higher education have focused on a single institution, without engaging in cross-organizational comparisons. We felt that, because of the diversity in American higher education, no single case study could possibly be representative of the whole. Major universities are quite different from state colleges; local community colleges are different from private liberal arts colleges. One of our major concerns, therefore, was to obtain comparative data, using identical research instruments in a wide variety of institutions across the country.

Third, we designed the project to be truly *representative* of the full range of American colleges and universities. Unfortunately, many well-known works in the field of academic management and governance have an elitist bias. Blau's book, *The Organization of Academic Work* (1973), simply excludes the analysis of two-year colleges altogether, as did Pace's *The Demise of Diversity?* (1974). Parsons and Platt's *The American University* (1972) was written at Harvard, and its analyses often appear to apply only to that rarefied atmosphere. Baldridge's *Power and Conflict in the University* (1971) was a case study of an atypical institution, New York University. Clark (1970) analyzed Reed, Swarthmore, and Antioch colleges, three small elite institutions that have little in common with main-line American higher education. Cohen and March's *Leadership and Ambiguity* (1973) is weighted in the direction of large, wealthy schools and excludes two-year colleges from the sample. In short, previous examinations of colleges and universities are usually case studies in which only a single institution is described or are nonrepresentative surveys that exclude some major bloc of colleges.

Fourth and finally, we used *historical materials* to round out the picture. We include historical material on governance patterns and trace contemporary institutional characteristics back to their origins. This material provides depth and perspective and thereby promotes an understanding of the development and growth of the academic patterns we currently see around us.

The Samples

For our contemporary analysis, we required two kinds of samples. First, we needed a representative sample of all colleges and universities in the nation. Second, we needed a sample of faculty members and administrators within each institution.

The Institutions. In 1970 there were 2,592 schools on the College Entrance Examination Board's (CEEB) list of colleges and universities in the United States. We singled out all those institutions that: (1) had a freshman class; (2) awarded at least an associate (two-year) degree; and (3) were not federal military service academies. From this reduced list we drew a sample of approximately 250 American colleges and universities.

A completely random sample would have included a large proportion of community colleges, with too few large universities for statistical analysis. To correct this, we undersampled community colleges by one half their normal proportion then weighted them double later in the procedure. Finally selected were 185 four-year schools plus 64 community colleges, for a total of 249. When the community colleges were weighted double, the adjusted *weighted sample* was 300, the number we will use throughout this book.

To check for representativeness, we compared our 300 institutions with the totality of 2,592 schools in the nation in six respects, data for which were available from the College Board: (1) highest degree offered; (2) location by CEEB geographic region; (3) location by national geographic section; (4) an admission selectivity rating developed by the CEEB; (5) sex of the student population (coeducational or single sex); and (6) size. The final study sample was also compared with several other large study samples drawn for major research projects conducted in the 1960s and early 1970s. The comparisons showed that our final institutional sample was representative (in the six selected areas) of these institutions throughout the nation.

The Individual Sample. It was not possible to include in our survey all of the 57,000 faculty members found in our sample of institutions. To obtain a representative and manageable faculty sample, we stratified institutions according to size and drew different proportions of individuals from schools of different sizes, with larger proportions from smaller schools. Faculty lists were obtained from college catalogues. Five administrators were included from each school: the president, and vice-presidents for academic affairs, student affairs, business affairs, and development (or their equivalents when these titles were not used).

The Individual Questionnaire. Once the institutional and individual samples were selected, we began gathering information from a variety of sources. An Individual Questionnaire was the primary source of raw data for the study. Careful pretesting was very important because the questionnaire was to be answered by individuals from very different institutions, academic backgrounds, and positions. Seven months, therefore, were spent in developing, pretesting, and revising the questionnaire.

A total of 17,296 individuals were randomly selected from college catalogues. Several waves of questionnaires and follow-up letters were mailed in the spring of 1971. The return rate was 53 percent, with 9,237 people returning complete, usable questionnaires. As they were analyzed, the stratified samples were weighted so we could estimate the probable results if everyone had been questioned. Thus, most tables show about 57,000 respondents, the *weighted individual* total.

In addition to revealing *individual* characteristics, the questionnaire responses could also be aggregated to give *institutional* patterns. For example, we can compare two institutions on the question of "percentage of individuals joining a union." In this manner we can obtain an *institutional* score based on *aggregated individual* responses.

Once we had received our returned questionnaires, we were able to compare our individual samples against known national statistics in a number of important areas, such as age, sex, publication rates, rank, tenure, and subject matter field. The sample was representative in almost every respect.

Four other sources of information were used: (1) *College Entrance Examination Board data,* which contains elaborate institutional information such as size, student selectivity, type of administrative and professional (formal) control, and geographic location of almost every college and university in the country; (2) *College catalogues* of all schools sampled, which provided a key source of information and lists of faculty members and administrators; (3) *The College Blue Book* (Russell, 1970), which contains descriptive information about all accredited institutions of postsecondary education in the United States, and which used to double-check all of our data on such items as library size, tuition cost, number of faculty members, and number of students enrolled, by classes and by degree programs; and (4) *College Presidents' Questionnaire,* from which we obtained information about the relationship between institutions and their social and political environments through a questionnaire sent to each college president. Second and third requests were mailed in several instances, and a telephone call was placed to presidents who did not respond. Every college and university in the sample eventually returned the questionnaire.

In 1974, the staff decided to gather additional information on faculty collective negotiations. We resampled all the institutions we originally surveyed in 1971 and found twenty-nine of them now unionized. In addition, we surveyed all other unionized institutions except for a few excluded because of their extremely specialized character. This additional unionized group included 300 institutions, for a total of 511 (240 in original 1971 sample plus 300, minus the overlapping 29). These samples provided a valuable contrast between a random sample of (1) *all* colleges and universities and (2) only those institutions with faculty unions. In this phase, we again used two questionnaires: one for presidents, the other for the faculty chairpersons of unions at the unionized institutions. More than 65 percent of these questionnaires were returned.

In addition to these questionnaire surveys, we conducted intensive *case studies* at seven institutions, diverse in background and governance, where collective bargaining was in different stages of development: (1) Central Michigan University, a public four-year institution unattached to a larger system and which has had a union since 1969; (2) the City Colleges of Chicago, a two-year system that has had a militant union since 1966; (3) Rutgers, the State University of New Jersey, with three campuses in close proximity to one another; (4) the State University of New York (SUNY) and (5) the City University of New York (CUNY), both with several years of strong collective bargaining experience; (6) the University of Hawaii, a public institution with one main campus, several outlying units, and a stormy, inconclusive history of attempted collective bargaining that did not result in a ratified contract until mid-1975 after several union elections and the ouster of one union by another; and finally, to help round out the picture, (7) Hofstra University, a private university in the New York suburb of Hempstead, Long Island.

Special Thanks

The research for this book was conducted under the auspices of three organizations: (1) the Stanford Center for Research and Development in Teaching, (2) the Higher Education Research Institute, Los Angeles, and (3) the Laboratory for Research in Higher Education, University of California, Los Angeles. Their assistance, as well as that of the National Institute of Education, is gratefully acknowledged. In addition, the research staff of the College Entrance Examination Board in Palo Alto were most cooperative in letting us use their CEEB data deck of institutional information.

So many people have ably participated in this project at so many different times that there is an obvious danger of forgetting someone in the list of thanks. In rough chronological order, these are people to whom we owe especially great debts:

Elizabeth Cohen and Terrance Deal, directors of the R & D Center Environment for Teaching Program, who provided both excellent administrative leadership and professional collegial relations.

Sharon Renee Tolbert, upon whose work Chapter Eight is dependent.

Frank R. Kemerer, whose solid research and hard work was central to our understanding of collective bargaining, and who helped with Chapter Seven.

Patricia Miller, who was extremely helpful in preparing Chapter Nine with her insightful ideas about the financial crisis' future impact on academic governance.

Janet Wheeler, whose editorial guidance and good ideas helped make sense of sociological jargon.

Valerie Familant, who cheerfully helped in the overwhelming load of secretarial work.

Penny Jordon and the gang in the methodology center, who made the numbers fit our ideas.

Lewis B. Mayhew and James Gardner March, from whom we all learned much about higher education and complex organizations.

Alexander W. Astin and Lewis Solmon, whose support at the Higher Education Research Institute made the writing time possible.

Allan M. Cartter, who served as mentor and friend to many of us, and whose untimely death impoverished the field of research on higher education.

Carol Feldman, who graciously helped in typing manuscripts.

And finally, to our wives and lovers—who kept us sane and happy when it might easily have been otherwise.

November 1977

J. VICTOR BALDRIDGE
DAVID V. CURTIS
GEORGE ECKER
GARY L. RILEY

Contents

The Authors

J. Victor Baldridge is senior research sociologist at the Higher
Education Research Institute in Los Angeles. He also teaches in the
higher education program at the University of California, Los
Angeles.

Baldridge received the B.A. in sociology from Lambuth College (1963) and then the B.D. in social ethics (1966), M.A. in sociology (1967), and Ph.D. in sociology (1968) from Yale University. His
specialties are administration, organization theory, and sociology of
education. He was a faculty member at Stanford University (1968–
1974) and Assistant Vice-President for Academic Affairs at the
California State University, Fresno (1974–1976).

Baldridge has published several books, including *Power and
Conflict in the University* (1971); *Academic Governance* (1971);
and *Unions on Campus: A National Study of the Consequences of
Faculty Bargaining* (with F. R. Kemerer, 1975). He has also
authored over twenty-five articles and book chapters on higher
education administration and organization theory.

Victor Baldridge and his wife, Patricia L. Miller, live in
Malibu, California.

DAVID V. CURTIS is executive associate to the president and university professor of political science at Governors State University in Illinois, where he has been since 1971. He received the B.A. in political science from the University of California, Riverside (1963), the M.A. in university administration from the University of Denver (1965), and the Ph.D. in organization studies and higher education administration from Stanford University (1972). One of the original researchers on the Stanford Project for Academic Governance, he has co-authored a number of articles dealing with that research. Additionally, he has spoken on the implementation and evaluation of innovative and nontraditional educational efforts.

Curtis is a consultant and evaluator for the North Central Association and has also been the chief negotiator for Governors State University in collective bargaining negotiations with the American Federation of Teachers.

He is married to Jean Curtis, has two children, and resides in Park Forest South, Illinois.

GEORGE ECKER is assistant professor in the Academic Faculty of Educational Administration at Ohio State University, a position he has held since 1974. A native of Concord, Massachusetts, he earned the B.A. in sociology from Cornell University (1964). After two years with the U.S. Army Intelligence Corps in Orléans, France, he returned to Cornell, where he served as Assistant Dean of Students and received the M.A. in higher education administration (1970). He received the Ph.D. in the sociology of education from Stanford University (1973) and spent the 1973–74 academic year at Stanford as a post-doctoral fellow in the National Institute for Mental Health Training Program in Organizational Research.

Ecker's research interests are organizational sociology, organizational behavior, and administration. His work has been published by the *Journal of Higher Education, Change,* and the Center for Educational Research at Stanford. He is a member of the American Sociological Association, the American Educational Research Association, the American Association of University Professors, and the Association for the Study of Higher Education.

His hobbies are skiing, hiking, and singing, and he is a member of the Appalachian Mountain Club and the National Ski

Patrol System. He is married to Cheryl North, and they live in Columbus, Ohio.

GARY L. RILEY is assistant professor of higher education at the University of California, Los Angeles. He received the B.A. from Gonzaga University (1965), the M.A. from Washington State University (1967), and the Ph.D. in higher education and sociology of organizations at Stanford University (1972). Prior to receiving an academic appointment at UCLA, he served as director of Planning and Development in the Pasco, Washington, school system; as a research associate on the Stanford Project on Academic Governance; and as a project administrator in student personnel services at Big Bend Community College in Moses Lake, Washington.

His current research activities at the University of California, Los Angeles, include a national longitudinal study of community college academic governance, investigations into the impact of academic collective bargaining on governance and personnel policies, and patterns of institutional research and evaluation in higher education. In 1975, he participated in a national study of higher education in Iran with Allan M. Cartter and others from the University of California.

Gary Riley is co-editor of *Governing Academic Organizations* (1977) and the author of several articles on academic governance; changes in the roles of students, administrators, and trustees in academic decision-making; and evaluation practices in educational systems. He and his wife, Kathleen M. Erickson, have co-directed a number of field studies in Washington and California, employing photo-ethnographic and interview techniques to assess the impact of special educational programs upon learners, school organizations, and community environments. They live in Sherman Oaks, California.

Publications Related
to the Stanford Project
on Academic Governance

Books

J. Victor Baldridge, *Power and Conflict in the University* (New York: Wiley, 1971).

Frank R. Kemerer and J. Victor Baldridge, *Unions on Campus* (San Francisco: Jossey-Bass, 1975).

J. Victor Baldridge (Ed.), *Academic Governance* (Berkeley: McCutchan, 1971).

J. Victor Baldridge and Terrance Deal (Eds.), *Managing Change in Academic Organizations* (Berkeley: McCutchan, 1975).

Gary L. Riley and J. Victor Baldridge (Eds.), *Governing Academic Organizations: New Issues, New Perspectives* (Berkeley: McCutchan, 1977).

Articles and Book Chapters

J. Victor Baldridge, David V. Curtis, George Ecker, and Gary L. Riley, "The Impact of Institutional Size and Complexity on Faculty Autonomy," *Journal of Higher Education,* 1973, *44,* 532–547.

J. Victor Baldridge and Robert Burnham, "Organizational Innovation: Individual, Organizational, and Environmental Impacts," *The Administrative Science Quarterly,* 1975, *20,* 165–176.

J. Victor Baldridge, David V. Curtis, George Ecker, and Gary L. Riley, "College Size and Professional Freedom," *Change,* 1973, *5*(4), 11–12, 63.

J. Victor Baldridge, "The Analysis of Organizational Change: A Human Relations Strategy Versus a Political Systems Strategy," *Educational Researcher,* 1972, *1*(1), 4–10.

J. Victor Baldridge and Frank R. Kemerer, "The Impact of Collective Bargaining on Academic Senates," *Journal of Higher Education,* 1976, *47*(4), 391–412.

J. Victor Baldridge, Sanford M. Dornbusch, Joseph W. Garbarino, and Richard M. Jacobs, "Faculty Evaluation: A Tool for Eliciting Desired Behaviors," *Journal of Dental Education,* 1976, *40*(8), 528ff.

J. Victor Baldridge, David V. Curtis, George Ecker, and Gary L. Riley, "Diversity in Higher Education: Professional Autonomy," *Journal of Higher Education* (in press).

J. Victor Baldridge, "Faculty Activism and Influence Patterns in the University," in J. Victor Baldridge (Ed.), *Academic Governance* (Berkeley: McCutchan, 1971).

J. Victor Baldridge, "Models of University Governance: Bureaucratic, Collegial, and Political," in *Academic Governance* (Berkeley: McCutchan, 1971).

James Stam and J. Victor Baldridge, "The Dynamics of Conflict on Campus: A Study of the Stanford April Third Movement," in *Academic Governance* (Berkeley: McCutchan, 1971).

J. Victor Baldridge, "Environmental Pressure, Professional Autonomy and Coping Strategies in Academic Organizations," in *Academic Governance* (Berkeley: McCutchan, 1971).

J. Victor Baldridge, "The Future for Academic Change and Innovation," in Frank R. Kemerer and Ron P. Satryb (Eds.), *Facing Financial Exigency* (Lexington, Mass.: Lexington Press, 1977).

J. Victor Baldridge, David V. Curtis, David Ecker, and Gary L. Riley, "Alternative Models of Governance in Higher Education," in Gary L. Riley and J. Victor Baldridge (Eds.), *Governing Academic Organizations* (Berkeley: McCutchan, 1977).

J. Victor Baldridge, David V. Curtis, George Ecker, and Gary L. Riley, "Diversity in Academic Governance Patterns," in Gary L. Riley and J. Victor Baldridge (Eds.), *Governing Academic Organizations* (Berkeley: McCutchan, 1977).

Other Publications from the Project

Five doctoral dissertations and over a dozen research and development memoranda based on the project's effects were also published. The Stanford Center for Research and Development, Stanford, California 94305, can furnish information about these publications.

Policy Making and Effective Leadership

A National Study
of Academic Management

Chapter 1

Summary of
Major Conclusions

As colleges and universities have grown to be central institutions in our society, concern and controversy over their decision and governance processes have increased. This book explores these processes from two basic standpoints. First, it describes, as concretely as possible, major developments in academic management and governance—including roles of the faculty, styles of administrative leadership, the functions of policy-making bodies, the efforts toward unionization, and control by state systems. Second, it expands traditional organization theory and applies it to colleges and universities.

Such a volume would be timely at almost any point, but it is even more timely now. This is a period of significant change in the social role, financing, and governance of educational institutions. We are at a critical stage in the development of these institutions, which is why we have chosen to examine, at this juncture, their enormously diverse patterns of management, leadership, and institu-

1

tional decision making. This chapter will outline our principal findings.

First, though, let us test your knowledge of these issues. The following are questions answered by our research. If you answer all of them correctly, you are ready to perform your own research without reading later chapters. If not, you might want to read the book. (If you do not care to take the test now you can skip over it; the text continues with little break.) The *answers* are given immediately following the test.

1. According to the ratings of professors on different campuses, the type of institution with the *least* amount of bureaucracy and red tape directly affecting the professor's teaching and research is:
   - ———— a) large public universities
   - ———— b) small, nonelite liberal arts colleges
   - ———— c) public community colleges
   - ———— d) private junior colleges

2. Of the following people, who do faculty believe has the broadest range of influence (that is, strong decision influence over more issues)?
   - ———— a) president
   - ———— b) trustees
   - ———— c) department heads
   - ———— d) deans
   - ———— e) a and d tied

3. Who is more likely to want faculty collective bargaining?
   - ———— a) males
   - ———— b) females
   - ———— c) about the same (less than 2 percentage points difference)

4. Which of the following faculty groups is *least* likely to favor collective bargaining?
   - ———— a) humanities
   - ———— b) natural sciences
   - ———— c) social sciences

———— d) professional

———— e) vocational/technical

5. Of the following groups of faculty members, which ones reported that they were basically "inactive" in faculty governance—participated very little in departmental activities, committees, or faculty organizations?

———— a) full professors

———— b) associate professors

———— c) assistant professors

———— d) lecturers or instructors

6. When presidents of colleges responded to our survey, what percentage agreed with the following statement: "Faculty collective bargaining will result in more conflict in the governance process"?

———— a) 30%

———— b) 50%

———— c) 70%

———— d) 90%

7. In what type of institution do faculty members report spending the *largest* amount of time on committee and administrative work?

———— a) community colleges

———— b) private elite universities

———— c) middle-quality state universities

———— d) private liberal arts colleges

8. In what type of institution is the *least* amount of time spent in community service activities?

———— a) private liberal arts colleges

———— b) public community colleges

———— c) middle-quality state colleges

———— d) large elite public universities

9. In what type of institution do faculty report that most of the evaluation for promotion and tenure is done by administrators?

———— a) large public universities

———— b) private junior colleges

———— c) public community colleges
———— d) private liberal arts colleges

10. In what type of institution do faculty want *undergraduate* teaching to get more weight in evaluating them for promotion and tenure?
———— a) public community colleges
———— b) private elite universities
———— c) small liberal arts colleges
———— d) middle-quality state colleges

11. When faculty members are up for promotion and tenure the faculty has some say over who is rewarded. In elite private universities the percentage of people who report high faculty influence is greater than in public community colleges. How much difference do you think there is?
———— a) 10% more report high influence
———— b) 20% more report high influence
———— c) 30% more report high influence
———— d) 40% more report high influence

12. The type of institution that gives the academic department the most freedom and most control over the hiring of new faculty members is:
———— a) private liberal arts colleges
———— b) public community colleges
———— c) elite private universities
———— d) large elite public universities

13. In what type of institution does a department have the most control over its departmental budget?
———— a) public community colleges
———— b) private liberal arts colleges
———— c) middle-quality state colleges
———— d) private elite universities

14. In what type of institution do faculty members report they had to sign very rigid, inflexible personnel contracts?
———— a) large elite public universities
———— b) private liberal arts colleges

———— c) public community colleges

———— d) elite private universities

15. Which of the following factors tends to make the most difference on the degree of bureaucratization and red tape that the faculty have to deal with?

———— a) the quality of academic programs and the training level of the faculty

———— b) whether the institution is public or private

———— c) whether the institution is urban or rural

———— d) whether the institution is church-related or secular

16. Which of the following types of institutions give the most "professional autonomy" to its faculty—that is, faculty feel less supervision, report less red tape, and feel more in control of their professional lives?

———— a) large institutions (over 300 faculty)

———— b) medium sized institutions (101–299 faculty)

———— c) small institutions (under 100 faculty)

17. In which type of institution are the faculty most likely to report that they do not want to leave the institution—they prefer to stay where they are?

———— a) elite private universities

———— b) middle-quality state colleges

———— c) public community colleges

———— d) large elite public universities

18. In which of the following institutions are faculty most likely to be unhappy and distrustful of their administrators?

———— a) large elite public universities

———— b) public community colleges

———— c) private junior colleges

———— d) middle-quality state universities

19. Which of the following types of institutions is most likely to have faculty members who are highly *satisfied* with working conditions on their campus (salaries, office space, students)?

———— a) large institutions (over 300 faculty)

———— b) medium sized institutions (101–299 faculty)

———— c) small institutions (under 100 faculty)

20. Which of the following types of institutions is the most likely to have a high percentage of faculty *dissatisfied* with their working conditions?

   ——— a) state institutions

   ——— b) church-related institutions

   ——— c) institutions run by local school districts

   ——— d) private but not church-related

21. On what type of campus would people be more likely to say that the president is a "petty tyrant"?

   ——— a) church-related liberal arts colleges

   ——— b) middle-quality state campuses

   ——— c) large elite public universities

   ——— d) high quality liberal arts colleges

22. More women faculty members in the United States are located in one type of institution than in any other. Which type is it?

   ——— a) elite private universities

   ——— b) middle-quality state colleges

   ——— c) private liberal arts colleges

   ——— d) public community colleges

23. In most types of colleges and universities men and women do roughly the same amount of research, with women doing slightly less. However, in one type of institution men faculty members do fully twice as much as the women, with the women being largely confined to undergraduate teaching. Which type of institution is more likely to have this enormous difference in research activities between men and women?

   ——— a) elite private universities

   ——— b) small liberal arts colleges

   ——— c) elite public universities

   ——— d) middle-quality state colleges

24. In terms of participation in departmental activities and faculty committee work, are women more or less likely to participate than men?

   ——— a) more active than men

   ——— b) roughly the same as men

   ——— c) less likely to participate than men

25. Compared to men, what level of confidence do women have in the top administration of their institutions?

———— a) considerably less confidence than men

———— b) about the same confidence as men—less than 3% difference

———— c) considerably more confidence than men

26. Faculty members in different types of institutions are very similar in their attitudes toward faculty unionism.

———— a) true

———— b) false

27. There is little difference in attitude toward collective bargaining between presidents of unionized schools and presidents of nonunionized schools.

———— a) true

———— b) false

28. Small liberal arts colleges are much more "collegial" in their decision processes than large public universities.

———— a) true

———— b) false

29. In spite of common sense ideas about differences, there are really very few differences among institutions in their styles of administrative leadership.

———— a) true

———— b) false

30. Small liberal arts colleges are surprisingly bureaucratic in character when compared to large public universities.

———— a) true

———— b) false

How did you score on the test? The answers are (1) a; (2) d; (3) b; (4) d; (5) d; (6) c; (7) a; (8) b; (9) b; (10) b; (11) d; (12) d; (13) b; (14) b; (15) a; (16) a; (17) c; (18) c; (19) a; (20) b; (21) a; (22) d; (23) c; (24) c; (25) a; (26) false; (27) false; (28) false; (29) false; and (30) true. Did you guess correctly that the *least* amount of bureaucracy and red tape affecting teaching and research occurs at large public universities? That faculty believe *deans* have the broadest range of influence over issues? That *women* want collective bargaining more than men? That faculty in the *professional* schools are least likely to favor collective bargaining? That *lecturers and instructors* are least active in faculty governance? That *70* percent of presidents believe that collective bargaining will result in more conflict in governance? That *community college* faculty report spending more time on committee work and administrative work than those of any other type of institution? Or, skipping to the last three questions, that small liberal arts colleges are *not* more "collegial" in their decision processes but are surprisingly bureaucratic in character when compared to large public universities, and that there really are differences among institutions in their styles of administrative leadership?

We picked questions that we thought were sensible and not deliberately tricky—but neither were they simply "common sense." Why did we open this book with such questions? Because we believe the patterns of leadership and styles of management in colleges and universities are not as well known as people believe. We open this way to combat a phenomenon common to most social scientists—the "Ho-Hum Problem." This refers to the tendency, *after* the research has been reported, for intellectually active people to then build a rationalization for why the results are "obvious."

This sociologist's hobgoblin is particularly found in class, where students can argue persuasively and powerfully for almost any side of an issue *before* the facts are known. But the same students then reverse themselves *after* the research results are known while still contending that the results are "obvious." Sophisticated observers of higher education, as the readers of this book are likely to be, may also fall victim to the "Ho-Hum" phenomenon. The test was an attempt to show that common-sense ideas like these may not be as obvious as they sometimes seem. We have found that the average person taking this test, even if knowledgeable about higher education, does not score very well. If you answered most of the questions correctly you are in the minority.

Below is a brief overview of our central findings. Some may be obvious to a sophisticated observer, some may not be.

1. *There are major differences between academic institutions and other kinds of organizations.* Over the past two decades, social

scientists from many disciplines have been analyzing the dynamics of complex organizations such as business firms, hospitals, military organizations, government agencies, and educational institutions. Information is now copious on organizational processes from inter-personal and environmental relationships to institutional structures. As discussed in detail in Chapter Two, the organizational character-istics of academic institutions are so different from other institutions that traditional management theories do not apply to them. Their goals are more ambiguous and diverse. They serve clients instead of processing materials. Their key employees are highly professional-ized. They have unclear technologies based more on professional skills than on standard operating procedures. They have "fluid par-ticipation" with amateur decision makers who wander in and out of the decision process.

As a result, traditional management theories cannot be applied to educational institutions without carefully considering whether they will work well in that unique academic setting. Some traditional theories, particularly in the decision-making area, apply well to academic settings; others fail miserably. We therefore must be extremely careful about attempts to manage or improve higher education with "modern management" techniques borrowed from business, for example. Such borrowing may make sense, but it must be approached very carefully.

2. *A "political" model of decision making is useful for un-derstanding academic governance.* Organizational theorists often try to condense complex decision processes by adopting a summarizing paradigm or shorthand terminology that captures complicated events in a brief image. Writers on academic governance have coined various terms: "collegium" (Millett, 1962, Goodman, 1962), "bureaucracy" (Stroup, 1966), "organized anarchy" (Cohen and March, 1974), and "federated professionalism" (Clark, 1970). In Chapter Two we review the paradigm of "political systems" as an overall image that summarizes the decision processes in colleges and universities. Baldridge, senior author of this book, first proposed this political paradigm in *Power and Conflict in the University* in 1971. In this book, some modifications to it are outlined.

Any *specific decision* process resembles a political struggle: interest groups are formed, influence tactics are used against decision makers, coalitions are constructed, legislative bodies are pressured, viable compromises are negotiated. But, over time, these individual decisions create *power structures,* with various groups gaining long-range power and control until changing events undermine their position. These long-range patterns of political dynamics and power differ in various types of academic organizations.

3. *There are major organizational differences and much diversity among colleges and universities.* We have already stated that academic organizations are different from most other types; to that we must hasten to add that within the academic world there are many variations, as well. In our study we examined three major areas of difference. One, we examined differences in *environmental relationships,* such as formal control structures, the political environment, the financial base, and the client pool from which the institution draws. Two, we examined the sharp variations in the *professional task,* such as the structure of the disciplines, the degree of faculty professionalization, and the diversity of institutional goals. Three, we looked at the enormous influence that institutional *size and complexity* have on decision making, strongly influencing the institution's degree of centralization and the involvement of faculty and other groups in governance activities.

We will often return to these three clusters of variables, for they help explain why colleges vary so much among themselves in styles of management, leadership, and governance. Some colleges and universities are highly dependent on their environment and are closely controlled by churches or states. Others are relatively free from direct control, have their own financial bases, and pit outside pressure groups against each other to gain a measure of independence. The professional tasks of some institutions mix graduate teaching, research, and undergraduate teaching. Other institutions are fairly homogeneous, concentrating on undergraduate teaching. In addition, there are major differences among them in size and complexity, with massive multiversities at one end of the spectrum and simple liberal arts colleges at the other. We explore many of these differences in Chapter Three.

4. *Distinctive types of institutions have evolved as the result of environmental, professional, and organizational pressures.* The vast differences mentioned above produce a bewilderingly complex

panorama of colleges and universities. To simplify the picture somewhat, in Chapter Three we categorize institutions into eight institutional types: Private Multiversities, Public Multiversities, Elite Liberal Arts Colleges, Public Comprehensives, Public Colleges, Liberal Arts Colleges, Community Colleges, and Private Junior Colleges. These institutional types vary consistently in three basic organizational characteristics—environmental relations, professional task, and size/complexity. Their governance patterns have roots deep in the history of higher education, and a special section after Chapter Nine recounts the evolution of these types and their patterns of governance.

5. *Governance and management vary systematically in different types of institutions.* Many critical issues concerning governance, decision making, faculty morale, unionization, and other key political dynamics are systematically related to major differences in the eight types of institutions listed above. To tell the story of academic leadership and management, therefore, we found we often had to tell a *different* story for each type. The failure to distinguish according to these important differences has been, in our opinion, a major shortcoming of most research in college management, leadership, and governance.

We find that the farther we progress from Community Colleges to Public Colleges to Elite Liberal Arts Colleges to Multiversities, (1) the more the faculty are influential, (2) the less the administrators dominate, (3) the less the environmental influences affect the institution's autonomy, and (4) the less likely it is that unions will be elected. Chapter Four discusses these patterns.

6. *There are substantial differences in the way institutions promote professional values and autonomy—or frustrate them with bureaucratic regulations and control.* Some institutions are tight bureaucracies, while others seem to be loose confederations of departments with considerable autonomy. For example, faculty in the large, more prestigious institutions are allowed more "peer evaluation" than their colleagues in smaller, less research-oriented schools. In assessing work and handing out promotions and rewards, the faculty tends to be most influential in larger colleges, administrators in smaller ones (see Chapter Five).

7. *Larger, more prestigious institutions give academic de-*

*partments more autonomy and control over curriculum and person-
nel policies.* Professors identify strongly with their disciplines, and
their loyalty is lodged in academic departments. In larger, research-
oriented institutions characterized by a high degree of faculty expertise and strong academic departments, more discretion is allowed
the department in selecting its faculty, controlling its courses, and
arranging for promotions and tenure. Very few departments have
much control over money, however; budgets are administratively
controlled in most institutions (see Chapter Five).

8. *Surprisingly, there is less bureaucracy and regulation in
large, more prestigious schools.* Most academic professionals seek
independence from organizational controls and bureaucratic red
tape. Large, complex universities with highly trained faculty afford
professionals greater freedom from bureaucratic regulations and
"standard operating procedures." Such institutions have fewer
regulations over professional travel and consulting, are less likely to
specify the courses faculty are required to teach, and have more
flexible, open-ended, personnel contracts (see Chapter Five).

9. *Faculty morale and satisfaction with working conditions
vary significantly.* Decision processes in universities and colleges are
essentially a form of political dynamics. Political scientists who have
studied political activities in the larger society find that attitudes
such as morale and satisfaction are central in determining people's
political action. We extensively analyzed the morale and satisfaction
rates of faculty in various institutional settings and tried to determine the organizational factors that influence those attitudes. In
addition, we examined the relation between *attitudes* faculties held
and the *action* they were likely to take—for example, whether they
were likely to join a union, be apathetic, or work "within the
system" (see Chapter Six).

10. *About 60 percent of all faculty members possess a high
degree of trust in their administrators.* The majority believe their
administrators are competent, share faculty professional values, and
work to enhance the academic programs of the campus. There are
some interesting differences among institutional types: the highest
degrees of faculty trust are found in Elite Liberal Colleges (72
percent) and Private Multiversities (66 percent); the lowest were in

Community Colleges (54 percent) and Public Comprehensives (55 percent); the rest hovered at about 63 percent (see Chapter Six).

11. *About 66 percent of all faculty were highly satisfied with their working conditions.* They believed their offices, salaries, students, and teaching load were reasonable. There were enormous differences in responses, however, among different types of institutions: the level of satisfaction was highest in high prestige institutions (about 80 percent in Multiversities and Elite Liberal Arts) and lowest in the two-year colleges (around 50 percent). The level of satisfaction probably corresponded closely to the actual working conditions.

12. *A number of factors seem to explain the level of trust and satisfaction among a particular faculty:*
• *Objective working conditions*—the better the conditions in terms of salary, students, and teaching load, the higher the satisfaction stated by the faculty.
• *External pressure*—the more the faculty felt threatened by powerful outside groups (trustees, church officials, legislators) the lower the morale.
• *Reference groups*—the level of morale partly depended on a faculty's "reference group." For example, community college faculty, who might be viewed by some people as in less desirable positions, compared themselves favorably with high school teachers and consequently had higher morale than might be expected. On the other hand, some privileged groups were not particularly high in morale; they had many advantages but learned to expect even more!
• *Policy participation*—faculty groups with a direct role in decision making had higher morale; those who felt they lacked influence had lower morale. This was true even when factors such as institutional quality and size were taken into account (see Chapter Six).

13. *Morale is closely related to militancy and unionism in the faculty.* The more widespread the feelings of dissatisfaction and distrust on a campus, the more that faculty members tend to join unions or express union sympathies (see Chapter Six).

14. *Collective bargaining is realigning many major power*

blocks in the traditional academic setting. Traditionally, senior professors and administrators have dominated the decision-making activities of most colleges and universities. Faculty collective bargaining is seriously challenging that pattern of governance, because it is the junior and part-time faculty who most frequently join unions to make their voices heard. If these more dissatisfied members of the faculty are successful in their unionization efforts, they will upset the traditional political processes of academic governance. Further, students—who until now have been gaining more voice in governance practices at most institutions—will also find their influence diminishing.

One of the most interesting aspects of this shifting political scene is the position of administrators. It is clear that their lives will become enormously more complicated when faculty members unionize. But it is also clear that many decisions formerly made in faculty committees will now be pressed upward to the administrators. In short, it seems likely that administrators will have more power because of faculty unionization but they will have a harder time using it (see Chapter Seven).

15. *Faculties are using unions for two different purposes: (1) to establish stronger faculty participation in institutions that never had a strong tradition of faculty governance and (2) to preserve their role in governance where they once were strong but are now being challenged.* The administrative dominance that is so characteristic of many community colleges and small liberal arts colleges will undoubtedly be tempered by healthy faculty unions. Another possible advantage is that unions can work to eradicate discrimination against women and minority groups; whether they will succeed or not is somewhat questionable, however; it is not clear whether minorities and women will be any more successful in mounting the necessary pressure within unions than they have been within their institutions (see Chapter Seven).

16. *Faculty unionization will add another strong interest group to campus politics, further complicating the decision-making process and constituting a potential veto to beneficial organizational change.* Unions, formed to fight administrative bureaucratization and centralization of power, will themselves generate substantial

amounts of red tape and concentrated control. Procedural *regularity* will often be balanced by endless procedural *restrictions*. The concentration of power in the hands of union executives will unquestionably undermine some traditional faculty governance processes. Moreover, off-campus administrative power will burgeon as state systems become unionized and state governments build ever greater off-campus educational bureaucracies to match those of the unions. All of these factors can be expected to accompany and complicate unionization (see Chapter Seven).

17. *Women are distributed very differently than men within the higher education system.* Women are *over*represented in community colleges, in less prestigious private liberal arts colleges, and in large nonprestigious public institutions. By contrast, women are *under*represented in the major graduate centers and the elite multiversities. When we examine the distribution of women by academic discipline, we confirm the generally accepted idea that women are concentrated in the humanities and traditional women's professions. They are underrepresented in physical sciences, social sciences, engineering and high-pay professional schools (see Chapter Eight).

18. *On the national average, styles of professional activity differ between men and women.* Women are much less likely to have doctorates than are men. They also teach more undergraduate and fewer graduate students and research and publish less than men.

19. *Women are not as heavily involved in institutional governance.* They are drastically underrepresented in administrative positions, and when they are administrators they are in very traditional "women's" areas, such as nursing and home economics. Women serve on proportionately fewer committees, report their committee work to be "trivial," and rarely assume leadership roles on committees. Even within their departments women feel powerless compared to their male colleagues. Women express some hope that unions may redress their problems—but they join them less than men. And male dominance of unions may be just as great as male dominance of administration (see Chapter Eight).

20. *In light of these dismal conclusions, it is no great surprise to find that women have lower morale and are less satisfied with their working conditions.* Women are slightly more inclined to dis-

trust administrators, although both men and women have fairly high trust levels. But women are *much* more inclined to be unhappy with their working conditions—offices, students, salaries, colleagues, teaching loads. Nonetheless, women are less likely to want to move out of their current situation. This is probably a reflection of family constraints and inability to move in a tight market (see Chapter Eight).

21. *These facts suggest that the position and attitudes of women are quite different from those of men in higher education.* However, the gross national differences between men and women narrows substantially *within* institutional groups. That is, women act quite similar to men in similar settings. Women in elite institutions act more like men in elite institutions. Women at community colleges act more like men at community colleges. To be sure, even within those types there are still significant differences—but nowhere near the huge differences that show up in gross national figures. In short, some differences are found simply because women have different activity styles *within* the same settings. But even more of the gross national difference is due to the *concentration* of women in less prestigious institutions—where they act quite similar to the men in those same institutions (see Chapter Eight).

22. *Several trends are significantly changing academic governance.* In Chapter Nine we shift gears, from analyzing how things are to speculating on where things are *going*. Let us preview a few of our tentative forecasts. Faculty influence is being severely undermined on many campuses, and unions have been created to protect faculty interests. Both of these have happened partly because outside agencies—legislatures, state coordinating boards, governors, and state administrators—are playing greater roles than ever before. Campus presidents find their power threatened by unions on one side and state administrators on the other. Meanwhile, student influence, on the upsurge a decade ago, has foundered on the rocks of centralized authority, faculty militancy, and unionism, as well as student apathy toward governance. Another important development is that the courts have entered the governance process on an unprecedented scale. Decisions once reserved to faculty committees and administrative councils—especially personnel matters—are in-

creasingly settled off the campus in the halls of law. All these trends will be discussed in Chapter Nine.

    23. *"Collegial" management is probably dying—if it ever existed at all.* In some ways, the trends mentioned above are depressing because they are movements that are likely to undermine whatever vestiges of professional decision making and collegiality that still exist. Some observers are predicting even more bureaucratization, collective bargaining, state control, and centralization of power. There is widespread fear that the governance of higher education will be more like that of high schools, with strong centralized administrative power and very little student or faculty participation. We suspect that for a substantial part of higher education these predictions are correct. Collegiality, the ideal of so many, was probably never dominant in modern higher education outside of a few departmental activities. But social trends will probably undermine even the limited collegial influence that once existed (See Chapter Nine).

    We close the book after Chapter Nine with a special study section on the historical development of management and governance in higher education. This section traces the development of the styles of management that we find on the current scene. Chronological order suggests that this study, dealing with the *past* as it does, should be placed at the front of the book followed by the bulk of the text, which deals with current conditions, then Chapter Nine, which projects future trends. We put the historical section at the end however, because we suspected that most readers are more concerned with where we are now—and where we might be going—than how we got here.

    The history section is not a general history of higher education; it is a specific history that focuses sharply on historical patterns of academic management, governance, and leadership. The study seems to answer three questions: (1) What were the organizational features of colleges in different periods, in terms of size, environmental relations, and professional tasks? (2) Which of the eight types of institutions existed in different periods, and how did they develop? (3) What were the patterns of academic management, governance, and leadership in different periods?

So, placed last or not, we urge the reader to read this history. It offers valuable insight for understanding the present. We performed the study to make certain we did not give a shallow contemporary picture of academic management without awareness of deep-rooted historical developments. We are glad we did. We found the study to be extremely helpful in understanding how we got where we are, and where we might be going.

Chapter 2

Organizational Characteristics of Colleges and Universities

⟨❦⟩⟨❦⟩⟨❦⟩⟨❦⟩⟨❦⟩⟨❦⟩⟨❦⟩⟨❦⟩⟨❦⟩⟨❦⟩⟨❦⟩⟨❦⟩⟨❦⟩⟨❦⟩

Organizations vary in a number of important ways: they have different kinds of clients; they employ workers with varying skills; they work with various types of technologies; they develop divergent styles of structure, coordination, and governance; and they have differing relationships to their external environments. To be sure, there are some common elements in the ways that colleges and universities, hospitals, prisons, business firms, and government bureaus are operated. No two organizations are really the same, however, and any adequate theory of decision making and governance must take their differences into account.

This chapter deals with the organizational characteristics of colleges and universities and with how these characteristics shape their decision processes. The basic argument can be summed up simply. Colleges and universities are unique kinds of professional organizations, differing in major characteristics from industrial organizations, government bureaus, and business firms. These critical differences force us to develop new images of organizational decision making; a "political" model will be offered to supplement the more common "bureaucratic" model.

Colleges and universities are complex organizations. They have goals, hierarchical systems and structures, officials that carry out specified duties, decision-making processes for setting institutional policy, and routine bureaucratic administration for handling day-to-day work. Although colleges and universities share many characteristics with other complex bureaucracies, in this section we will explore some critical differences that make it necessary to construct revised theories of decision making if we are to analyze academic governance.

Goal ambiguity is common in academic organizations. Most organizations know what they are doing. Business firms seek to make a profit, government agencies perform tasks specified by law, hospitals try to cure sick people, and prisons attempt to incarcerate and rehabilitate. Since they know where they are going, they can build decision structures to get them there. By contrast, colleges and universities have vague, ambiguous goals, and they must build decision structures that grapple with uncertainty and conflict over those goals.

What are the goals of a university? That is a difficult question, for the list of possibilities is long and each has a strong claim: teaching, research, service to the local community, administration of scientific installations, housing for students and faculty, support of the arts, solving social problems. In their book *Leadership and Ambiguity,* David Cohen and James G. March comment: "Almost any educated person could deliver a lecture entitled 'The Goals of the University.' Almost no one will listen to the lecture voluntarily. For the most part, such lectures and their companion essays are well-intentioned exercises in social rhetoric, with little operational content. Efforts to generate normative statements of the goals of the university tend to produce goals that are either meaningless or dubious" (1974, p. 195).

"Goal ambiguity" is one of the chief characteristics of academic organizations. Not only do they often try to be all things to all people but they rarely have a single mission. Because their preferences are unclear, they also find it hard to decline additional goals. Edward Gross and Paul V. Grambsch (1968, 1974) analyzed the goals of faculty and administrators in a large number of American universities. The result was remarkable in that both administrators and faculty marked as important almost every one of 47 goals listed by Gross and Grambsch. To be sure, they ranked some higher than others—academic freedom being one near the top. But the point is, people seem to feel the university should be doing almost everything. Under these circumstances, it is difficult to see how it can do anything.

Not only are academic goals unclear, they are also highly *contested*. As long as goals are left ambiguous and abstract, people agree; as soon as they are concretely specified and put into operation, disagreement arises. This link between clarity and conflict may help explain the prevalence of meaningless rhetoric in academic speeches and policy statements. If you talk in general terms about academic virtues—the scholarly counterparts of motherhood and apple pie—everybody nods wisely. If you talk specifically about how these virtues are to be translated into operational policy, conflict erupts. The choice seems difficult: rhetoric brings agreement; serious discussion creates conflict.

Academic organizations are client-serving institutions. Like public school systems, hospitals, and welfare agencies, colleges and universities are "people-processing" institutions. Society feeds clients with specific needs into the institution and the institution acts upon them then returns them to the larger society. This is an extremely important fact, for the clients demand and often obtain a significant amount of influence over the decision-making processes of the institution. Even powerless clients such as small school children usually have protectors such as parents who demand a voice in the operation of the organization. This client-serving character of academic organizations raises another issue: what kinds of technology and personnel does the organization need to do its multifaceted job.

Problematic technologies. Because they serve clients with disparate, complicated needs, client-serving organizations often have problematic technologies. An organization that manufactures steel develops a specific technology that can be segmented and made routine. Unskilled, semiskilled, and white collar workers can be used without a heavy reliance upon professional expertise. But it is difficult to construct a simple technology for dealing with minds, bodies, and spirits. Serving clients is difficult to accomplish, to evaluate, and show short-term successes. Considering the entire person is a holistic task that cannot be easily separated into small, routine technical segments. If, at times, colleges and universities do not know *what* they are doing, they furthermore often do not know *how* to do it. A holistic, unclear, and nonroutine technology demands a highly professional staff.

High professionalism dominates the academic task. What does a client-oriented organization usually do when its goals are unclear and contested, and its technology is nonroutine? Usually, it solves this problem by hiring expertly trained professionals. Hospitals employ doctors and nurses, social welfare agencies employ social workers, public schools employ teachers, and colleges and universities employ faculty members. These highly-trained professional groups deal with the complex, nonroutine problems of clients using a broad repertoire of the skills necessary for the task. Instead of permitting the routine subdividing of the task, assembly-line style, professional work tends to require that a range of skills be encapsulated in a single professional employee.

Sociologists have suggested a number of important facts about professional employees, whether they work in hospitals, schools, law firms, or universities: (1) Professionals demand *work autonomy* and freedom from supervision; they base their work on skill and expertise and demand to be left alone to apply them. (2) Professionals have *divided loyalties;* they have "cosmopolitan" tendencies, and their loyalty to peers in their discipline around the nation sometimes conflicts with their "local" tendencies to be good employees for their organization. (3) There are strong tensions between *professional values* and *bureaucratic expectations* in an organization; these can intensify conflict between professional employees and organizational managers. And (4) professionals demand peer evaluation of their work; they feel only colleagues can judge their performance, and they reject the evaluations of noncolleague managers, even if those managers are technically "superior" in the hierarchy.

All of these characteristics undercut the traditional bureaucracy, rejecting its hierarchy, control structure, and management procedures. As a consequence, we can expect a distinct management style in a professional organization.

Colleges and universities tend to have "fragmented" professional staffs. In some organizations, there is one dominant professional group—for example, doctors in hospitals. In other organizations the professional staff is fragmented into subspecialities, with no one of them dominating—the faculty in a university provides a clear case. Burton R. Clark comments on fragmented academic professionalism:

> The internal controls of the medical profession are strong and are substituted for those of the organization. But in the college or university this situation does not obtain; there are twelve, twenty-five, or fifty clusters of experts. The experts are prone to identify with their own disciplines, and the "academic profession" over-all comes off a poor second. We have wheels within wheels, many professions within a profession. No one of the disciplines on a campus is likely to dominate the others. . . . The campus is not a closely-knit group of professionals who see the world from one perspective. As a collection of professionals, it is decentralized, loose, and flabby. The principle is this: where professional influence is high and there is one dominant professional group, the organization will be integrated by the imposition of professional standards. Where professional influence is high and there are a number of professional groups, the organization will be split by professionalism. The university and the large college are fractured by expertness, not unified by it [1963, pp. 37–51].

The governance processes in colleges and universities are highly influenced by the presence of these diverse professional staffs. In fact, this is one of the dominant features of academic organiza-

tions and justifies viewing the faculty as critical to the decision-
making process—as we have done throughout our research for the
Stanford Project on Academic Governance.

*Colleges and universities are becoming more environmentally
vulnerable.* All complex organizations are vulnerable to outside
pressure; there is simply no completely "independent" or "autonomous" organization. But they vary a great deal on how much the
outside world controls them, with some institutions having considerably more freedom of action than others. The degree of autonomy that an organization has in regard to its environment is one
of the critical determinants of how it will be managed.

In a free market economy, for example, business firms and
industry have a substantial degree of autonomy. Although they are
regulated by countless government agencies, they essentially are free
agents responsive only to market demands. At the other extreme,
there are a number of organizations that are virtually "captured"
by their environments. Professionals in many government agencies
such as public school districts feel the constant scrutiny of the entire
community.

Colleges and universities are somewhere in the middle of this
continuum from "independent" to "captured." In many respects
they enjoy substantial insulation from the environment. Recently,
however, powerful external forces have been applied to them.
Particularly in the 1970s have the conflicting wishes, demands, and
threats of dozens of interest groups been made known to the administrations and faculties of academic organizations.

What impact does this kind of environmental pressure have
on the governance of colleges and universities? When they are well-
insulated from the pressures of the outside environment, then professional values, norms, and work definitions dominate the character
of the organization. On the other hand, when high external pressure
is brought to bear on these colleges and universities, the operating
autonomy of the academic professionals is significantly reduced;
faculties and administrators lose control over the curriculum, the
institution's goals, and the daily operation of the college. Under
these circumstances, the professionals within the organization are
frequently reduced to the role of hired employees doing the bidding
of bureaucratic managers.

Although colleges and universities are not entirely captured by their environments, they are steadily being penetrated by outside forces. As this vulnerability grows, the institutions change significantly in their management patterns. This is a major difference between academic organizations and traditional industrial bureaucracies that are relatively free from environmental constraints.

A Summary Image: "Organized Anarchy"

To summarize, academic organizations have several unique organizational characteristics. They have unclear and contested *goal* structures; almost anything can be justified, but almost anything can be attacked as illegitimate. They serve *clients* who demand input into the decision-making process. They have a *problematic technology,* for in order to serve clients the technology must be holistic and nonroutine. As a result, academic organizations are important instances of *professionalized organizations* where professionals serving the clients demand a large measure of control over the institution's decision processes. Finally, academic organizations are becoming more and more *vulnerable to their environments.*

What image captures the spirit of such a complex organizational system? Surely the standard term "bureaucracy" misses the point. "Bureaucracy" implies rigidity and stability; academic organizations seem more fluid, changing, and confused. "Bureaucracy" implies clear lines of authority and strict hierarchical command; academic organizations have autonomy-demanding professionals and the lines of authority often become blurred and confused. "Bureaucracy" suggests cohesive organization and unified goals; academic organizations are splintered and fragmented around an ambiguous, changing, and contested set of objectives. In sum, although the imagery of bureaucracy adequately describes certain aspects of colleges and universities—business administration, plant management, capital outlay, and auxilliary services, for example—at the heart of the academic enterprise, in their policy-making and professional teaching/research tasks, academic institutions do not resemble bureaucracies.

What useful shorthand terminology can be used to exemplify academic organizations? Cohen and March, in their book *Leader-*

ship and Ambiguity have suggested the term *organized anarchy.*
They see a confused world with very little organizational coordination and central goal making: "In a university anarchy each
individual in the university is seen as making autonomous decisions.
Teachers decide if, when, and what to teach. Students decide if,
when, and what to learn. Legislators and donors decide if, when,
and what to support. Neither coordination . . . nor control are
practised. Resources are allocated by whatever process emerges but
without explicit reference to some superordinate goal. The 'decisions'
of the system are a consequence produced by the system but intended by no one and decisively controlled by no one" (1974, pp.
33–34).

     To summarize Cohen and March, the image of organized
anarchy differs radically from the well organized bureaucracy. It is
an organization in which people talk past each other, in which
generous resources allow people to go in different directions without
coordination, in which leaders are relatively weak and decisions are
arrived at through the non-coordinated action of individuals. Since
goals are ambiguous, nobody is quite sure where the organization is
going or how it will get there. The situation is fluid. Decisions are
often by-products of activity that is unintended and unplanned.

     In such fluid circumstances, presidents and other institutional
leaders serve primarily as catalysts. They do not so much lead the
institution as they channel its activities in subtle ways. They do not
command, they negotiate. They do not plan comprehensively, they
try to nudge problems together with preexisting solutions. They are
not heroic leaders, they are facilitators of an ongoing process.

     Decisions are not so much "made" as they "happen"—they
are events in which problems, choices, and decision makers happen
to coalesce to form temporary solutions. In a sense, then, a decision
situation is a "garbage can" into which problems, decision makers,
and preconceived solutions are poured and jostled around until a
solution emerges that at least temporarily satisfies the organization's
needs. Cohen and March suggest that university decision processes
are "sets of procedures through which organizational participants
arrive at an interpretation of what they are doing and what they
have done while they are doing it. From this point of view, an organization is a collection of choices looking for problems, issues and

feelings looking for decision situations in which they might be aired, solutions looking for issues for which they might be the answer, and decision makers looking for work" (1974, p. 81).

In many ways, the organized anarchy image is an exceptionally strong and persuasive concept. It breaks through much traditional formality that surrounds discussions of decision making. The imagery of organized anarchy helps capture the spirit of the confused organizational dynamics in academic institutions: unclear goals, unclear technologies, and environmental vulnerability.

To some people, the term *organized anarchy* may seem overly colorful, suggesting more confusion, disarray, and conflict than is really present. This may be a legitimate criticism. The term may also carry negative connotations to those who are not aware that it applies to specific organizational characteristics rather than an overall view of the entire campus community. Nevertheless, the term helps to expand our conceptions, dislodge the bureaucracy image, and suggest a looser, more fluid kind of organization. These virtues persuade us to adopt a modified version of Cohen's and March's (1974) organized anarchy image to summarize some of the unique organizational characteristics of colleges and universities: (1) unclear goals, (2) client service, (3) unclear technology, (4) professional staffing, and (5) environmental vulnerability. In the next section we will try to answer a new question: What do decision and governance processes look like in an organized anarchy?

Governance of Organized Anarchies

People tend to reduce the confusing complexity of their world to simple symbols. Administrators, organization theorists, students or professors—almost everyone who has looked at academic governance—have developed one summarizing image after another to capture the essence of this complex process. We look at the bewildering detail of this process and summarize it as "collegial," or as "political" or "professional," "participatory" or "oligarchical." These images dominate our thinking, organize the way we see the world, and determine how we will go about analyzing the process. Our metaphors and images are not innocent, for the way we view the world and summarize it with models helps determine the way we act. If we believe the system is political, then we form coalitions and exert pressure on decision makers accordingly. If we think the situation is collegial, then we try to persuade people and appeal to reason. If we suspect the system is bureaucratic, then we employ legalistic formalities to gain our ends.

In one sense, the search for an all-encompassing model is simplistic, for no one model can delineate the intricacies of decision processes in complex organizations such as universities and colleges. On the other hand, there is a pleasant parsimony about having a single model that summarizes a complicated world for us. This is not bad except when we allow our models to blind us to important features of the organization. For example, earlier we insisted that the term *bureaucracy* was inadequate, by itself. That does not mean there are no bureaucratic features of colleges; we only mean that bureaucracy *alone* is not an adequate term to describe everything that is happening.

In the past few years, as research on higher education has increased, images describing academic governance have also proliferated. Three models have received widespread attention, more or less dominating the thinking of people who study academic governance. We will examine briefly each of these models in turn: (1) bureaucratic, (2) collegial, and (3) political. Each has strong points, and together they can be used to examine slightly different aspects of the governance process.

Bureaucracy and the "Rational" Theory of Decision Making

One of the most influential descriptions of complex organizations was Max Weber's momumental work on bureaucracies (1947). Weber identified the characteristics of bureaucracies that separated them from other, less formal work organizations. In skeleton form, he suggested that bureaucracies are networks of social groups dedicated to limited goals and organized for maximum efficiency. Moreover, the regulation of the system is based on the principle of "legal-rationality," as contrasted with informal regulation based on friendship, loyalty to family, or personal allegiance to a charismatic leader. The structure is hierarchical and is tied together by formal chains of command and systems of communication.

Weber's description included such characteristics as tenure, appointment to office, and competency as the basis of promotion. Most of his ideas are well known and need little elaboration.

Several authors claim that university governance may be more fully understood by applying this bureaucratic paradigm. For example, Herbert Stroup (1966) points out some characteristics of colleges and universities that fit Weber's original discussion of the nature of bureaucracy. Stroup's conclusions about colleges include the following:

- Competence is the criterion used for appointment.
- Officials are appointed, not elected.
- Salaries are fixed and paid directly by the organization rather than determined in "free-fee" style.
- Rank is recognized and respected.
- The career tends to be exclusive; little other work is done.
- The style of life is centered around the organization.
- Security is present in a tenure system.
- Personal and organizational property are separated.

Stroup is undoubtedly correct in saying that Weber's paradigm can be applied to universities, and most observers are well aware of the bureaucratic factors involved in university administration. Among the more prominent of these are the following:

State charter. The university is a complex organization chartered by the state, and in this respect it is like most other bureaucracies. This seemingly innocent fact has major consequences, especially as states increasingly exercise control.

Formal hierarchy. The university has a formal hierarchy, with offices and a set of bylaws that specify the relations between those offices. Professors, instructors, and research assistants are members of this bureaucratic hierarchy in the same sense as are deans, chancellors, and presidents.

Communication channels. There are formal channels of communication that must be respected, as many a student or young professor finds out to his dismay.

Authority relations. There are definite bureaucratic authority relations, with some officials exercising authority over others. In a university, authority relations are often blurred, ambiguous, and shifting, but they nonetheless exist.

Rules and regulations. There are formal policies and rules that govern much of the institution's work. Library regulations, budgetary guidelines, and procedures of the university senate are all part of the system of regulations and procedures that hold the university together and control its work.

People processing. Bureaucratic elements are most vividly apparent to students in the "people-processing" aspects of record keeping—registration, graduation requirements, and a thousand other routine, day-to-day activities that are designed to help the modern university handle its masses of students. Students often complain that these requirements and procedures result in impersonality and callousness, but they are necessary if the university is to cope with its overwhelming influx of students.

Decision processes. Decision-making processes are most often bureaucratic when routine decisions are at stake and being made by officials who have been given the responsibility by the formal administrative structure. Admissions actions are formally delegated to the dean of admissions; procedures for graduation are routinely administered by other designated officials; research policies of the university are supervised by officials specified in the rules of the university; financial activities are usually handled in a bureaucratic manner by the finance office.

In many ways, however, the bureaucratic paradigm falls short of explaining university governance, especially if one is primarily concerned with decision making processes. First, the bureaucratic model tells us much about "authority"—legitimate, formalized power—but not much about power based on nonlegitimate threats, mass movements, expertise, and appeals to emotion and sentiment. The Weberian paradigm is weak when it attempts to deal with these nonformal types of power and influence. Second, the bureaucratic paradigm explains much about the formal *structure* but little about the dynamic *processes* of the institution in action. Third, the bureaucratic paradigm deals with the formal structure at one particular time, but does not explain changes over time. Finally, the bureaucratic model does not deal extensively with the crucial task of policy formulation. The paradigm explains how policies may be carried out most efficiently after they are set, but it says little about the process by which policy is established in the first place. It does not deal with political issues, such as the efforts of groups within the university to force policy decisions favoring their special interests. In these ways, then, the bureaucratic paradigm falls far short of explaining policy making in the university.

University Collegium

Many writers have consciously rejected the bureaucratic image of the university and instead have declared the university a "collegium," or "community of scholars." This is found to be a rather ambiguous concept when closely examined. In fact, there seem to be at least three different themes running through the literature based on this concept.

One theme is that *academic decision making should be like the hierarchical processes in other bureaucracies;* instead, there should be full participation of the members of the academic community—especially the faculty—in its management. Only a few small liberal arts colleges exist as actual examples of such "round table" democratic institutions, but the concept persists nonetheless. Under it the "community of scholars" administers its own affairs, with bureaucratic officials having little influence (see Goodman, 1962).

John Millett, one of the foremost proponents of this model, has succinctly stated this view: "I do not believe that the concept of hierarchy is a realistic representation of the interpersonal relationships which exist within a college or university. Nor do I believe that a structure of hierarchy is a desirable prescription for the organization of a college or university. . . . I would argue that there is another concept of organization that is just as valuable a tool of analysis and perhaps even more useful as a generalized observation of group and interpersonal behavior. This is the concept of community. The concept of community presupposes an organization in which functions are differentiated and in which specialization must be brought together, or the coordination, if you will, is achieved not through a structure of superordination and subordination of persons and groups but through a *dynamic of consensus*" (1962, pp. 234–5).

A second theme concerns *the "professional" authority of faculty.* Talcot Parsons (1947) was one of the first to call attention to the difference between the "official competence" derived from one's office in the bureaucracy and "technical competence" derived from one's ability to perform a given task. Parsons concentrated on technical competence of the physician, but others have extended this logic to other professionals who hold authority on the basis of what they *know* and can *do,* rather than on the basis of their official positions. The scientist in industry, the military advisor, the expert in government, the physician in the hospital, and the professor in the university are all examples of professionals whose influence depends on their knowledge rather than on their formal positions.

The argument for collegial organization is strongly supported by the literature on professionalism, for it emphasizes the professional's ability to make his own decisions and his need for freedom from organizational restraints. Proponents of this argument hold, therefore, that a collegium is the most reasonable method of organizing the university. Parsons, for example, notes that when professionals are organized in a bureaucracy "there are strong tendencies for them to develop a different sort of structure from that characteristic of the administrative hierarchy . . . of bureaucracy. Instead of a rigid hierarchy of status and authority there tends to be what is roughly, in formal status, a company of equals . . ." (1947, p. 60).

A third theme carries with it *a utopian operational prescription.* Supporters of this thesis argue that contemporary society is increasingly discontented with the impersonalization of life exemplified by the multiversity with its thousands of students and huge bureaucracy. The student revolts of the 1960s and perhaps even the widespread apathy of the 1970s have been symptoms of a deeply felt alienation between the average student and the massive educational establishment. This discontent and anxiety are well summed up in the now-famous sign worn by a Berkeley student: "I am a human being—do not fold, spindle, or mutilate."

In response to this impersonal bureaucratized educational system, many critics are calling for a return to the "academic community," with all of that concept's accompanying images of personal attention, humane education, and "relevant confrontation with life." Paul Goodman's work in *The Community of Scholars* (1962) appeals to many seeking to reform the university, citing the need for more personal interaction between faculty and students, for more "relevant" courses, and for educational innovations to bring the student into existential dialogue with the subject matter of his discipline. The number of articles on this subject, in both the mass media and the professional journals, is astonishingly large. Indeed, this version of the collegial, academic community is now widely advocated as one answer to the impersonality and meaninglessness of today's large multiversity. Thus conceived, the idea of the collegium and the academic community is more of a revolutionary ideology and a utopian projection than a description of the real shape of governance at any university.

How can we evaluate these three themes running through the collegial model? The calls for the professor's professional freedom, for consensus and democratic consultation, and for more humane education are all supported by legitimate and appealing arguments. Few would deny that our universities would more truly be centers of learning if we could somehow implement these objectives. However, there is a misleading simplicity about these otherwise persuasive arguments because they gloss over many of the realities of a complex university. Several of these weaknesses of the collegial model should be mentioned.

The collegial literature often confuses *descriptive* and *normative* enterprises. Are the writers saying that the university *is* a collegium or that it *ought* to be a collegium? Frequently, the discussions of collegium are more a lament for paradise lost than a description of present reality. Indeed, the collegial idea of round-table decision making does not accurately reflect the actual processes in most institutions, as our data in later chapters will clearly show. To be sure, at the department level there are many examples of collegial decision making, but at higher levels it can be found only in some aspects of the committee system. Of course, the proponents of the collegial model may be proposing this as a desirable goal or reform strategy rather than a present reality that helps us to understand the actual workings of universities.

The collegial model also fails to deal adequately with the problem of *conflict*. When Millett emphasizes the "dynamic of consensus," he neglects the prolonged battles that precede consensus and the fact that the consensus actually represents the prevalence of one group over another. Collegial proponents are correct in declaring that simple bureaucratic rule making is not the essence of decision making, but in making this point they take the equally indefensible position that major decisions are reached primarily by consensus. Neither extreme is correct, for decisions are rarely made by either bureaucratic fiat or simple consensus. What is needed is a model that can include consensus factors and bureaucratic processes, and that can also grapple with power plays, conflict, and the rough-and-tumble politics of many academic institutions.

The Political Model

In *Power and Conflict in the University* (1971), Baldridge proposed a "political systems" model of university governance. Although the other major models of governance—collegial and bureaucratic—offer genuine insights, we believe that their analyses can be strengthened by insights from this political model.

The political model assumes that complex organizations can be studied as miniature political systems, with interest group dynamics and conflicts similar to those in city, state, and other political situations. The political model has several stages, all of which center around the university's policy-forming processes. Policy formation was selected as the central focal point because major policies commit the organization to definite goals, set the strategies for reaching those goals, and in general determine the long-range destiny of the organization. Policy decisions are critical decisions, those that have a major impact on the organization's future. In any practical situation it may be difficult to separate the routine from the critical, for issues that seem minor at one point may later be of considerable importance, or vice versa. In general, however, policy decisions are those that bind the organization to important courses of action.

Since politics are so important, people throughout the organization try to influence their formulation in order to see that their own special interests are protected and furthered. Policy making becomes a vital focus of special interest group activity that permeates the university. Just as the political scientist often selects legislative acts in congress as the focal point for his analysis of the state's political processes, organization theorists may select policy decisions as the key for studying organizational conflict and change. With policy formation as its key issue, the political model then makes a series of assumptions about the political process.

One assumption is that *inactivity prevails*. To say that policy making is a political process is not to say that everybody is involved. Quite the contrary. For most people most of the time, the policy-making process is an uninteresting, unrewarding activity, so they allow administrators to run the show. This is characteristic of political processes not only in colleges but also in the larger society. Voters do not vote, people do not attend city council meetings, school boards usually do what they please, and by and large the decisions of the society are made by small groups of elites.

A second assumption is that of *fluid participation*. Even when people are active they move in and out of the decision-making process. Individuals usually do not spend very much time on any given issue; decisions, therefore, are usually made by those who persist. This normally means that small groups of political elites govern most major decisions because only they invest the necessary time in the process.

A third assumption is that colleges and universities, like most other social organizations, are *fragmented into interest groups* with different goals and values. These groups normally live in a state of armed co-existence. When resources are plentiful and the environment congenial, these interest groups engage in only minimal conflict. They mobilize and fight to influence decisions, however, when resources are tight, outside pressure groups attack, or other internal groups try to take over their goals.

A fourth assumption is that *conflict is normal*. In a fragmented, dynamic social system, conflict is natural and not necessarily a symptom of breakdown in the academic community. In fact, conflict is a significant factor in promoting healthy organizational change.

A fifth assumption is that *authority is limited*. In universities, the formal authority prescribed in a bureaucratic system is severely limited by the political pressure that groups can exert. Decisions are not simply bureaucratic orders, but are often negotiated compromises between competing groups. Officials are not free simply to issue a decision; instead they must jockey between interest groups hoping to build viable positions between powerful blocks.

A sixth assumption is that *external interest groups are important*. Academic decision making does not occur in a campus-bound vacuum. External interest groups exert a great deal of influence over the policy-making process. And external pressures and formal control by outside agencies—especially in public institutions—are powerful shapers of internal governance processes.

Often the bureaucratic image of organizational structure is accompanied by a decision approach that can be called the "rational" strategy. It assumes not only that the structure is hierarchical and well-organized but also that decisions are made through clear-cut, predetermined steps. This traditional decision theory for bureaucracies starts with a basic premise: Mr. X (the dean, president, or whoever) must make a decision and, from conflicting advice, must therefore form a judgment. This formalistic theory suggests that a definite, rational approach will lead to the optimal decision. Once the problem is recognized (difficult in itself), then a number of steps are proposed: (1) setting *goals* to overcome the problem, (2) selecting *alternatives* to reach the goals, (3) assessing the *consequences* of various alternatives, (4) *choosing* the best alternatives, and (5) *implementing* the decision.

The rational model appeals to most of us who like to interpret our actions as essentially goal-directed and rational. Realistically, however, we should realize that the rational model is more an ideal than an actual description of how people act. In fact, in the confused organizational setting of the university, political constraints can seriously undermine attempts to arrive at rational decisions. A political interpretation suggests that this theory must be rethought in the light of actual decision processes if it is to amount to more than a formalistic, impractical scheme. Baldridge outlined the argument in *Power and Conflict in the University:*

> The first new question posed by the political model is *why* a given decision is made at all. The formalists have already indicated that "recognition of the problem" is one element in the process, but too little attention

has been paid to the activities that bring a particular issue to the forefront. Why is *this* decision being considered at *this* particular time? The political model insists that interest groups, powerful individuals, and bureaucratic processes are critical in drawing attention to some decisions rather than to others. A study of "attention cues" by which issues are called to a community's attention is a vital part of any analysis.

Second, a question must be raised about the right of any person or group to make the decisions. Previously the *who* question was seldom raised, chiefly because the decision literature was developed for hierarchical organizations in which the focus of authority could be easily defined. In a more loosely coordinated system, however, we must ask a prior question: Why is Dean Smith making the decision instead of Dean Jones, or why is the University Senate dealing with the problem instead of the central administration? Establishing the right of authority over a decision is a political question, subject to conflict, power manipulation, and struggles between interest groups. Thus the political model always asks tough questions: Who has the right to make the decision? What are the conflict-ridden processes by which the decision was located at this point rather than at another? The crucial point is that often the issue of *who* makes the decision has already limited, structured, and pre-formed *how* it will be made.

The third new issue raised by a political interpretation concerns the development of complex decision networks. As a result of the fragmentation of the university, decision making is rarely located in one official; instead it is dependent upon the advice and authority of numerous people. Again the importance of the committee system is evident. It is necessary to understand that the committee network is the legitimate reflection of the need for professional influence to intermingle with bureaucratic influence. The decision process, then, is taken out of the hands of individuals (although there are still many who are powerful) and placed into a network that allows a *cumulative buildup* of expertise and advice. When the very life of the organization clusters around expertise, *decision making is likely to be diffuse, segmentalized, and decentralized.* A complex network of committees, councils, and advisory bodies grows to handle the task of assembling the expertise necessary for reasonable decisions. Decision making by the individual bureaucrat is replaced with decision making by committee, council, and cabinet. Centralized decision making is replaced with diffuse decision making. The process becomes a far-flung network for gathering expertise from every corner of the organization and translating it into policy [Baldridge, 1971, p. 190].

The fourth new question raised by the political approach concerns the choice of alternative solutions to the problem at hand. The rational decision theory suggests that all possible options are open within easy reach of the decision maker. A realistic appraisal of decision dynamics in most organizations, however, suggests that by no means are all options open. The political dynamics of interest groups, the force of external power blocs, and the opposition of powerful professional constituencies may leave only a handful of viable options. The range of alternatives is sharply limited; the realistic choices are narrow. Just as important, the time and energy available for seeking new solutions most likely is extremely short. Although all possible solutions *should* be identified under the rational model, administrators in the real world have little time to grope for solutions before deadlines are upon them. Again, Baldridge's argument is applicable:

These comments may be summed up by proposing a "political process" model of decision making. The political model suggests the following. First, powerful political forces—interest groups, bureaucratic officials, influential individuals, organizational subunits—cause a given issue to emerge from the limbo of on-going problems and certain "attention cues" force the political community to consider the problem. Second, there is a struggle over locating the decision with a particular person or group, for the location of the right to make the decision often determines the outcome. Third, decisions are usually "pre-formed" to a great extent by the time one person or group is given the legitimacy to make the decision; not all options are open and the choices have been severely limited by the previous conflicts. Fourth, such political struggles are more likely to occur in reference to "critical" decisions than to "routine" decisions. Fifth, a complex decision network is developed to gather the necessary information and supply the critical expertise. Sixth, during the process of making the decision political controversy is likely to continue and compromises, deals, and plain head cracking are often necessary to get any decision made. Finally, the controversy is not likely to end easily. In fact, it is difficult even to know when a decision *is* made, for the political processes have a habit of unmaking, confusing, and muddling whatever agreements are hammered out.

This may be a better way of grappling with the complexity that surrounds decision processes within a loosely coordinated, fragmented political system. The formal decision models seem to have been asking very limited questions about the decision process, and more insight can be gained by asking a new set of political questions. Thus the decision model that emerges from the university's political dynamics is more open, more dependent on conflict and political action. It is not so systematic or formalistic as most decision theory, but it is probably closer to the truth. Decision making, then, is not an isolated technique but another critical process that must be integrated into a larger political image [Baldridge, 1971, pp. 191–192].

If the decision process is really as fluid and complex as we suggest, then a more complex analytic framework is needed than the "rational" theory affords. As Baldridge described it in *Power and Conflict in the University* (1971), the political model offers an analytical scheme for describing and mapping the political events around individual organizational decisions.

The sociologist examining academic policy making wants to know how the social structure of the college or university influences the decision processes, how political pressures are brought to bear on decision makers, how decisions are forged out of the conflict, and how formulated policies are implemented. Thus, the political model has five points of analysis:

Social structure. Academic organizations are splintered into groups with basically different life styles and political interests. Those differences often lead to conflict, for what is in the best interest of one group may damage another. It is important to examine this social setting, with its fragmented groups, divergent goal aspirations, and conflicting claims on decision makers. Academic organizations have particularly pluralistic social systems because groups both inside and out are pushing in dissimilar directions according to their own special interests. One need only glance at the various outside "publics" of a college or university to see how diverse are the elements of its external social context; a glance inward reveals an internal social structure composed of similarly fragmented interest groups. Many of the current conflicts on campus have their roots in the complexity of this academic social structure, and in the complex goals and values held by these divergent groups.

Interest articulation. Attempts at political intervention come from external groups, faculty, student, staff, and administration. In this political tangle the articulation of interests is a fundamental process. A group must somehow effectively influence favorable action by decision-making bodies. How does a powerful group exert pressure, what threats or promises can it make, and how does it translate its desires into political capital?

The legislative stage. University legislative bodies respond to pressures on them, and attempt to transform the conflict into politically feasible policy. Committees meet, commissions report, negotiators bargain, and powerful people haggle over the eventual policy. In the process, negotiations are undertaken, compromises are forged, and rewards are divided. Not only must we identify the different types of interest groups involved and the methods they use to bring pressure to bear but we must also clarify the translation process by which all of these pressures are negotiated into formal policy.

Formulation of policy. All articulated interests have now gone through conflict and compromise stages, and the final legislative action is taken. The resulting policy is the official climax to the conflict, and represents an authoritative, binding decision to commit the organization to one set of possible alternative actions, one set of goals and values.

Execution of policy. The battle is now officially over and the resulting policy is turned over to the bureaucrats for its routine execution. This may oversimplify things, but it is remarkable the way yesterday's vicious confrontation may become today's boring bureaucratic chore. This may not be the end of the conflict, for the losers may take up arms again for a new round of "interest articulation." Too, execution of the new policy may generate new tensions, with new vested interests instigating a renewed cycle of political conflict.

In summary, the broad outline of the academic organization's political system looks like this: there is a complex social structure that generates multiple pressures, there are many sources and forms of power and pressure that impinge on decision makers, there is a legislative stage that translates these pressures into policy, and there is a policy execution phase that generates feedback and potentially new conflicts.

This approach forces us to place several factors under close scrutiny. First, and primarily, we should examine the mechanics of goal setting and the conflict over values rather than the question of efficiency in achieving goals. Second, we should analyze change processes and the adaptation of the organization to its changing internal and external environment; political dynamics are constantly shifting, pressuring the university in many directions and forcing change throughout the academic system. Third, we should closely analyze conflict and conflict resolution, a crucial component of a political study. Fourth, we should explore the role that interest groups play in pressuring decision makers to formulate certain policy. Finally, we should give considerable attention to legislative and decision-making phases—the processes by which pressures and power are translated into policy. Taken together, these emphases are the bare outline for a political analysis of governance.

The Revised Political Model: an Environmental and Structuralist Approach

Since it originally appeared in *Power and Conflict in the University* (1971), our political model of governance has received a number of comments. Some have suggested that it provides a dynamic and useful view of academic governance. But it is important to comment on several of the approach's shortcomings, because a revised political model is the basis for the Stanford Project on Academic Governance.

First, our original political model probably underestimated the impact of routine bureaucratic processes. Many decisions are made not in the heat of political controversy but because standard operating procedures dominate in most organizations. The political description in *Power and Conflict in the University* was based on a situation in which there was extremely high conflict. New York University (NYU) was confronted with two crises, a student revolution and a financial disaster. The political model developed from that study probably overstresses the role of conflict, bargaining, and negotiating as elements in standard decision making since those were the processes that were most apparent then. In our current research we have more carefully considered routine procedures as part of the governance process.

Second, our political model, limited to one case study of a unique institution at a unique point in history, certainly did not do justice to the range of contrasting political activity that might occur in different kinds of institutions. Many of the intense political dynamics may have been exaggerated in a huge, troubled institution such as NYU, particularly during the heated conflicts of the late 1960s. Surely NYU is quite different from Oberlin College, for instance, and they are both distinct from a local community college. To meet these criticisms, in the Stanford Project on Academic Governance we surveyed a large random sample of all institutions after most of the campus tensions and discord of the 1960s had passed.

Third, we want to stress even more strongly the central role played by environmental factors. The NYU analysis clearly showed that conflict and political processes were tied to environmental competition from the public universities and to the environmental factors that caused NYU's financial crisis. The Stanford Project on Academic Governance has enlarged its view of the political model by explicitly taking into account these external factors. We carefully studied financial bases, political relationships, university linkages to the state system and religious bodies, and a host of other environmental factors for each institution sampled. In addition, we built a theoretical framework to link internal political processes to the environmental context.

Fourth and finally, the political model developed in *Power and Conflict in the University* suffered from an "episodic" character. That is, the model downplayed long-term patterns of decision processes and neglected the way institutional structure shaped and channeled political efforts. It slighted such things as centralization of power, the growth of decision councils, long-term patterns of professional autonomy, the dynamics of departmental power, and the growth of unionization. Our current research has concentrated more on long-term patterns of decision processes. What groups tend to dominate decision making over long periods of time? Do some groups seem to be systematically excluded from the decision-making process? Do different kinds of institutions have different patterns of political processes? Do institutional characteristics affect the morale of participants so they engage in different kinds of decision-influencing activities? Do different kinds of institutions have systematic patterns of faculty participation in decision making? Are decision processes highly centralized in different kinds of institutions?

In our current research, therefore, we are still asking political questions such as where is the conflict, who participates in it, who influences decisions, how are decision outcomes affected by structure? But three basic readjustments to the political model are being made:

1. *The scope of the model's application has been enlarged.* We are trying to account for the diversity of political processes by taking a large cross-sample of all American colleges and universities.

2. *A strong environmentalist theme has been introduced.* We are explicitly incorporating a discussion of the impact of external factors on the political process.

3. *A concern for long-term decision patterns and structures has been introduced.* We are shifting the focus away from the description of a single decision event.

This political model is not a substitute for the bureaucratic or collegial models of academic decision making. In a very real sense each of those addresses a separate set of problems and they often provide complimentary interpretations. The political model

also has many strengths, however, and we offer it as a strong con-
tender for interpreting academic governance.

Images of Leadership
and Strategies of Management

So far in this chapter we have made two basic arguments:
(1) colleges and universities are unique among institutions in many
of their organizational characteristics, and, as a consequence, it is
necessary to build new models of organizational structure, governance, and decision making; and (2) because of these different
organizational characteristics, it is helpful to add the insights to be
gained from a "political" model to the interpretations offered by
other images. In this last section of the chapter, we will suggest that
these unique characteristics and political processes make it necessary
for us to consider alternative models of leadership and management
approaches.

*Under the bureaucratic model the leader is seen as the hero
who stands at the top of a complex pyramid of power.* The hero's
job is to assess the problems, consider alternatives, and make rational
choices. Much of the organization's power is held by the hero, and
great expectations are raised because people trust him to solve problems and fend off threats from the environment. The imagery of the
authoritarian hero is deeply ingrained in the mentality of most
nations and the philosophy of most organization theorists.

We expect leaders to be technically knowledgeable of their
organizations and uniquely skilled at solving its problems. Often
proposed as tools for accomplishing the latter are such "scientific
management" methods as Planning Programing Budgeting Systems
(PPBS) and Management by Objectives. Generally, schools of
management, business, and educational administration teach such
courses to develop the technical skills that the hero-planner will
need for leading the organization.

Although the hero image is deeply imbedded in our culture's
concepts of leadership, the hero's place in organizations such as
colleges and universities is not at all as all-powerful as many assume
it to be. Power is more diffuse, lodged with professional experts and
fragmented into many departments and subdivisions. Under these

circumstances, high expectations of leadership performance are often disappointed—the leader has neither the power nor the information to consistently make heroic decisions. Moreover, the scientific management procedures prescribed for organizational leaders quickly break down under conditions of goal ambiguity, professional dominance, and environmental vulnerability—the organizational characteristics of colleges and universities. They break down because they are founded on several basic assumptions: (1) that goals are clear; (2) that the organization is a "closed" system insulated from environmental penetration; and (3) that planners have the power to execute their decisions. These assumptions seem unrealistic in the confused and fluid world of university management.

Leadership in the collegial model contrasts strongly with the hero-bureaucrat image. The collegial leader is at most a "first among equals" in an academic organization supposedly run by professional experts. Essentially, this is management according to what John Millett calls the "dynamic of consensus in a community of scholars." The basic idea of the collegial leader is less to command than to listen, less to lead than to gather expert judgments, less to manage than to facilitate, less to order than to persuade and negotiate.

Obviously, the skills needed by a collegial leader differ from the scientific management principles employed by the hero. Instead of technical problem-solving skills, the collegial leader needs both professional expertise to insure high esteem among his colleagues and interpersonal abilities for developing the professional consensus needed to carry out organizational goals. Whereas the hero is always expected to make the decisions and take responsibility for them, the collegial leader is not so much a star standing alone as the developer of consensus among the professionals who must share the burden of the decision. In the university, therefore, expectations are more modest, more realistic, and more widely shared among the organization's members. Clearly, negotiation and compromise rather than authoritarian dictates are the strategies most employed by the collegial leader.

Under the political model, the leader is a mediator, a negotiator, a person who jockeys between power blocs trying to establish viable courses of action for the institution. Such was not always the case. But unlike the autocratic president of the past who ruled with an iron hand, the contemporary academic president must play a more political role, pulling together coalitions to fight for desired changes. The academic monarch of yesteryear has almost vanished, but in his place is not the academic "hero-bureaucrat," as many suggest, but the academic "statesman." Robert Dahl paints an amusing picture of the political maneuvers of Mayor Richard Lee of New Haven and the same description applies to the new academic political leaders: "The mayor was not at the peak of a pyramid but rather at the center of intersecting circles. He rarely commanded. He negotiated, cajoled, exhorted, beguiled, charmed, pressed, appealed, reasoned, promised, insisted, demanded, even threatened, but he most needed support and acquiescence from other leaders who simply could not be commanded. Because the mayor could not command, he had to bargain" (1961, p. 204).

The political interpretation of leadership can be pressed even farther, for the governance of the university more and more comes to look like a "cabinet" form of administration. The key figure today is not the president, the solitary giant, but the political leader surrounded by his staff, the prime minister who gathers the information and expertise to construct policy. It is the "staff," the network of key administrators who actually make most of the critical decisions. The university has become much too complicated to be ruled by any one person, regardless of stature. Cadres of vice-presidents, research men, budget officials, public relations men, and experts of various stripes combine with the leader to reach collective decisions. Expertise becomes more important than ever, and leadership increasingly amounts to the ability to assemble, persuade, and facilitate the activities of knowledgeable experts.

Summary

Colleges and universities are distinctly different from most other kinds of complex organizations. Their goals are more ambiguous and contested, they serve clients instead of working for profit, their technologies are unclear and problematic, and professionals dominate the work force and decision-making process. Thus, colleges and universities are not standard "bureaucracies" but can best be described as "organized anarchies" (see Cohen and March, 1974).

What do the decision and governance processes look like in an institution characterized as an "organized anarchy"? Does the decision process look like a bureaucratic system, with rational problem solving and the application of standard operating procedures? Does it resemble a "collegial" system, in which the professional faculty participate in a "community of scholars"? Or does it appear to be a "political" process, with various interest groups struggling for influence over the setting of organizational policy? A case can be made for each, but we are convinced that policy making in an organization protrayed as an organized anarchy can be best explained by a political model.

If colleges and universities have unique organizational features like organized anarchies, and if their decision processes resemble political dynamics, then we must seriously question the standard images of leadership and management applied to those institutions. Classic leadership theory based on a bureaucratic model suggests the image of the hero and the use of scientific management processes. We suggest that the leadership image should be that of the academic statesman, while the management process should look more like strategic decision making instead of scientific management.

In the coming chapters we will use the political model to analyze academic governance in the United States. First, we will examine material to show how environmental and institutional processes led to the emergence of certain kinds of governance patterns. Later, we will report on the long-term political patterns which are evident in contemporary American higher education.

Chapter 3

Diversity in the
Academic System

An analysis of academic governance in the United States shows the bewildering diversity of institutional patterns. There are many different organizational forms, different sets of environmental pressures, different professional configurations, and different goals in American higher education. There is startling diversity in the range from major universities to community colleges, medical schools to technical schools, institutions with graduate schools to liberal arts colleges without them, massive multiversities to proprietary business schools. It is virtually impossible to make reasonable statements about college institutional patterns that apply universally.

Not only do these institutions have widely differing structures and purposes, but they also widely vary in the degree of professional autonomy they allow their faculties. In some instances, faculties are highly autonomous professionally, determining their own work processes and controlling their own personnel practices. In other situations, faculties are merely hired employees with very little professional autonomy.

Decision processes also vary substantially. Some institutions are dominated by strong presidents. Some have strong faculty and collegial participation. Some allow students a strong voice in the decision-making process. Some are bound by state system regulations and have little decision-making latitude. Some are virtually dominated by the local communities they serve.

These major differences among institutions seem obvious even to the most naive observer. And any adequate understanding of American higher education must take this hodgepodge of situations into account. Nevertheless, most studies of academic governance have been extremely narrow in scope, often ignoring the subject's complexity. Research on academic governance has characteristically fallen into two patterns: (1) case studies of a single institution and its decision-making processes and (2) slightly broader studies based on small, nonrepresentative samples covering only a small segment of higher education. Of course, focusing on a single segment permits one to investigate it in depth. But the richness and depth of the data provided by narrowly focused studies should more often be supplemented by studies based on samples that cover the whole spectrum of American higher education. To obtain this additional scope, the Stanford Project on Academic Governance surveyed the entire higher educational spectrum, from community colleges through elite institutions with graduate schools. We can preview the major conclusions of this chapter in several statements:

1. In spite of many public pronouncements of growing homogeneity, we still believe that the American higher education system is incredibly diverse and perhaps growing even more so. Because of this diversity, we cannot apply a single theory of decision making or management to all situations; instead, we must design unique management strategies for different kinds of institutions.
2. Because institutions are so different we found it necessary to build an institutional typology. We divided the whole spectrum of American higher education into eight types.
3. Three basic organizational characteristics seem to be important in distinguishing colleges and universities: size and complexity,

nature of the academic task, and relationship to the external environment. In this chapter, we define each of these characteristics, show how we measured them, and demonstrate how they systematically vary within the various types of institutions.

4. We believe that differences among colleges in organizational features will make substantial differences in the nature of their governance processes, faculty morale levels, and dominant patterns of policy activities. To put it briefly, each of the different types of institutions was predicted to have a different governance pattern, and the study results verify this prediction.

The Argument that Diversity Has Declined

The assertion that American higher education is extremely diverse and complex is challenged by several contemporary observers and national commissions. These critics suggest that there is now a tendency toward increasing homogeneity. It may be useful to summarize the pros and cons of the argument, since in addition to their theoretical interest they have important *policy implications.*

At least three factors have been identified as promoting more homogeneity in higher education. (1) "institutional imitation," a process by which institutions lower on the academic pecking order try to imitate those above; (2) the shift from private education to public; and (3) the movement into the mainstream of previously unique institutions that have served specialized clienteles, and the opening of their doors to a broader spectrum of students.

Institutional Imitation. In *The Academic Revolution* (1968), Christopher Jencks and David Riesman argue that there is a strong pattern of imitation in higher education. Institutions with less prestige tend to imitate those with more. Community colleges frequently expand their programs to offer a bachelor's degree; four-year colleges expand to offer a master's degree; and colleges with master's degree programs look forward to the day they can offer the doctorate.

Jencks and Reisman suggest that until recently there were many forces promoting diversity in institutions and their clienteles, including religious, political, ethnic, social class, and geographic differences. They believe that today, however, there are strong economic and professional pressures gradually obscuring this diversity. In order to prepare people to enter the economic mainstream, colleges have tended to imitate each other, gradually developing similar programs and similar clienteles. Observing the history of higher education, Jencks and Riesman argue:

> The local college was local first and a college second; the Catholic college was Catholic first and a college second; the Negro college was Negro first and a college second, and so forth. But as time went on these disparate institutions took on lives and purposes of their own. Undergraduates thought of themselves less as future women, Baptists, or teachers and more often simply as students, having a common interest with students in all sorts of places called colleges rather than with girls, Baptists, or teachers who were not students. Similar changes have taken place at the faculty level. Even the college president of today often thinks of himself less as the president of a college in San Jose, a college catering to the rich, or a college for Irish Catholics than as president of an academically first-rate, second-rate, or third-rate college. Such a man's reference group is no longer the traditional clientele and patrons of his institution or the trustees who will speak for them, but the presidents of other colleges, many of which had historically different origins and aims. The result is convergence of aims, methods, and, probably, results [1968, p. 25].

Jencks and Riesman summarize their point by saying, "Our overall feeling is that homogenization is proceeding faster than differentiation" (p. 154).

The Newman Reports (Newman and others, 1971, 1973) agree that because of institutional imitation and other factors, American higher education is growing more homogeneous. The report argues that the options for American students are being closed, that academic programs are growing more similar all the time, and that new students with new interests cannot find a unique home in the increasingly similar American institutions:

American higher education is renowned for its
diversity. Yet, in fact, our colleges and universities have
become extraordinarily similar. Nearly all 2,500 institutions have adopted the same mode of teaching and learning. Nearly all strive to perform the same generalized
educational mission. The traditional sources of differentiation—between public and private, large and small,
secular and sectarian, male and female—are disappearing.
Even the differences in character of individual institutions are fading. It is no longer true that most students
have real choices among differing institutions in which
to seek a higher education. . . . Colleges and universities
are, to be sure, not the only American institutions which
have become homogenized; changes in American society
have dramatically altered the mission, size, and character
of many important institutions. But the growing uniformity of higher education institutions should command
special attention [1971, p. 96].

The Shift from Private to Public. Many observers also argue
that homogeneity may also be promoted by the shift from private
to public institutions. Over the last fifty years there has been a steady
movement of students from the one sector to the other. In 1900 the
majority of students in higher education were enrolled in private
institutions; today about two thirds are enrolled in public institutions. Many observers argue that the diversity of American higher
education is being correspondingly reduced, that the unique programs offered by private institutions are gradually being obliterated,
and that state schools display disconcerting similarity. Thus the shift
toward state dominance of higher education may reinforce the trend
toward homogeneity that institutional imitation has already started.

*The Movement of Distinctive Colleges into the Academic
Mainstream.* In his book *The Demise of Diversity?* (1974),
C. Robert Pace compared a group of people who had graduated
from college in 1950 with a group who had graduated in 1970. He
concluded that the 1970 group had had a more homogeneous education than the 1950 group. He also examined several different
types of colleges and suggested that many of them have lost their
unique character and moved into the mainstream of American

higher education. In particular, he noted that the elite liberal arts colleges and the state colleges have grown less distinctive in their missions and programs.

Some of Pace's findings seem debatable, however. First, his sample totally excluded community colleges, thus eliminating a very diverse student population. Second, he admits that students' *experiences in college* have become more homogeneous, but the *outcomes* in terms of student attitudes and skills have actually become more diverse. It is hard to see how an argument can be made that homogeneity has increased if the outcomes are actually more heterogeneous. Pace suggests that "the case for arguing that there has been a general decline in diversity and distinctiveness does not on the surface appear to be strongly convincing. But beneath the surface there is reason for believing that the case is more convincing" (p. 30). In general, we find the former part of Pace's statement to be more convincing than the latter. It appears that his own data indicate a strong element of complexity and diversity in American higher education.

The Argument That Diversity Has Increased

The argument that educational homogeneity is increasing may seem persuasive to many students of higher education. There is, indeed, much institutional imitation; state institutions are increasingly displacing private ones; and many distinctive types of institutions have now moved into the academic mainstream. In spite of these facts, however, we believe there are strong counter-arguments.

Historical Trends. In the history of higher education, as some institutions have moved up the ladder of academic prestige, other institutions have proliferated below. The widespread growth of community and junior colleges in this country over the last two decades is hardly a sign of increasing homogeneity. In addition, there are many new kinds of technical institutions, expanding education in industrial settings, and an upsurge of proprietary institutions. These developments are simply not consonant with a trend toward educational homogeneity. Thus, in spite of imitation and state control, we believe the differences between institutions are *increasing* rather than decreasing.

It was because of the obvious differences between colleges that the Carnegie Commission on Higher Education felt compelled to commission in-depth studies of unique segments of American academic life. In that effort, Pace (1972) developed a profile of Protestant colleges; Astin and Lee (1972) examined small, private institutions with limited resources, which they called the "invisible colleges"; Bowles and DeCosta (1971) examined Negro higher education; Fein and Webster (1971) examined medical education; Dunham (1969) compiled a profile of state colleges and regional universities; and Greeley (1969) focused on Catholic higher education. To be sure, there were some signs of increased homogeneity (the Catholic colleges, for example, were losing some of their distinctiveness), but on the whole there were plenty of signs of a robust, dynamic, institutional diversity.

Of course, as we enter a period of steady enrollments and diminished resources, the proliferation of new institutions may slow. The thrust toward diversity still seems strong, however, especially in the proprietary institutions and the community colleges. The future *may* bring more homogeneity, as critics are predicting. But the historical trends have moved in the opposite direction.

Diversity Within Institutions. Not only has there been substantial diversity *among* institutions but there has also been a growing diversity *within* institutions. In fact, since the Second World War there has been an astonishing proliferation of technical training efforts, academic subjects, research efforts, and degree-granting programs within institutions. Increased size has been a major factor in this internal differentiation, for a large enrollment makes it possible to support specialized programs. Those who speak of institutional homogeneity have been short-sighted in failing to examine the proliferation of options *within* the multiversity campuses. We do not agree that program and career options have been decreased within institutions. On the contrary, any systematic examination of college catalogs from twenty years ago and today would suggest just the opposite.

International Comparisons. It might also be pertinet to consider the matter from an international point of view. A cursory examination reveals that the American higher educational system is more diverse than any system elsewhere in the world. No other system has so high a percentage of students from such diverse socioeconomic, racial, and academic backgrounds as the United States. No other system approaches the institutional diversity to be found in the American system, with its complex multiversities, state colleges, liberal arts colleges, community colleges, and private junior colleges. No other system has such diverse sources of funding as the American system, which is supported by federal, state, foundation, tuition, and church money combined. In short, by any reasonable measure the American higher educational system is more complex, diverse, and fragmented than any other higher educational system in the world.

The Effects of Public Control. The critics say that more public control over higher educational institutions will lead to more homogeneity, but this is not necessarily true. Surely there is enormous diversity in both the public and the private sector now, and the mere bookkeeping fact that more students are attending publicly supported institutions does not necessarily mean those institutions will exhibit less diversity. *In fact, there is strong reason to suspect that increasing public control may actually lead to more diversity.*

This possibility is very real. The phenomenon of institutional imitation is more apparent in private than in public universities. As state university systems have developed, states have generally tried to formulate policies that enforce some degree of diversity among their public institutions of higher learning. For example, the California Master Plan defines the unique roles of the community colleges, the state colleges and universities, and the University of California system. In other states with strong higher education system management, such as Illinois and Wisconsin, state management has played a central role in promoting diversity among its educational institutions. In many ways too, the state systems are major *promoters* of diversity, because of the greater ability of private institutions to imitate institutions with more prestige.

Of course, we should not be so naive as to believe that state master plans alone are sufficient to enforce diversity. We are well aware that there is great pressure for imitation in state systems— everybody in California wants to be Berkeley and UCLA. And of course, some California state colleges recently changed their names to "universities." But we still believe that state-wide planning efforts help enforce much more diversity than the private sector would have generated. For example, in spite of their strong desire to emulate the University of California system, the huge state colleges in California are still not permitted to offer the doctorate (with one minor exception). Private institutions of similar size and complexity almost universally do—they are able to imitate more readily. In short, we believe the shift to public institutions may not be as disastrous to institutional diversity as most writers suggest.

Factors on Which Diversity Is Measured. One of the biggest problems presented by the literature is a confusion over what factors are being measured. Do the critics mean that higher education has a more *homogeneous clientele* than it once did—that students are drawn from a narrower segment of society? We would hope not, for the student population is clearly more diverse than it has ever been. Do the critics mean that the *programs* offered within institutions have become more homogeneous—that is, more limited? This interpretation would not be supported by a survey of catalogues. Do the critics mean that the *outcomes* of education all seem the same—that graduates now have a narrower range of skills and job opportunities than they once did? Again, this would not be supported by the evidence. Do the critics mean that the *governance patterns* in education have grown similar—that decision-making processes and formal control systems are all alike? Our research and many other studies have clearly demonstrated otherwise.

We do not believe that the system has grown less diverse in any of these ways, or in any other important way that we can identify. Part of the problem seems to be imprecise terminology. For example, some observers such as Jencks and Riesman have pointed to the phenomenon of institutional imitation as evidence of increasing homogeneity. If one looks at the *total* system of higher education, however, it seems apparent that there is a strong proliferation of new institutions as others move up in the system. To say that an *individual institution* has become more like other institutions is not necessarily to say that the *whole system* has become more homogeneous. We believe that this confusion is at the heart of the debate. Certainly we have seen individual institutions change missions in imitation of others. On the whole, however, the system has still retained a remarkably vigorous ability to spawn new institutions and generate new options.

It is important to note that almost everyone entering the debate over diversity has an important policy implication at the back of his mind. Those arguing that the system is becoming more homogeneous may see themselves as the liberal vanguard, demanding more diversity in order to meet the needs of more students, create more job opportunities, and achieve new social goals. They see themselves fighting against an entrenched, conservative academic system that tends to force everyone into a similar academic mold. This point of view is implicit in, for example, the Newman Reports (1971), the Carnegie Commission Studies (1973), and studies by K. Patricia Cross. The cry that the system is becoming more homogeneous is basically a plea for more diversity in order to accommodate more students with new interests and needs—a worthy goal, indeed. Coupled with these concerns is the implicit—and often explicit—call for more federal money to promote that diversity.

In that sense, the complaint that the American system is becoming more homogeneous is primarily a plea for planning, federal money, and suport for the diversity needed to accommodate new students from different racial and socioeconomic backgrounds, and with different job aspirations. In view of these policy goals, we agree with these powerful social critics that increasing diversity is necessary, and it should be supported by whatever means are consonant with academic values.

But we also believe that the supporting argument should be phrased differently. Let us not base the demand for more diversity on the empirically incorrect statement that homogeneity is increasing. Instead, let us argue that historically and internationally, the American educational system has been the most diverse in the world and we should maintain that momentum, even increase it. In other words, "We've got a good thing going—let's support it."

Diversity and Public Policy about Governance. This debate over diversity in higher education is an issue that at first may not seem to have much to do with academic governance. We believe it is critical to it, however. If American higher education has become as homogeneous as many critics would have us believe, then decision-making and policy planning approaches could change substantially, and it becomes theoretically more possible to impose uniform management and decision-making systems on it. For example, a master planner in state government could propose faculty work patterns, evaluation procedures, decision processes, mechanisms of faculty participation, and patterns of student involvement in governance without regard to particular institutional settings and circumstances.

This possibility illustrates a danger in the debate over diversity. Those who argue that the American system has become homogeneous are trying to maximize the opportunities offered for new kinds of students. But their efforts could have the unfortunate side effect of convincing policy planners in state and federal government that homogeneous management and budgetary policies are appropriate for these homogeneous institutions. By placing so much emphasis on the development of homogeneity, many leading critics in the educational field may have unwittingly created an atmosphere in which policy planners can begin to enforce even more homogeneity through their management policies, evaluation systems, and accounting processes.

Diversity and the Conduct of Research. The debate over diversity also has critical research implications. If researchers believe that higher education is homogeneous, they will look for one basic pattern of professional behavior, faculty work patterns, and academic governance. This is, unfortunately, what most researchers have done. On the other hand, if researchers believe that there is broad diversity in higher education, then they will be sensitive to the complexity of their subject and will plan for systematic comparisons across different types of institutions. Because we believe that the system is diverse, we have taken the latter course.

Contemporary Diversity: Establishing a Typology of Institutions

One major task of the Stanford Project on Academic Governance was to establish a meaningful typology that would aid in comparing diverse kinds of institutions. The task was a perplexing one. Where does one draw the line between various kinds of institutions? Obviously, the answer to that question depends on one's interests and the issues that are being explored. One category system makes sense for one purpose; another makes sense for another purpose. We wanted a category system that would serve two functions. First, we wanted to be intuitively meaningful to those who work in American higher education. Second, we wanted it to make theoretical sense to the organizational researcher.

The Carnegie Commission on Higher Education had already established a typology based on the clustering of similar institutional characteristics: size, degree offerings, financial support, aspects of the student body, and prestige of research. The Carnegie typology covers the range of American higher education institutions, from elite multiversities with doctoral programs to small, specialized, proprietary colleges. It is a relatively complex structure, consisting of twelve categories with minor subdivisions and further distinctions between public and private—a total of thirty-two distinct categories (Carnegie Commission on Higher Education, 1973).

In the Stanford Project on Academic Governance we thought that there would be a great advantage in using the Carnegie typology, since adopting this standard would allow comparative work by other researchers. But we found that its complexities and fine nuances did not serve our purpose. We accordingly reduced the twelve Carnegie categories to eight, maintaining the overall outline of the Carnegie typology while reducing its categories to a more manageable number. Every higher educational institution in the United States had been categorized by the Carnegie Commission, and by using their data we could easily determine which of our enlarged categories each institution fitted into. Each category is described as follows:

Private Multiversity. Among the most elite institutions in the country, the Private Multiversities are large, highly prestigious institutions that by the Carnegie definition awarded at least 20 doctor of philosophy (or doctor of medicine if the medical school is on the same campus) degrees and received at least $3 million in federal financial support in 1970–1971. These institutions have an elite faculty with complex research and teaching responsibilities. Their graduate programs are the leading ones in the country, and their extensive research programs are highly regarded. Examples are Cornell, Harvard, Princeton, Stanford, and Yale universities.

Public Multiversity. At the apex of the state systems stand the giant and prestigious Public Multiversities—the Universities of California, Illinois, Michigan, Minnesota, Washington, Wisconsin, and so on. They are extremely large, they receive enormous amounts of federal research money, and they have highly prestigious graduate programs and elite faculties.

Elite Liberal Arts College. In American higher education, there have always been some small private liberal arts colleges that are outstanding, with highly trained faculties and high-quality degree programs. Although they do not receive as much federal research money as the multiversities, they nevertheless are strong scholarship and research centers. Normally they are best known for high-quality bachelor's programs, but most of them offer some master's degrees and even a few doctor's degrees. Examples of institutions in this category are Dartmouth, Reed, Smith, Swarthmore, and Vassar.

Public Comprehensive. We established two categories for the middle-range public institutions. The Public Comprehensives make up the upper part of that middle group. These are the solid, middle-quality state institutions that are to be found throughout the United States. In general, their strong point is their bachelor's program, but almost all of them offer some master's or professional programs, and many offer a few doctor's degrees as well.

Public College. The Public Colleges are among the least prestigious of the public group, less distinguished in faculty quality, student selectivity, and strength of degree programs. Little research is carried out in these institutions, for their chief mission is to provide undergraduate programs for the average American college student. In addition, most of these colleges do offer at least one professional or occupational program such as nursing or teaching. We used this category as a catchall for public institutions above the community college level but not qualifying for the category of Public Comprehensive.

Private Liberal Arts College. The best of the private institutions were included in the category Elite Liberal Arts College, above. Remaining liberal arts colleges offering at least a bachelor's degree were included in a category called Private Liberal Arts College. There are more institutions of this kind in the country than any other.

Community College. Although they are relative newcomers, the public "open-door" Community Colleges are the fastest growing segment of American higher education. These institutions offer associate in arts degrees, with both transfer programs into other colleges and technical programs for terminating students. The funding for these institutions is provided either by local districts or by the state, or by a combination of both. Usually no more than a fourth of the faculty at these institutions have doctorates, and teaching, not research, is their exclusive occupation.

Private Junior College. Once a thriving segment of higher education, in the last few decades these institutions, which offer associate in arts degrees, have been dying out or expanding to offer four-year programs. Most are either church-sponsored institutions serving a church-based clientele, or so-called "finishing schools." The formal training of the faculty in these institutions is the lowest in the whole spectrum of American higher education; about 10 percent have doctorates.

This institutional typology may not be satisfactory to everyone. It is not entirely satisfactory to us. Clearly, where to categorize any particular institution often becomes a problem. There are borderline cases. There are situations where the data are not clear. The line might be drawn slightly differently and several institutions recategorized. Still, the distinctions we make are certainly not arbitrary, and it is surprising how different schemes—of which we developed several—come out with essentially similar placements for institutions. And, on the positive side, this eight-segment breakdown has several virtues. First, it is *intuitively meaningful*. Most people would recognize these institutional types and generally feel that the major segments of American higher education have been covered adequately. Second, there are relatively *few categories*. Eight might be a rather large number to work with in some respects, but that is substantially better than the huge number the Carnegie Commission originally specified. Finally, the most important virtue is the scheme's *theoretical importance* for our organizational theory interests—a topic that deserves a little more discussion in the next section.

Basic Diversity: Some Measures

We believe the differences among institutions in the various categories are substantial. We believe they have not all become alike, as many people claim. Of course, this is a matter of perspective.

Whether a glass is half full or half empty depends on the viewer's concern, not the glass. Whether colleges in these categories are significantly different is a question of judgment and perspective. We believe they are really different.

What organizational features are most important in influencing the diverse patterns that emerge in these various institutions? The potential list is long, but three features stand out as particularly important. First, we must understand the *environment* in which an institution exists. The environmental context of financial support, formal control, and relations with other social institutions is an extremely important determinant of institutional decision-making processes. Second, the nature of the *professional task* often shapes the degree of professional autonomy. Institutions with a limited range of tasks, such as colleges that concentrate on undergraduate teaching, have professional work patterns and governance processes that differ radically from institutions with an extremely diverse and complicated range of tasks. Third, the *size* and administrative *complexity* of an institution greatly affect its patterns of activity. Small, homogeneous colleges have governance and professional work patterns significantly different from those of huge multiversities.

Are the eight types of institutions identified above really diverse in their environmental relations, professional task, and complexity? Or are they, as so many have insisted, really homogeneous? We believe the facts clearly support the diversity argument. Tables 1 and 2 show scores for different types of institutions on a wide variety of institutional characteristics, derived from the College Entrance Examination Board's data files and from a national survey of faculty we conducted in 1971. Let us look briefly at these differences.

Environmental Relations. It is increasingly obvious that many of the most critical decisions for colleges and universities around the nation are being made outside the institutions themselves—in Congress, the governor's office, the state system office, the foundation director's office, to name only a few of the powerful external forces impinging on the academic community from all sides. The student revolution and subsequent public reaction in the mid 1960s weakened the fabric of many academic institutions. The financial crises and faculty unions of the 1970s raised new challenges. Growing state higher education networks are currently looming large on the environmental horizon. In short, any useful study of higher education today must take environmental factors into account.

It is obvious from an examination of Table 1 that the different types of institutions in the Stanford typology vary systematically in most of these environmental variables. When we examine *funding sources,* we find a systematic variation in different types of institutions. First, there is a fairly sharp distinction between public and private institutions, as might be expected. In general, public institutions get somewhat over half their funds from the state, while private institutions depend much more on tuition and foundation money. The private multiversities are almost unique in their dependence on federal research money. Only a handful of institutions receive much support from the churches, even among those that are formally associated with religious denominations. In general, the funding pattern is just as one might expect: private institutions obtain most of their funds from tuition, and state institutions obtain most of theirs from the state. Federal research money goes primarily to the elite multiversities.

In general, the institutions at the upper end of the typology obtain their funds from a *wider variety* of sources (they have a higher "Varied Sources" rating), they are more affluent, they pay their faculties better, and they are more selective in their student admissions. They vary considerably in age and endowment, the private multiversities and elite liberal arts colleges being the oldest and most heavily endowed. All of these different characteristics have been drawn together in the combined factor "institutional heritage."

Finally, the last column in Table 1 shows the External/Internal Influence Ratio, a measure of the influence of outsiders versus that of insiders. This measure is a scale constructed from several questions on our faculty questionnaire. A higher score indicates more external influence. In general, the figures in this column suggest two patterns: (1) state-related institutions are subject to more outside influence than others; and (2) institutions at the lower end of the typology are subject to more outside influence than those at the

Table 1. Environmental Characteristics: Breakdown by Institutional Types.

	N	Funding Sources									Institutional Heritage				External/Internal Influence Ratio
		State Money	Public/Private	Tuition Money	"Varied Sources" of Funding[a]	Federal Research Money	Endowment	Local Money	Church Money	Foundation Money	Affluence: $ per Student	AAUP Mean Salary ($1,000s)	Student Selectivity Scale[b]	Age of Institution	External/Internal Influence Ratio
All 300 Institutions		31%		41%	.10	1.9%	3.5%	9.5%	3.4%	1.4%	2,428	11.0	2.6	60	.62
Private Multiversity	6	2	PRI	35	1.00	27.0	21.0	.2	2.5	6.1	9,997	15.0	4.5	142	.54
Public Multiversity	13	51	PUB	21	.70	10.0	2.3	.3	0	1.6	4,914	13.2	3.8	101	.68
Elite Liberal Arts	25	1	PRI	70	.30	2.1	13.5	0	1.4	2.5	4,907	11.8	4.5	104	.49
Public Comprehensive	40	65	PUB	26	.27	1.5	.8	1.7	.1	.1	2,530	11.1	2.9	69	.66
Public College	16	76	PUB	20	.18	1.3	.3	.1	0	.3	3,273	11.7	3.6	55	.52
Private Liberal Arts	85	1	PRI	63	.09	.3	4.8	.2	7.2	3.1	2,894	9.8	3.1	74	.61
Community Colleges	96	50	PUB	15	.02	.9	.4	28.5	.3	0	1,771	11.5	1.3	24	.68
Private Junior College	19	1	PRI	68	.00	.7	4.1	0	16.6	1.0	2,183	8.4	2.6	64	.65

[a] 0 = highly concentrated funding sources, 1 = extreme variety in funding sources.
[b] Student Selectivity Scale; The College Entrance Examination Board's rating; the higher the score the more selectivity.

higher end. Once again we find that the environmental characteristics vary systematically by the different types of institutions.

Characteristics of the Professional Task. We assume that one
of the critical differences among higher educational institutions is
the nature of their professional tasks. In the academic world there
are many different professional tasks, including teaching, research,
and community service, among others. This makes it difficult to
measure the totality of activity in a college or university. In general,
however, it can be measured by the number of academic degree
programs offered and the breadth of professional qualifications
among the faculty. Clearly, this is not the only way to classify the
different tasks of a college or university, but it is an appropriate and
significant one. Institutions that offer doctoral programs and have
a very high percentage of faculty members with doctoral degrees
are generally carrying out complex research, graduate training, and
policy analysis as well as undergraduate teaching. At the other
extreme, community colleges offering associate in arts degrees generally have an entirely different activity pattern, one confined almost
exclusively to undergraduate teaching.

Different types of institutions vary systematically in professional tasks they are involved in, as Table 2 shows. The institutions at the upper end of the typology offer doctoral degrees; over
three fourths of their faculty members have a doctoral degree; their
entering freshman students have extremely high Scholastic Aptitude
test (SAT) scores; and their faculties have high publication rates.
Those at the lower end of the typology—the Community Colleges and
Private Junior Colleges—offer only the associate in arts degree; few
of their faculty members have a doctoral degree; their students have
the lowest SAT scores; and there is very little publication by their
faculties. Between these two extremes, the complexity of the professional task usually increases with every step up the typology.
There is a strong correlation between an institution's place in the
typology and its requirements for professional expertise (see professional task expertise indicators in Table 2).

Institutional Size and Complexity. Organization theorists in
recent years have intensively studied the impact of an organization's
size on its decision making processes and structural features (see
Blau, 1973; Boland, 1971). It is now well established that the

Table 2. Some Characteristics of Different Types of Institutions.

| | | | Professional Task Expertise | | | | | Institutional Size and Complexity | | | | |
	N	Highest Degree Offered[a]	Faculty with Ph.D.	Combined Student SAT Scores	Faculty with Published Book	Faculty with Published Article	Number of Faculty	Number of Students	Number of Departments	Number of Schools and Colleges	Number of Structural Units
All 300 Institutions	300	2.0	39%	929	16%	12%	193	3,010	21	7	27
Private Multiversity	6	4.0	82	1223	48	49	1248	11,710	61	9	60
Public Multiversity	13	4.0	77	1010	33	38	1110	17,920	65	10	82
Elite Liberal Arts	25	2.7	69	1185	26	18	143	1,880	22	5	23
Public Comprehensive	40	3.0	53	917	19	13	272	5,100	25	5	31
Public College	16	2.6	55	999	20	13	204	2,220	20	3	19
Private Liberal Arts	85	2.2	44	937	15	12	84	1,130	17	3	17
Community College	96	1.0	15	828	10	5	111	2,200	17	0	30
Private Junior College	19	1.0	12	889	61	7	39	600	9	0	7

[a] 1 = A.A.; 2 = B.A.; 3 = M.A.; 4 = Ph.D.

larger an organization is, the more complex its decision-making processes and departmental and administrative structures are likely to be. Size and complexity greatly affect the amount of decentralization in an organization, the degree of conflict between subunits, the development of complex decision-making networks, and other aspects of its decision-making processes.

This is borne out by the data in Table 2. In general, institutions at the higher end of the typology are larger, though the Elite Liberal Arts Colleges tend to be somewhat smaller than the public institutions just below them. Aside from that one exception, there is a strong correlation between an institution's place in the typology and its size and complexity.

Summary

Not only are academic organizations different from other organizations but they are different from each other—especially on the three key factors of *environmental relations, professional task,* and *size/complexity.* Some institutions are heavily dependent on their environments while others have a great deal of autonomy. Some have relatively simple tasks while others grapple with a kaleidoscope of objectives. Some are small and simple while others are massive and complex.

Because of the huge differences, it is necessary to study academic organizations in meaningful groups rather than in one massive block. We believe—contrary to many current writers—that the American system is extremely complex and diverse and that governance processes are, and should be, different. This is why, though we have simplified the complex Carnegie Commission typology, we have still provided for eight institutional types.

We have found that institutions categorized according to the Stanford Project's typology vary systematically on the three basic organizational characteristics we have identified—environmental relations, professional task, and size/complexity. This regularity simplifies much of our task of presenting data analysis in this book. As we begin to make predictions about how organizational characteristics will affect governance, we can generally simplify matters by showing the relation between the *typology* and governance pat-

terns, instead of having to take each of the organizational characteristics individually. From time to time we will look at individual
variables to clarify details, but generally the major story is told
when we examine governance patterns within each institutional
category.

It is important to understand that these organizational features
have a direct impact on governance patterns. In general, we find
high faculty autonomy and decision participation in institutions that
are independent of their environment, have complex professionalized
tasks, and are large in size. At the other pole we find virtual administrative and/or trustee dominance in small, less complex institutions
that are highly dependent on their environment. American higher
education has not one but many patterns of governance and management. The remainder of this book essentially is devoted to explaining this complex diversity.

Chapter 4

Patterns of
Management and
Governance

Most people have a very simplistic notion of how organizations are managed. There is a widespread belief that organizations are simple bureaucracies characterized by neat pyramidal hierarchies with the president at the top, clear "chains of command," and careful patterns of formal communication. People higher on the organizational hierarchy are assumed to be the bosses of the people under them in the chain of command. People at the top perform long-range planning and budget management and the people down the line execute those decisions. This view of the organizational world is common, and in some situations is fairly accurate. Military organizations and routine government bureaucracies such as the Postal Service probably come fairly close to operating in this fashion.

The management of colleges and universities, however, is not nearly so neat and simple. The previous chapter suggested there is a subtle mix of bureaucratic factors, collegial and professional influences, and political dynamics at work in academic institutions. These confusing organizational situations—"organized anarchies" as Cohen and March call them—are much more complex in their management than simple theories of bureaucracy can describe. March has playfully suggested that the management of educational organizations is like a crazy, untraditional soccer match: "Imagine that you're either the referee, coach, player or spectator at an unconventional soccer match: the field for the game is round; there are several goals scattered haphazardly around the circular field; people can enter or leave the game whenever they want to; they can throw the balls in whenever they want to; they can say 'that's my goal' whenever they want to, as many times as they want to, and for as many goals as they want to; the entire game takes place on a sloped field; and the game is played as if it makes sense" (quoted by Weick, 1976, p. 2).

In some respects these academic organizations are very similar to other bureaucracies. They have officials who go about their organizational business just like other bureaucrats. And sometimes, on some issues, under some circumstances, there are fairly clear chains of command. At other times, however, the collegial processes loom very large. Faculty committees meet and haggle, superstar professors demand and get special privileges, and the professional experts hold most of the winning cards. At other times the political processes take over, and interest groups pressure and jockey for power. In addition, there are many different actors involved in the process: faculty members, trustees, students, administrators, legislative committees, and state officials. The management picture is much more complex than a simple bureaucratic model suggests.

The first chapter of this book outlined several theoretical models of academic governance. This chapter will explore some of the complex processes involved in the governance of colleges and universities. In doing so, it will also show some patterns of governance that showed up in our research.

Power Fragmentation

We wanted to chart the patterns of decision-making power in different institutional settings. On our questionnaire, therefore, we asked this question: "On a scale from one to five, rate the influence of departmental faculties, department heads, college-wide faculty committees, deans, presidents, and trustees in the following situations: (1) appointment of a faculty member, (2) selection of a new department head, (3) long-range institutional planning, (4) general or 'global' influence." The results of the national survey are given in Table 3. What did we learn from these ratings of influence?

For one thing, we found that influence patterns in colleges and universities differ by internal level; there are different issues and different decision processes at the departmental level, at the college level, and at the university level. Groups in colleges and universities generally carve out "spheres of influence" for themselves and thus sometimes avoid conflict. The faculty claims primary influence over such issues as curriculum and degree requirements; the administration claims matters such as budgets, long-range planning, and building programs. In other words, everybody does not try to control everything. In the complex process of university politics, much conflict is avoided simply by dividing up influence over specific issues among different groups.

The spheres of influence claimed by different groups show up clearly in Table 3. Instead of one dominant power elite there seems to be a fragmented system of influence. *Trustees* heavily influence long-range and budgetary planning, and have considerable "global" influence. The *central administration's* influence is strongest in long-range planning and the "global," area, and is much less weighty in curricular and personnel matters. *Deans* seem to have a remarkable range of power and influence, with quite high influence ratings on almost all issues and the highest on faculty appointments. Deans are obviously the links between faculty and central administrations. This central, key position gives deans an enormous amount of power but also subjects them to a great deal of political pressure.

Table 3. "Spheres of Influence" Ratings of Influence of Certain People/Groups Over Different Issues.

			Issues		
Groups/People	Curriculum Development	Faculty Appointment	Selection of Department Head	Long-Range Planning	"Global" or General Influence
1. Department Faculty and Committees	4.2	2.8	3.1	2.5	2.2
2. Department Heads	3.9	3.9	2.4	3.0	2.6
3. College-Wide Faculty Committees	3.1	2.3	1.8	3.5	3.5
4. Deans	3.2	4.1	3.8	3.8	3.6
5. President and Staff	2.1	2.2	2.6	4.5	3.7
6. Trustees	1.2	1.4	1.2	4.0	3.1

Note: On a scale of 1 to 5, 1 is low and 5 is high.

Faculty and *departmental* influence, on the other hand, is primarily over matters that most intimately concern professional duties: curriculum, faculty appointments, and the selection of department heads.

The overall pattern suggests that power is highly "issue specific." Different groups carve out spheres of influence around the issues that are most germane to their professional concerns. The confusing soccer game that James March used as an analogy seems to have different mini-games occurring on that sloped playing field. It is no wonder that traditional bureaucratic models, with their neat hierarchies of power, fail to describe the buzzing, booming confusion of academic decision making.

There are several problems in discussing spheres of influence. First, a survey such as this is able to describe how people think influence is distributed, but their perceptions may or may not be accurate. Moreover, the survey shows how people think influence is arranged but not necessarily how it ought to be distributed. The configuration of influence that is thought to exist is not necessarily the most efficient or the most politically fair arrangement. Nor does the distribution shown in the survey remain stable. As events change, spheres of influence change. In fact, later in this chapter we will discuss changes we saw in the case studies which might result in a redistribution of spheres of influence. Most importantly, spheres of influence look different in different types of institutions—a point we will also discuss later.

Power is not necessarily divided *equally* among the different spheres of influence in academic organizations. Obviously, some people have more influence than others. Both our survey and our case studies showed that administrators have enormous influence over a wide variety of issues. Presidents have enormous power, and their ratings of "global" influence is consistently high. The campus interviews suggested that presidents had even more power than our survey results would lead us to believe. Deans also were considered very powerful. The influence of deans is probably the broadest spectrum of any. Moreover, those high ratings for deans and presidents remained constant regardless of type of institution.

In some institutions the administrators were virtually dominant in the decision-making process. Administrative influence was extremely high in nonelite Liberal Arts Colleges, Community Colleges, and Private Junior Colleges. Our research team vividly recalls an interview with a senior faculty man at a small liberal arts college. His name and institution shall remain anonymous, for obvious reasons: "That 'spheres of influence' idea you guys have discussed with me is a pretty good notion. But don't get carried away with it. On this campus the administrators pretty well dominate the process. You want to talk about budgets—then you better talk about the administrators. You want to talk about faculty raises and money—then you better talk about the administrators. You want to talk about expanding or cutting back on an academic department—you have to talk about administrators. You want to talk about relations to the outside world or a new building or a special curriculum project—then you damn well better talk to the administrators. In fact, as I think about it, this college (and most others like it) are run by what I call PPT's—petty pissant tyrants. Administrators run this place!"

This view is rather harsh, and did not represent the majority of the faculty we talked to. In fact, most faculty nationally expressed fairly high confidence in their administrators. (An extended discussion of this subject can be found in Chapter 6.) Nevertheless, the feeling that administrators dominate the process is certainly consistent with many of our interviews. Presidents, in particular, were felt to have enormous influence at smaller institutions, and at many of the nonelite state colleges.

Faculty Role in Academic Governance

What is the faculty's role in the decision-making and governance processes of higher education? This matter has been much debated. Groups such as the American Association of University Professors (AAUP) have long stressed the need for collegial decision making and for full faculty participation. In many ways, these are merely statements of who *ought* to have power. However, we felt that our research team's job was not to join the debates over who should have power but to try to determine as clearly as possible how much influence the faculty actually has. Some of our conclusions are outlined in the following sections.

This discussion is aptly led off by a quote from Robert Dahl: "It would clear the air of a good deal of cant if instead of assuming that politics is a normal and natural concern for human beings, one were to make the contrary assumption that whatever lip service citizens may pay to platitudes, politics is a remote, alien, and unrewarding activity" (1961, p. 279).

Dahl, a political scientist, had in mind citizen participation in local governments but might just as well have been talking about university professors. The constant discussion of faculty involvement in decision making masks an important point. Most faculty are really interested in teaching and research, and would just as soon leave the administration of the institution to the administrators. On our questionnaire we asked the following question: "Some people are simply not interested in academic 'politics' to any serious extent. These people prefer to do their teaching and research and leave the policy activities to the administrators and other faculty members. Of course, such a person does do a minimum amount of committee work and does participate to some degree in the department's activities. But by and large, such a person simply does not get heavily involved in institutional decision making. *Is this a fairly good description of your behavior?*"

Fifty-four percent of the faculty agreed that this was a good characterization of their behavior. In the political processes of the university, like those in the larger society, many people simply are not involved, and do not want to be. For the most part, the dominant governance pattern among American college and university faculty members is *lack* of participation.

If many people are inactive and apathetic about governance processes, who *does* run the institution? Obviously the administrators do most of the decision making. But small groups of faculty also are involved in the process. Like most organizations, there is a decision-making elite—the senior professors, the department chairmen, and a handful of "faculty politicians" who get deeply involved. Our questionnaire tried to discover who these faculty politicians were by asking the following question: "Some people undertake more policy-making activities and serve on a great many committees. They see this as an interesting, important function that they really must do. These people take more than their share of committee assignments and actively work to influence policy decisions in the college or university. *Would you say that you engage in this kind of activity?"*

Eighteen percent of the faculty said they "frequently" participated in this manner; they would probably characterize themselves as academic politicians. We did a statistical analysis of that 18 percent.

Who are the faculty heavily involved in the policy-influencing activities? Are they younger or older, tenured or non-tenured, men or women? As shown in Table 4, we found that the marginal members of the academic community, the instructors and lecturers, are the least active within *formal* channels, and the least likely to take committee leadership. This makes sense, because their lack of professorial rank excludes these individuals from many formal avenues of participation. Perhaps for the same reason, professors are more active than associate professors, who are in turn, more active than assistant professors. It appears that increased rank brings a requirement for active formal participation in institutional affairs. Thus we are not surprised to see that men, who generally outrank women, are more active than women. Formal participation also appears to increase with higher earned degrees, so again, the "senior" people dominate decision making. There are also minor differences by subject matter specialization, with social scientists and humanists reporting the highest "formal" participation, the lowest "inactive" level, and the highest rate of committee leadership.

In short, we find a small, strong "power elite" among the faculty and a mass of inactive people who are not involved. In this respect, colleges and universities are like most other organizations. Long ago, Robert Michels advanced the theory of the "iron law of oligarchy," which suggests that all organizations develop active elites while the masses remain inactive. Michels' study of European socialist parties showed that elites inevitably arose even in these supposedly model democratic organizations. Michels commented, "the appearance of oligarchical phenomena in the very bosom of the revolutionary parties is a conclusive proof of the existence of imminent oligarchical tendencies in every kind of human organization" (1915, in 1949 reprint, p. 14). The political scientist James Bryce said it in even more sweeping terms: "In all assemblies and

Table 4. Faculty Participation in Governance.

		Inactive[a]	Much formal Involvement[b]	Led Faculty Committee	"Strategic" Activity[c]	Urge Collective Negotiation
I.	Rank					
	Professor	44	27	61	28	27
	Associate Professor	49	19	55	31	33
	Assistant Professor	60	12	44	27	36
	Lecturer/Instructor	70	7	28	20	44
	2 year Ranks	56	21	50	35	54
II.	Sex					
	Male	52	19	52	29	25
	Female	59	13	43	28	37
III.	Degree Earned					
	Masters	57	16	46	31	43
	Professional	58	21	44	23	29
	Doctorate	50	20	55	27	30
IV.	Subject Areas					
	Humanities	51	18	52	38	40
	Natural Sciences	55	17	44	23	31
	Social Sciences	51	20	58	30	36
	Professional	54	17	52	22	30
	Vocational/Technical	57	18	42	29	44
V.	National Average	54	18	50	28	29

[a] *Inactive*—minimal participation in committees, department activities, or associations.
[b] *Much Formal Involvement*—heavy involvement in governance, committees, and "institutional politics." Percent of people answering "frequently."
[c] *"Strategic" Activity*—little formal participation, but work in "outside" channels such as AAUP or unions. Includes percent of faculty answering "frequently" or "sometimes."

groups and organized bodies of men, from a nation down to the committee of a club, directions and decisions rest in the hands of a small percentage, less and less in proportion to the larger and larger size of the body, till in a great population it becomes an infinitesimally small proportion of the number. This is and always has been true of all forms of government" (1921, p. 542).

So far, we have discussed two types of faculty activity. Most people are inactive and simply do the minimal amount of committee work in their departments. Another small group, composing less than one fifth of the faculty, is a "power elite" of senior people who participate heavily in "formal" activities such as committee member-ships and academic senate deliberations. There is a third style of activity, which we call "strategic." The survey question pertaining to this read: "Sometimes people work in faculty organizations out-side the formal committee system, such as the AAUP, faculty unions, etc. (Incidentally, we are not talking about professional associa-tions, but about organizations which are directly influencing local policy decisions within the college.) *How often do you engage in this type of activity: frequently, sometimes, rarely?*"

We also tried to determine the willingness of faculty to go outside regular channels to use unions for influencing institutional policy. Our question here was: "Do you agree that collective negotiations are one of the best ways for the faculty to deal with the administration?"

The responses to these two questions indicate that roughly one fourth of the faculty engage in activities outside regular channels of influence, and 28 percent of the faculty report they "sometimes" or "regularly" work with unions or other organizations to influence policy. About the same percentage (29 percent) urges collective bargaining as an appropriate strategy for dealing with the administration.

Who is it that seeks influence through these faculty organiza-tions outside regular channels? Our guess is that it is the people who are excluded from the normal channels but who chose not to become inactive. Table 6 shows that people who are low on "formal" in-volvement tend to be higher on "strategic" activities, and vice versa. The difference shows up most vividly when we compare people in different academic ranks. Under the two columns dealing with "formal" and "strategic" involvement, we see a clear pattern: formal activities go *down* as rank goes down; but "strategic" activity goes *up* as rank goes down. The evidence is fairly persuasive: most people who participate in unions are probably outside the formal system; the power elite in the formal system has very little need for unions. If you examine the column on "urging collective negotiations" in Table 4, the difference between faculty ranks is particularly sharp. Each successive step down the ranks from full professor shows a marked *increase* in favorable sentiment toward unions.

Incidentally, the way we asked our questions probably confused the results somewhat. We combined "participation in unions" with "participation in the AAUP." Later we realized that, since the AAUP tends to be a senior faculty club, this probably obscured the differences between ranks. If we had asked only about unions we probably would have gotten an even sharper difference between the senior and junior faculty. Independent information from surveys taken in 1976 show the percentage of people favoring unions to be much higher in that year than is shown in the 1971 data. However, the evidence suggests that the *relative* distribution is about the same; everybody favors unions at a higher rate, but assistant professors still favor them more than associate professors, and associates more than full professors. The same is true for college differences. Everywhere, the 1977 percentages show more faculty in favor of collective bargaining than in 1971. But the *relative difference* between community colleges and elite multiversities, for example, is still about the same, with the community colleges having double the rate of the multiversities. When examining our data on unions, then, the reader must be aware that the *absolute* percentages are much higher today, but that the *relative* differences between groups and institutions remain about the same.

Academic Senates: "Tinkertoys" or Powerful Influences?

We have been discussing the variety of ways in which the faculty participate in decision making and governance. On most campuses the real faculty influence occurs in the department, an issue we will discuss at length in Chapter 5. However, the average campus also has an all-campus organization, typically known as the academic senate or academic forum. These organizations vary amazingly. Some include faculty only, others are a mixture of administrators and faculty, and still others include students and support staff. There has been a continuing discussion in higher education about the effectiveness of academic senates. Some people believe they are powerful, others believe they are shams. The chairman of the academic senate in one of our case studies made the following observation: "Sometimes I wonder why in the world I waste my time working on the academic senate. We hold dozens of meetings, most of which never have a quorum. When we do have a quorum, we rubber stamp some administrative initiative. The committees report, but usually it has taken so long to 'study the issue' that the matter is long past! Our academic senate is basically a tinkertoy, a make-believe world that allows faculty politicians to make speeches and pretend that they are doing something significant. And in the meantime, the real activity goes on in the departments. Or else, the administrators just run the place. Important decisions can't wait for faculty games."

We examined these senates rather carefully in all of our studies. On both the 1971 and 1974 surveys we incorporated questions about senates, and in developing our seven case studies we interviewed people about the effectiveness of senates. Our basic conclusion is that senates have many problems, and on most campuses are ineffective and weak.

The problems of senates can be seen in a few simple facts. Most campuses included in our study have senates, though nearly 75 percent of those at two-year institutions are reported as eight years old or less. On the other hand, only 25 percent of public and private multiversities reported recently forming a senate, so senates at those institutions have most likely been there quite a while. Overall, the less prestigious the institutions, especially if it is unionized, the less likely it is to have a faculty representative senate. The significance of all this is that the absence of a strong tradition of this kind of faculty participation in governance may promote the growth of faculty collective bargaining; this seems to be the case at two-year and less prestigious four-year public colleges we surveyed.

The survey results showed that the faculty senate no longer represents only the faculty at a majority of institutions. Over 60 percent of those institutions with senates include administrative representation in them, nearly 50 percent have student representation, and almost a third have nonacademic staff representation. Our interviews also suggest that broad-based senates expend much of their energy on campus-wide problems, with faculty interests ceasing to be a primary concern.

Senates operate on delegated authority and depend on institutional appropriations and staffing. Because faculty senates are dependent bodies, their power to affect decision making is granted by the grace of the governing board and the administration. Historically, the elite, high prestige institutions have encouraged faculty input in decision making and consequently are more likely to preserve the influence of faculty senates. But younger senates may find environmental pressures reducing their role in shared governance. A spokesman active in senate affairs at Central Michigan University has noted, "We became aware that we enjoyed the benefits of our hard-won battles purely at the pleasure of the board of trustees." Senates are therefore susceptible to being labelled "company unions." In addition, since administrators are often included in senate membership, senates are not really representative of the faculty as faculty.

Let us turn now to the question of actual senate influence in academic governance. Our 1974 survey asked presidents of institutions to rate the influence of their senate on several issues. It must be pointed out that campus presidents are likely to rate a senate's influence higher than it really is. Hodgkinson, for example, concluded from his study of broadly representative senates that "administrators by and large are more euphoric about the performance and potential of campus senates than those who are directly involved in these bodies on a daily and weekly basis" (1974, p. 194). In any case, according to the perceptions of the respondents in our study, senates at unionized campuses are heavily involved in academic areas. The highest ratings presidents gave senates are over issues of degree requirements and curriculum. Issues concerning faculty promotion are also reported as strongly influenced by senates at all types of institutions except two-year colleges, which tend to follow the secondary school model of school administration. In economic areas such as faculty salaries, department budgets, and faculty workload, senates were given far lower ratings. A similar pattern was evident for senates at institutions which are part of a state system of higher education.

For years the lack of real decision-making power by senates over economic issues, and over personnel policy at public two-year institutions, has caused many academicians to consider senates ineffective. In 1969 the Carnegie survey asked respondents to indicate the effectiveness of their senates; 60 percent of the 60,000 respondents answered "fair" or "poor" (Carnegie, pp. 98–99). In Hodgkinson's 1974 study of 688 broad-based senates, campus presidents most frequently rated the influence of the senate in campus affairs as "advisory," with the second most frequently mentioned role being "no responsibility at all." Hodgkinson also found that instead of "shared governance" the presidents stressed a senate's value to faculty members as its offering "the possibility of access" to decision-making channels (pp. 29 and 136).

These reservations particularly apply to the institutions where unionization has generally occurred—the community colleges, state colleges, and some less prestigious liberal arts institutions. Because these institutions rarely had effective faculty governance, it is difficult to determine how much unions have affected the process.

In light of these problems, we frankly believe the importance of senates has been overstressed in the literature on academic governance. It is very doubtful indeed that the senates at most institutions deal effectively with matters of real substance. The critical issues are generally handled by the faculty at the departmental level (curriculum, student relations, faculty hiring, firing, and promoting) or by the administration at other levels (budgets, overall staffing, physical plant, long-range planning). The average academic senate, we suspect, deals with relatively minor issues, and more readily responds to administrative than faculty leadership.

The Clash Between Unions and Senates

When a campus has both a senate and a union, what areas of decision and policy does each influence? What are the factors that promote or diminish conflict between senates and unions? Since unions have usually emerged on campuses with weak senates, we cannot predict what may happen to healthier senates in institutions with a long history of faculty governance. We are cautious, therefore, in projecting our conclusions much beyond the colleges and universities with weak senates, where unionization has occurred. The results may be entirely different if unionization comes to the prestigious colleges and universities. These words of caution are not meant to downgrade the importance of union-senate interaction but to be realistic; public discussions of senates and union impact on them probably overstress the issue.

Our 1974 survey asked people on unionized campuses to rate union and senate influence over a broad spectrum of issues. Figure 1 suggests a number of conclusions. Presidents and union chairpersons are basically similar in their assessments of influence. They agree that unions strongly outperform senates in influencing economic issues, particularly faculty salaries, promotions, and working conditions. Meanwhile, senates retain influence over academic issues such as degree requirements and curriculum. Senates and unions share a joint area of influence over personnel issues such as faculty hiring, promotion, and tenure policy. Neither senates nor unions influence department budgets or long-range planning. It is interesting to note that there is little difference on all these issues between single-campus unions and multicampus unions, or between two-year and four-year institutions.

Our survey results suggest that both presidents and union chairpersons believe senates and unions have staked out fairly unique territories. That is, senates are reported to have their greatest influence in academic areas, while economic matters are the province of unions. Where the lines of demarcation are unclear, such as in faculty working conditions and long-range planning, the union and senate converge on degrees of influence.

These findings more or less support an AAUP argument. The AAUP has argued that unions and senates should have separate areas of influence—the so-called "dual track" theory of bargaining. Dual track bargaining assumes two mutually exclusive areas of influence for senates and unions. The reactions of both presidents and chairpersons to our questionnaire were fairly consonant with dual track model predictions of influence areas. One qualification must be made, however, for much union and senate influence overlaps. At one end of the continuum, economic issues, influence lies far

Figure 1.

Ratings by Presidents:

Influence of Senates and Unions over Various Issues.

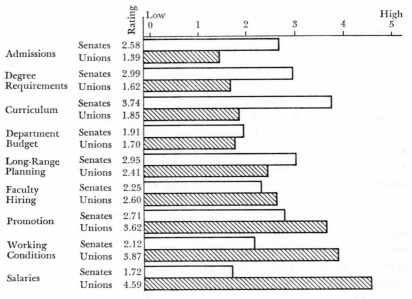

Note: Only unionized institutions included.

more with the union. With their legal backing and their legal right to economic information, unions undoubtedly have more power than senates to gain economic objectives. At the other end of the continuum—academic issues such as curriculum and degree requirements—the senate is far more influential. Between the two poles is a grey area where unions and senates share influence over department budgets, hiring policies, faculty promotion and tenure policies, faculty working conditions (student-teacher ratio, class load), and long-range planning. In most cases, the dual track model leaves *procedural* issues to the union but reserves policy affecting the *substance* of decisions to the senate.

There are, however, a number of serious threats to the stability of dual track bargaining. If the areas of senate and union influence remain stable, then dual track bargaining will continue as described. Many factors could cause a breakdown of the dual track, however, and encourage unions to expand into senate territory. Collective bargaining is a competitive political process. In order to maintain membership support, union leaders will necessarily press to expand the scope of bargaining. Who is to decide which issues belong to the senate or to the union? Furthermore, over a period of time even the difficulty of drawing fine lines of distinction between issues could create instability in the dual track system.

Several facts suggest that this breakdown in dual track bargaining and expansion of union influence is already occurring. Contracts negotiated by unions are one indicator of this trend. Research by John Andres (1974) shows that these contracts have essentially dealt with "working conditions"—workload, salaries, class size, and sometimes the selection of administrators. With each passing year, however, they are containing more items that were once the province of senates, such as teaching load, governance issues, and matters related to faculty bylaws and policies. There is a "creeping expansion" of union areas of influence.

Similarly, our survey found presidents and chairpersons predicting a bleak future for senates and expanding roles for unions. We asked people to agree or disagree with this statement: "Where it occurs, faculty collective bargaining will determine the influence of faculty senate or other established decision bodies." The presidents overwhelmingly agreed—74 percent of the presidents at nonunion colleges and 69 percent of the presidents at unionized colleges. Interestingly, only 36 percent of the union chairpersons agreed with the statement.

Do all these facts about encroaching unionism mean that senates are doomed in the face of union pressure? Not necessarily. Most of the unionized campuses had a weak tradition of faculty participation in governance. Unions on those campuses merely undercut already impotent senates. Senates, furthermore, are threatened by other forces as well—especially institutional growth, centralization, and powerful economic pressures. When unions and senates coexist, the health or weakness of the senate depends upon many variables other than faculty unionization.

For example, *budget cuts* and *declining enrollments* force into the open latent conflicts of interest among campus constituencies and undermine the spirit of cooperative decision making. We believe such fundamental differences are becoming common on all campuses as the economic and political climate for higher education worsens. Given the tendency of environmental pressures to exacerbate differences among campus constituencies, rapid institutional adaptation to changing times cannot be accomplished without great turmoil that directly threatens traditional modes of campus governance.

A second major factor determining the future of senates is the *legal situation*. Even a politically astute administration can do little to alter the effects of a multicampus unit determination establishing a statewide union that undermines local campus senates, or a court decision upholding a union's involvement in governance. Another legal question revolves around writing governance matters into the contract. Even where governance is not a mandatory subject for bargaining, an administration may agree to bargain about it. The long-term effects of writing governance into the contract are uncertain: it could strengthen formerly weak academic processes, but it could also subject governance activities to constant negotiation and potential undermining.

A third variable that will help determine the future of senates is the style and degree of *administrative support*. Woodrow Wilson once likened democracy to living tissue: it must be carefully protected and nourished to thrive. Senates possessing little *de jure* authority are extremely fragile and, like a democratic government, depend upon the willingness of individuals to work on their behalf. Unions can quickly move in to replace ineffective senates if administrators fail to respond meaningfully to faculty discontent with those bodies. Too often, administrators pay lip service to the senate while condemning the union—forgetting that both are creations of the faculty. As a result, unions grow more militant, senates become weaker, and faculties are torn by conflict. Furthermore, administrators who attempt to defeat a faculty union by negotiating with the senate on union matters also promote unionization. The most effective way for administrators to strengthen their senates is by supporting genuine, effective faculty participation in governance of all types.

In a sense, this last is a matter of clarifying proper roles, of restraining different interest groups from encroaching on the proper influence areas of others. This task is made difficult by the multiple, overlapping decision bodies on a campus. It is not unusual for a single campus to have most of the following: (1) department, school, and division committees; (2) faculty senate; (3) student senate; (4) broad-based senate; (5) faculty union (sometimes more than one representing academic employees); and (6) an administrative council. Drawing the boundaries around the spheres of influence for each organization can be very difficult. Nevertheless, because of its unique position of authority on campus, the administration should take the lead in establishing a workable governance scheme. Where conflict of interest is great, however, the chances for a stable consensus are diminished regardless of how adroitly the administration attempts to mediate.

At the same time, the increase in union power at the expense of the senates is often blamed on unsupportive administrators and on laws that arm the unions with legal weapons. But much of the future viability or failure of senates will be determined by the faculty themselves. Apathy is a major problem. Many junior faculty remain inactive in governance, concentrating instead on teaching and research in order to gain tenure. And many tenured faculty members find more satisfaction in their professional activities than in campus politics. Time and time again, people interviewed in our case studies reported that senates were ineffective because faculty members were not active participants.

If faculty do not become involved in both senate and union affairs, the ominous predictions about the demise of faculty governance may come true. Combined with other factors undermining dual track governance, faculty apathy can strike the final blow to traditional academic governance. On the other hand, faculty involvement, determination to pressure the best of traditional practices, and an insistence on responsible union leadership could be the factors that tip the scales toward genuine dual track bargaining—with strong unions and strong senates each doing what they do best.

To summarize, we really do not have enough experience to predict accurately the long-term impact that unionization will have on traditional faculty senates. This is especially true since, with a few exceptions, only institutions with weak senates have unionized, making it difficult to guess how unions might affect stronger senates. However, with these reservations in mind, there are several conclusions that can be drawn from the current situation.

First, the weakness of senates is a factor in promoting unionization in the first place. Moreover, senates are unlikely to convert successfully to become unions, because laws hinder such a change and senates attempting to do so would not be supported by national unions.

Second, coexisting senates and unions appear to divide their attempts to influence, with unions addressing economic issues and working conditions, and senates dealing with curriculum, degree requirements, and admissions. They jointly attempt to influence personnel issues such as hiring, promotion, and tenure. Finally, neither senates nor unions have much control over budgets, selection of administrators, overall staffing arrangements, physical plant, and long-range planning. In these areas, administrators remain in command.

Third, the dual tracks of influence may not remain stable, as union influence expands into traditional senate areas of influence. The survey responses, especially of presidents and to some degree of chairpersons, as well as an analysis of union-negotiated contracts, suggest that unions are expanding with each passing year.

Fourth, how far the dual track breakdown goes will depend on many factors, and unionism is only one. Conflicts of interest, the leadership of administrators, the legal context, and faculty participation are all critical elements that singly or together will determine the future viability of senates in the face of union challenges.

All in all, the evidence does not warrant the pessimistic view that senates will collapse with the arrival of collective bargaining, but serious problems definitely exist. Where senates and unions coexist, unions do curtail senate influence over economically related issues and to a varying extent share concurrent jurisdiction with senates in areas such as personnel decision making. But unions alone cannot be held responsible for the problems of senates. Many senates are also weakened by faculty apathy, administrative interference, and system-level power plays. Our primary conclusion is that the senates and other mechanisms of faculty governance are fragile, and, if not protected and supported, will be destroyed by the political winds now sweeping the campus.

Styles of Academic Governance in Different Institutions

We have been discussing national trends in governance and decision making, but if we have learned anything from this study it is that the diversity that permeates higher education produces significantly different management styles and decision-making patterns. In this section we will briefly describe the styles of governance and management that we believe are characteristic of each of the eight institutional types. This analysis is based on our surveys, our case studies, and our judgment. Not every institution within a group will have the exact patterns we describe, but we believe these characteristics are typical of the average institution in each type. Table 5 summarizes the governance patterns in the eight types of institutions. On the left of Table 5 are some styles of faculty involvement, and on the right are ratings for different groups on their "global" influence. These ratings are derived from the "spheres of influence" questions we discussed earlier in this chapter.

Private and Public Multiversities. Large, elite, research-oriented Public and Private Multiversities have a pattern of decision making, policy formulation, and governance that we might call "federated professionalism." These institutions have extremely strong faculties, and yet they are such complex organizations that they need strong administrators as well. There is an enormous amount of tension in these institutions. The faculties demand and receive control over departments and academic programs; the administrations exercise strong leadership in long-range planning, budgeting, and institutional programming. These are certainly not administratively dominated institutions, for the faculties are powerful and vocal. Still the latter are so fragmented among their departments that they have only moderate control over the institution as a whole. There is therefore a precarious balance of power between the highly influential faculties and the powerful administrators. As a consequence, we rate the degree of *administrative control* in these institutions to be "moderate," because administrative power is tempered by faculty influence.

Table 5. Governance Styles in Different Types of Institutions.

	Percent Faculty Participating in Each Activity					Ratings of "Global" Influence for Different Groups					
	Inactive	Formal Involvement	Led Faculty Committee	Strategic	Urge Collective Negotiations	Trustees	President	Institutional Faculty	Deans	Department Heads	Departmental Faculty
Private Multiversity	53	16	44	19	27	3.1	3.7	3.5	3.7	2.7	2.3
Public Multiversity	60	14	48	18	28	3.2	4.3	3.3	3.2	2.4	2.0
Elite Liberal Arts	44	22	53	31	24	2.6	4.1	3.9	3.4	2.4	2.3
Public Comprehensives	52	18	51	36	35	3.3	4.5	3.1	3.6	2.6	2.0
Public Colleges	46	20	57	33	36	2.8	4.3	3.4	3.4	2.8	2.3
Private Liberal Arts	49	23	52	34	29	3.1	4.4	3.2	3.8	2.6	2.2
Community Colleges	51	23	54	38	55	3.4	4.4	3.0	3.5	2.7	2.3
Private Junior Colleges	55	22	52	21	37	3.1	4.6	2.8	3.5	2.4	2.2

In these institutions, the influence of the external environment is considerable. But the high influence of the faculty, and the institution's enormous complexity and size, allow the development of strong departmental professional enclaves that are sheltered from direct environmental influence. Even in the state-controlled multiversities, the prestige, political power, and influence of the faculty serve as a shield against too much environmental influence. As a consequence, we rate the *external influence* from "low" in private multiversities to "moderate" in public multiversities.

What is the style of faculty involvement in governance in the multiversities? On the one hand, there is a high level of inactivity, for these institutions are simply too complex and bewildering for the faculty to get heavily involved in institutional governance. The administrators basically handle the running of the institution as a whole. On the other hand, the faculty has enormous influence over their professional enclaves, the academic departments. There is a high degree of fragmentation in these institutions, with the administrators carving out certain spheres of influence and the faculty carving out others.

The senates in these multiversities are only moderately strong. The academic departments are so strongly entrenched that senates find themselves unable to exercise much control over the curriculum. At the same time, however, this high respect given the faculty means that senates, themselves composed largely of faculty, can often balance administrative power. As a consequence, we would rate senate influence as "moderate." Faculty unions are almost nonexistent in these institutions. The faculty are the "fat cats" of the profession—highly paid, and highly influential in decision making. As a consequence, they have not turned to unions to gain influence.

Elite Liberal Arts Colleges. Usually small to medium in size, these high-quality, highly selective private institutions are characterized by a "semicollegial" governance pattern. We do not believe that any institutions are *purely* collegial in their governance. There is simply too much environmental pressure and administrative influence brought to bear to say that even these institutions are purely collegial. The Elite Liberal Arts Colleges come closer than anybody else, however, so we call them semicollegial.

In these institutions, administrative influence is moderate

and environmental influence limited. The administration works very closely with the faculty, and the faculty has a vested interest in institution-wide matters. The statistics in Table 5 suggest that this type of institution has the highest level of faculty participation in governance, the lowest level of faculty apathy, and the lowest percentage of faculty favoring collective negotiations.

Faculty participation occurs in both the departments and the influential senates. Furthermore, these institutions are small enough to make it feasible for the faculty actually to participate in institution-wide decision making. In many cases, the senate becomes the vehicle for this participation. In fact, this is the only type of institution where the senate seems to have a "high" level of influence. The academic departments are also very strong, and the institution to a great extent allows the professionals to control their own situations. The "global" influence of institutional faculty, shown in Table 5, is the highest of any institutional type. The likelihood of unions making headway in these institutions is small.

Where spheres of influence in massive Multiversities tend to be sharply defined, those in Elite Liberal Arts Colleges overlap considerably. By that we mean that the faculty and administration tend to work together more on all major issues. If there ever is a true "community of scholars" in higher education, it will probably be in these Elite Liberal Arts Colleges. The administrators usually come from the faculty, senior faculty members are usually very powerful in decision making, and faculty and administrators share decision-making activities. (For an excellent discussion of governance in these elite colleges, see Burton R. Clark, *The Distinctive College: Reed, Antioch, and Swarthmore,* 1970.)

Public Comprehensives and Public Colleges. These are the main-line American public colleges. Usually moderate to large in size, their faculties are at the median in training and expertise and their students of average academic ability. We believe that the administrative managers in these institutions have more power than in the massive Public Multiversities and that the external environment is more influential. The faculty still have moderately strong departments and senate organizations, but the outside influence of legislators and system-level controls is very strong. In short, the external environment often influences these institutions, and there are strong bureaucratic controls over the daily life of the faculty. The administrators are stronger, and their spheres of influence extend to a broader spectrum of activities. We call these "managed professionalism" institutions. By this we mean that there is still a moderately high level of professionalism, with moderately strong departments, but the managers exercise a much more prominent role.

In these institutions, the academic departments are important but not as strong as those in the elite multiversities. The spheres of influence are moderately dispersed; that is, the neat separation of power areas that occurs in the elite multiversities is blurred considerably in these less prestigious institutions. The reason is that the administrators and faculty have less clear domains, and administrators probably interfere to a greater degree. Faculty styles of participation tend to be highly *inactive*. The administration has most of the influence over institution-wide activities, and as a consequence the faculty governance activity level is considerably lower. In fact, aside from the few faculty members in the power elite—a phenomenon found in every type of institution—the typical mode of action for faculty members who get involved is "strategic." Unions are growing in these institutions as the faculty, shut out because of administrative dominance, turn gradually to unions for help.

In short, the Public Comprehensives and the Public Colleges stand somewhere in the middle of American higher education. Their administrators are very strong and external environmental forces penetrate to a larger degree. As a consequence, faculty influence is considerably weakened, although the departments certainly maintain some influence. It is a picture of strong administrations, high faculty apathy, weak senates, and a high likelihood of union growth.

Private Liberal Arts Colleges. Unlike their more elite sister institutions, these colleges have fairly weak faculties and strong administrations. In many cases these are church-affiliated with religious bodies sometimes exercising considerable control. The institutions are small enough to permit environmental forces that would hardly affect a larger institution to have significant impact here. As a result, there is a high level of bureaucratic control over the faculty in these colleges (as we will discuss in Chapter Five).

Senates in these institutions are notoriously weak and dominated by administrators. In fact, most of these institutions have not even had senates until very recently. These institutions could have unionized years ago under the Federal National Labor Relations Act. And all their characteristics would lead us to suspect that they would do so to counterbalance this strong environmental and administrative dominance. Surprisingly, though, up to this point they have not done so. As the union movement develops, however, we suspect they may eventually become union-organized.

Two-Year Colleges. The most numerous of institutions of higher education, these are the strongholds of administrative dominance. Faculties here are the weakest in professional expertise, and environmental forces are the highest in all of higher education. Given a relative weak faculty and high environmental influence, it is not surprising to find the administrators in control of almost all spheres of governance.

Faculty participation in governance is low—the lowest of any institutional group. There is an apathetic atmosphere, with only marginal participation by the faculty in the decision-making process. The levels of inactivity recorded in our survey were the very highest in these institutions. Faculty senates in these institutions are either nonexistent or extremely weak.

This clear administrative dominance, the weakness of faculty governance mechanisms, and the high degree of external control lead naturally to unionization as a means of counterbalancing these forces. This is why the vast majority of unionized campuses in the country are two-year institutions, and why it is here that faculty support for unionization is highest. The picture in these two-year colleges then, is of powerless faculties in administratively dominated institutions turning to unions as a countervailing force.

A Look at Some Future Trends

The institutional governance patterns we have painted thus far are primarily static pictures. However, academic governance is being reshaped rather significantly in the mid and late 1970s. Both decreased enrollments and lowered public support have caused a drastic change in the resources available to higher education. What effect will this tightening of resources have on academic decision processes and on the morale and political participation of faculty members? We can make some intelligent guesses about what happens to governance when institutions move from financial feast to famine.

Two general results are likely. First, most institutions will experience high levels of conflict as departments, schools, and units grapple for resources. In connection with this, personnel and tenure decisions will loom ever larger as sources of tension, and union activity will flourish as a protective strategy. Second, more and more power will be concentrated in a few central figures—deans, presidents, and, increasingly, trustees and legislators. Let us examine these trends in more detail.

A number of critical changes—the weakened job market, less research funds, and the encroachment of outside pressure groups—have diminished faculty influence over decision processes in most institutions. These changes have resulted in restricted budgets, frozen faculty salaries, the elimination of departments, and the execution of major decisions over the strong objections of faculties that feel increasingly impotent. This is particularly true of faculty members in local community college systems and in stringently regulated state college networks. It seems probable that many faculties sense a growing personal and professional threat.

From the 1940s through the early 1960s, college and university faculties obtained a high degree of influence over the governance of their institutions. They enhanced their professional status, reserved for themselves many critical decisions over curriculum, faculty, and student affairs, and gained power over many of the academic policy-making networks. The "Academic Revolution" described by Jencks and Riesman (1968) propelled the professor to the forefront of academic decision making. The growth of faculty power was selective—it happened in the elite institutions more than in the nonelite, and in the private institutions more than in the public ones. Nevertheless, the thrust of faculty control, power, and autonomy was felt to varying degrees in all areas of the academic professions.

Faculty autonomy and power developed when certain forces in the society converged: expanding enrollments; a public belief in education's ability to solve social problems; increased financial support; the growth of large-scale research requiring more faculty experts; and a shortage of qualified personnel. All these forces sharply increased a faculty's bargaining position. They also boosted higher education's governmental priority and strengthened the role of academic disciplines. Faculty influence then became institutionalized, within departments and disciplinary associations as well as through the growing force of academic senates and the American Association of University Professors.

Recent events, however, have begun to undermine this faculty power and elevated status of higher education. Lower enrollments and oversupplies of doctoral degrees have caused the public to question its support of higher education and has lessened the bargaining power of professors. Furthermore, basic attitudes are changing in a society that once unquestioningly accepted the legitimacy of higher education's claim for public support. Particularly has a crisis of public confidence been brought on by the student revolts of the 1960s, a growing disillusionment with the ideology that education can solve most social problems, a rising skepticism about education's contribution to occupational success, and the strident attacks on faculties by politicians. The impact of these factors is now commonly recognized: lower financial support, more state control of educational policy, and less research money.

The environmental factors listed above have quite different impacts on different colleges and universities. Some institutions still have enormous independence from their environment, based on a self-perpetuating board of trustees, wealth derived from endowments and research money, and a continuously high student application rate that ensures abundant tuition money. Faculties in these institutions are central in the policy-making processes, working through strong departments that are relatively free of bureaucratic rules and regulations. In other cases, however, institutions are virtually captured by their environmental setting. Such institutions are closely supervised by local community agencies and are almost exclusively dependent on one source of money, such as a church or legislature. In addition, their supply of tuition money is always precarious because of fluctuations in student demand. Whether an institution is highly independent or highly dependent is a critical factor in forming internal governance patterns.

As pointed out earlier, institutions that are virtual captives of strong environmental pressures have faculties that play a weak role in the governance process. Academic departments in such institutions have little control over selection and promotion of faculty, courses offered, and other academic issues. Faculty members have little autonomy concerning the courses they teach, and are highly regulated by strict rules and regulations. Faculty participation in the determination of institutional policy is also very limited.

Heavy environmental dependency also results in a "dominant coalition" of administrators. The more dependent a college is on its environment, the more likely the administrators are to take on great power. When the legislature demands "accountability" from the faculty, the administration is given the power to enforce it. When resources are short and a few powerful financial barons are controlling the purse strings, the administrators use that dependency to dictate educational policy. Is the supply of clientele drying up? Are resources scarce? Do a few outside agencies have a stranglehold? These kinds of problems always give administrators more power to determine educational policy, allocate resources, and make critical policy decisions. In short, dependency on the outside world concentrates power in the hands of administrators, and a "dominant coalition" of administrative elite emerges. Moreover, this dominant group of administrators is very likely to be in some central headquarters off the campus, in a state system office.

We suspect that presidential power on many campuses is still substantial, but it is being threatened by many new developments. Many presidents appear to be hemmed in by new controversies and crises. Although they have had and still have substantial power, they expressed in our interviews strong worry about the erosion of their influence. As powerful state systems have developed, many presidents have been placed in the awkward position of acting as middle managers. They are held responsible by everybody—the faculty below and the state above. Even in private colleges and universities there are strong outside pressure groups and enormous financial crises that have restrained the president's ability to act. In fact, Michael Cohen and James March, in their book *Leadership and Ambiguity: The American College President* (1974), have suggested that growing institutional complexity and increased outside pressures have produced a generation of presidents who are largely ceremonial figures with little opportunity to exercise real leadership. Although we doubt that college presidents are as impotent as Cohen and March suggest, it is nevertheless true that environmental, financial, and institutional forces have combined to make presidential power more complicated than it ever was before. This is particularly true as state systems pull power *off* the campus and faculty collective bargaining complicates power *on* it.

It may seem contradictory on the face of it to say at one point—as we did above—that power is being centralized, and at another point that presidential power is being complicated and undermined by external offices and unions. But those seemingly contradictory statements merely illustrate just how complex academic governance is becoming. The fact that these two events are occurring simultaneously has produced a governance situation that is highly complicated and filled with conflict.

Never particularly strong, the student role in academic governance has been sharply curtailed. Student revolutions of the sixties affected institutional decision making in a number of ways. On the one hand, they drew the wrath of the public in an almost unprecedented fashion. On the other hand, that revolutionary behavior opened up paths for exercising student influence and voicing concerns and demands. In the late 1960s and early 1970s it appeared that student influence in governance would indeed be significant. Students joined academic senates at hundreds of institutions, students were placed on departmental and institutional committees in great numbers, and student lobbies were formed around the legislatures of many states. It seemed that students would finally have a major voice in academic governance.

Then the roof fell in. The same pressure that has reduced *faculty* influence has also reduced *student* influence—the economic crunch with its attendant centralization of power. In addition, the steps that the faculty has taken to protect its own sphere, especially the formation of unions, have undercut the students. In another book (Kemerer and Baldridge, 1975) we have discussed extensively the impact of unions on students. It is enough to say here that faculty unions, with rare exceptions, have not been favorable to student influence and have effectively cut students out of the decision-making process on many unionized campuses.

Professionals in education have begun to consider collective bargaining as a vehicle for retaining faculty power where it exists, regaining power where it has been lost, and seizing power where it was never before theirs. A few short years ago there was virtually no union activity in American colleges and universities. Today, it is a potent and rising force. Competing union groups are vying for recognition, state networks are building negotiating systems, and bargaining laws are being drawn up in the legislatures. Some predict the union movement will sweep higher education; others suggest that it will not grow much more than it already has. In any event, collective bargaining in higher education must be reckoned with in any analysis of governance processes.

Obviously, governance patterns are quite different from campus to campus. Moreover, social and economic forces are working to change governance patterns on individual campuses. With such great diversity in governance styles, therefore, we might expect to find similar differences in campus climates—faculty attitudes, patterns of work and work behavior, and patterns of professionalism. These topics will be discussed in the following chapters as they relate to patterns of governance and decision making.

Chapter 5

Bureaucracy and Autonomy in Academic Work

@@@@@@@@@@@@@@@@@@@@@@@@@@@@@@

American higher education is permeated with a rich diversity of institutional characteristics and governance patterns, but nowhere is its complexity more obvious than in the *work patterns* of faculty. American colleges and universities have a bewildering variety of academic programs, research agendas, and community service projects. Faculty teach students, run hospitals, manage giant atom smashers, conduct public opinion polls, and write books. In this chapter we will explore this diverse work pattern of professors.

At the same time we want to study how the institutions manage all this diverse work. All organizations, whether military or government or business, face management problems. All must mold workers into an effective team, channeling the diverse activities of these workers so as to achieve the institution's goals. Some organizations—such as law firms—allow the worker much freedom. Others—such as the military—impose strict bureaucratic control carried out with complex systems of rules and regulations.

How do academic organizations control their faculty? Is the pattern more like that of a loose, nonbureaucratic, professional organization, or a rigid bureaucracy? In this chapter we will explore the autonomy of academic professionals and the efforts of the academic bureaucracy to control their work, considering both the professional's need for freedom and autonomy in his work, and the institution's need for control, regulation, and accountability. As usual, we find amazing diversity in the ways different colleges handle this issue.

We will try to answer several questions: (1) What are the work activities of faculty? What are the differences in institutional settings? (2) How is faculty work evaluated? What are the criteria that determine success? Who does the evaluation? (3) How do different institutions regulate work behavior? Are there significant differences in the level of bureaucratization? and (4) How do major institutional characteristics (such as size, level of faculty expertise, and environmental relations) influence faculty autonomy and the level of bureaucracy? Part of the reason for this is that the "profession" of being a faculty member is not a unified profession but a composite of diverse subcultures. And these subcultures themselves vary according to differences in work styles, institutional bureaucracy, and professional autonomy. Because of these factors; those working under the broad umbrella of "professor" are really engaged in many different and variable academic mini-professions.

Work Activities of the Faculty

Primarily, of course, professors engage in teaching, research, and community service. For the vast bulk of faculty members, in fact, teaching is their sole activity. Nevertheless, under the umbrellas of teaching, research, and community service there are found major variations in the work patterns of faculty in different institutions.

In our national survey we asked: "How much of your work time do you spend in the following activities: graduate teaching, undergraduate teaching, research, community service, institutional service? Table 6, showing the responses, reveals nothing startling. In general, the results are exactly as might be predicted.

The table does suggest a few trends. *First, undergraduate teaching dominates faculty work in all types of institutions.* This is true regardless of the institution, regardless of the person's sex, regardless of the institute's prestige or the professor's rank. Teaching undergraduates is *the* occupation of professors in all institutional setting and for professors of all ranks. In short, for all practical purposes, undergraduate teaching is the exclusive work of the bulk of higher education faculties.

When we examined teaching activities within different academic ranks, we found that full professors teach undergraduates almost as much as assistant professors do. Both men and women spend the majority of their time on undergraduate teaching, although women do so slightly more. And most disciplines spend about the same amount of time teaching undergraduates. In short, undergraduate teaching is the name of the game for professors of all ranks, sexes, and disciplines.

There were some variations to this pattern. In a few elite institutions, senior professors spend more time with graduate students and more time on research. In only two types of institutions, however, do professors spend less than a majority of their time teaching undergraduates—Private and Public Multiversities (32 and 34 percent respectively). In a few subject matter areas (such as advanced professional schools) the faculty teach only graduate students. But these are just a few exceptions to a pervasive pattern. This pattern strongly contradicts the widespread notion that undergraduates are being neglected while professors work on graduate research, high paid consultancies, grants for the government, and community activities. This notion would probably hold true only in a few tiny enclaves within higher education. The overwhelming majority of professors are undergraduate teachers—and little else.

This leads to our second major conclusion: *Graduate teaching and research account for only a very small percentage of faculty work.* Furthermore, graduate teaching and research are concentrated in a very limited range of institutions, as Table 6 shows. Only in the elite multiversities do college faculty members report spending a

Table 6. Faculty Work Activities.

	1 Average Time Spent in Undergraduate Training	2 Average Time Spent in Graduate Training	3 Average Time Spent in Research	4 Average Time Spent in Community Service	5 Average Time Spent in Committees and Administration	6 Average Number Articles Published in Last Four Years[a]	7 Average Number Books Published in Last Four Years[a]
Private Multiversity	32%	23%	25%	4%	16%	7.4	.9
Public Multiversity	34	21	22	5	18	6.8	.8
Elite Liberal Arts	59	6	14	3	18	3.2	.5
Public Comprehensives	58	10	10	5	17	2.5	.5
Public Colleges	59	9	10	4	18	2.7	.6
Private Liberal Arts	66	2	9	5	18	2.3	.3
Community Colleges	70	0	5	4	21	2.0	.3
Private Junior College	70	0	5	4	21	1.9	.3
National Average	52	12	14	4	18	4.3	.6

[a] Men faculty only.

healthy percentage of their time on research and graduate teaching—
(in Private Multiversities, 23 percent teaching graduate students,
25 percent research; in Public Multiversities, 21 percent teaching
graduate students, 22 percent research). Table 6 also shows that
publishing is highest where the percentage of graduate teaching and
research is high—a finding that is not particularly surprising.

The interesting conclusion overall is not that research, graduate teaching, and publication are concentrated, but how *totally*
those activities are concentrated in Private and Public Multiversities,
where publication rates are three to six times higher than in other
institutions. Higher education almost has two separate worlds. The
first exists in the complex multiversities, where graduate teaching,
research, and publication exist alongside ever-present undergraduate
teaching. The second world is found in the rest of higher education,
where undergraduate teaching is almost the only game in town.

*A third conclusion is that institutional service and admin-
istration account for a significant portion of faculty time.* Another
common myth says faculty members are burdened with enormous
amounts of administrative trivia, with endless hours of boring committees needed to manage the institutions. Our results show this
myth to be absolutely true! In all institutions the faculty spent
roughly one fifth of their time on committees and administrative
work. People in higher prestige institutions report doing less committee work, but the general trend is evident in all other situations.
Frankly, we suspect the time reported on this activity is higher than
it really is, but nevertheless the pain of sitting through boring
committees seems vivid in our respondents' minds.

*Fourth, community service does not consume much of the
faculty's time.* There is much talk about the heavy involvement of
professors in community service activities. But if our figures are
realistic there is very little action on that front—the average is pretty
consistently 4 or 5 percent. Surprisingly, the Community and Public
Comprehensive Colleges, where one might expect a much higher
level of community involvement, have about the same levels as
everybody else. The reason there seems to be very little community
service activity is probably that undergraduate teaching so dominates
the faculty's time that there is little left for outside activities.

Finally, there is substantial diversity among different types of institutions. Higher education is many different things, and faculties engage in many different activities. It is indeed true that, regardless of location, faculty members spend more time on undergraduate teaching than on anything else. Beyond that fact, however, the similarities lessen. Graduate teaching and research are concentrated in a narrow range of institutions, and the amounts of publication and research vary by type of institution. The differences are very regular and very large. There is five times as much research time spent in the elite institutions as in the two-year colleges, two and a half times more than in most public colleges. In short, people who call themselves professors actually engage in a wide range of activities. Their common bond is teaching undergraduates, but, starting from that base, they branch off in many different directions.

Evaluation Processes

All organizations evaluate work performance in some manner. In fact, some organization theorists (notably Scott and Dornbusch) argue that the evaluation process is a major management tool. According to them, organizations *control* work behavior by setting goals then evaluating performance against those goals (see Scott, Dornbusch, Busching, and Laing, 1964; and Dornbusch and Scott, 1975). They suggest that a good test of an organization's level of bureaucracy, regulation, and control is to determine how it evaluates performance. In highly bureaucratic organizations the evaluation is done by administrators, the superiors in the hierarchy. By contrast, performance is evaluated in "professional" organizations by professional experts. Higher education uses both approaches.

Academic evaluation is complicated by the vagueness of academic goals. Most organizations have clear-cut purposes. Business firms supply needed goods and services as a way of making a profit, government bureaus have tasks specified by law, hospitals try to overcome illness and injury, prisons try to "rehabilitate." By contrast, the goals of a college or university make a long, evaluatively amorphous list: teaching, research, serving the local community, administering scientific installations, housing students and faculty, supporting the arts, attacking social problems. When goals are finally specified in concrete terms and put into operation, disagreement promptly results. Thus, the problem is not only that academic goals are unclear, they are also highly contested once they are made clear.

Two important characteristics of academic institutions play an important part in determining goals. First, like schools, hospitals, and welfare agencies, academic organizations are "people-processing" institutions that serve clients—the students. Second, because their clients have disparate, complicated needs, these particular "people-processing" organizations frequently have no one "best" way of doing things. A company manufacturing steel or plastics develops a specific manufacturing process that can be divided into steps and routinized: unskilled, semiskilled, and white-collar workers can be employed without relying heavily on professional expertise. By contrast, academic institutions are dealing with the minds, bodies, and spirits of the nation's upper level students. Not only is it difficult to serve these clients, but it also is difficult to evaluate accomplishments and demonstrate even short-term successes. If, at times, colleges and universities do not know *what* they are doing, they often do not know *how* to do it either.

For these reasons, *performance standards* in a university are, to a large degree, inherently subjective. No matter how often tasks are specified, objectives listed, or performance criteria catalogued, the subtleties of the academic task will always remain to be dealt with. Like the job of the artist or statesman, the academic job is difficult to quantify, measure, or minutely supervise. Under these circumstances—vague goals, client service, professional tasks, and subjective criteria—it is extremely difficult to evaluate academic performance.

Still, it must de done, if only to make personnel decisions such as granting promotions and tenure. And, in fact, evaluation though difficult is not impossible. Professional organizations such as colleges, law firms, and hospitals have developed *peer evaluation* procedures that do work. In developing them, these organizations have had to take into account such factors as that most professionals demand that their colleagues, trained and inculcated with the values of both the profession and the institution, evaluate their work. Like other professionals, *academics tend to reject the evaluations of non-*

experts. Let us see how the academic evaluation process appears in our national survey.

Professionals demand the right to evaluate their own work behavior. As the experts, as the people who know right from wrong, they expect their performance to be judged only by other experts. Professionals reject evaluation by organizational bureaucrats or any other evaluation that is not directly related to their professional expertise. We decided that the way they were evaluated would be an excellent measure of the different work climates, so we asked a series of questions about evaluation processes. First we listed the major activities (teaching, research, and so on); second we asked who evaluated the work: trustees, administrators, students, faculty colleagues? We combined these different measures into a very simple one: for each activity, what percentage of the time were faculty colleagues the dominant evaluators?

Column one of Table 7 shows faculty responses. The differences among types of institutions are astonishing. "Who are the critical evaluators when it comes time for promotion and tenure?" In the elite institutions, faculty colleagues were often named. People such as deans, department chairpersons, and administrators were mentioned much less frequently. The faculty in Private Multiversities listed faculty colleagues 64 percent of the time, Public Multiversities 43 percent of the time, and Elite Liberal Arts Colleges 58 percent of the time.

In the rest of higher education, the percentage of faculty evaluators drops sharply. The highest score is in the Public Colleges, with 38 percent of the faculty listing their colleagues as the principal evaluators. In the two-year institutions, deans and department chairpersons loom dominant in the evaluation process. In fact, the Private Junior Colleges have an astonishingly low figure for faculty colleagues as evaluators—9 percent.

Earlier we noted that higher education seemed to be divided into two activity worlds: the world of undergraduate teaching coupled with research and publication, and the world of almost exclusively undergraduate teaching. It is interesting to note that the evaluation processes split exactly the same way. In the institutions where the research and graduate teaching occurs, faculty colleagues are the dominant evaluators. Deans, department chairpersons, and

Table 7. Evaluation Processes.

| | Who Evaluates? Percent Reporting Peers (Faculty Colleagues) are Prime Evaluators. | What Is Evaluated? Weight given to various activities. | | | | | | | | |
| | | Undergraduate Teaching | | | Graduate Teaching | | | Research | | |
	Column 1	2 Actual Weight[a]	3 Preferred Weight[b]	4 Difference[c]	5 Actual Weight	6 Preferred Weight	7 Difference	8 Actual Weight	9 Preferred Weight	10 Difference
Private Multiversity	64	21	28	−7	18	24	−6	42	31	+11
Public Multiversity	43	20	30	−10	16	21	−5	42	29	+13
Elite Liberal Arts	58	53	56	−3	4	5	−1	21	21	0
Public Comprehensives	29	49	51	−2	9	12	+3	16	15	+1
Public Colleges	38	49	55	−6	7	9	+2	17	15	+2
Private Liberal Arts	25	63	62	+1	2	2	0	10	13	−3
Community Colleges	23	60	62	+2	3	3	0	7	9	−2
Private Junior College	9	67	66	+1	0	0	0	2	4	−2
National Average	29	48	45	+3	10	13	−3	25	20	+5

[a] Actual Weight—The average percent of total influence the faculty felt this activity actually had in promotion and tenure matters.

[b] Preferred Weight—The weight they would have preferred.

[c] Difference—Gap between actual and preferred. Minus number suggests that in the faculty's opinion, the activity is not receiving enough emphasis; positive number suggests it is receiving too much.

other administrators play less important roles. But in the remainder—
the overwhelming majority of institutions—peers play far less of an
evaluative role. Does this mean that most of higher education does
not have that critical element of peer evaluation? And, remembering
that professionals demand the right to evaluate themselves, does it
mean that the level of professionalism is low in most of higher education? Our figures suggest that that is exactly the case.

*Now let us consider another issue: "What activities are
evaluated?"* Table 7 shows the faculty's judgment of how much
weight various tasks carry in promotion and tenure evaluations—
how much those activities *actually* affect evaluation, and how much
faculties would *prefer* they affected it. There are several interesting
facts in this table. First, with only two exceptions, undergraduate
teaching is rated quite high (Column 2). This is to be expected
considering the overwhelming role undergraduate teaching plays.
However, the high influence of teaching is rather surprising in light
of traditionally constant complaints from faculty members that
teaching is not rewarded. This table suggests that undergraduate
teaching is considered, and considered heavily, in the evaluation
process—a pattern that is constant throughout all the institutions,
with two major exceptions in Private and Public Multiversities.

Several other facts in Table 7 help explain the complaints
that teaching is not rewarded. First, in *every* type of institution,
undergraduate teaching is given less "actual" weight in the evaluation process than the percentage of time people spend on it (compare Column 1 of Table 6 with Column 2 of Table 7). In the elite
multiversities the disparity is quite large—people spend roughly 34
percent of their time on undergraduate teaching but it accounts for
only about 20 percent of their evaluation for promotion and tenure.
In other types of institutions the imbalance is not as heavy, but
undergraduate teaching still never gets its full weight in the
evaluation.

Second, research is greatly overstressed in the evaluation
process compared to actual time spent on it. Again, in *every* type of
college, research is evaluated higher than is justified by the time
spent on it (compare Table 6, Column 3, with Table 7, Column 8).
In general, the weight of research in evaluation is roughly one and
one half times greater than the percent of time spent on it—in *all*

types of institutions. Table 7 shows huge disparities between "actual" and "preferred" evaluation weights in multiversities. Faculty in those institutions feel uniquely pressured to research, but they would *prefer* a much lower emphasis on it. The "difference" columns in Table 7 are very revealing. They show the multiversities standing out with major gaps between "actual" and "preferred" evaluations, with research *over* evaluated, and undergraduate teaching *under* evaluated.

Third and finally, service and institutional service are not particularly important in evaluations for promotion and tenure. Although these activities are given some weight in Community Colleges and the Public Colleges, the ratings of their influence were so uniformly low that we did not include them in Table 7. The community may expect public service, and trustees may voice platitudes about the need for public service. But when the chips are down and evaluations are being made, public service and institutional service do not stack up as important issues.

In our seven case study institutions some problems about evaluation came up that were not apparent in the surveys. When we interviewed people on those campuses we found remarkable agreement about the *absence of meaningful evaluation*. In our questionnaire survey, we asked *what* was evaluated and *who* evaluated, but not whether the evaluation was *effective*. In our campus interviews we heard many complaints that the evaluation process was basically ineffective, that the stated criteria were only verbal platitudes, and that most promotion and tenure decisions were based largely on seniority. In addition, people often felt that the evaluation was capricious—that personality factors, departmental politics, and arbitrary administrative interference often dictated the outcome.

The problem of ineffective evaluation was highlighted when we interviewed people on unionized campuses. The tension over evaluation was severe. Administrators on those campuses were demanding more "accountability," more strict evaluation of the faculty's quality. The unions were responding by demanding more careful and more systematic evaluations. What long-term impact will unionism have? Unions have many goals, but during a financial crisis the prime goals are job security and economic benefits. These goals pose a dilemma for academic professionalism because they complicate the faculty's traditional responsibility to evaluate professional competence and performance.

Will unions dilute faculty quality by providing legal and procedural barriers behind which incompetency can hide, or can unions preserve quality even as they protect job security? Can unions shelter academics from arbitrary administrative meddling in personnel decisions, or will unions tie up the system so that effective administration is impossible? These questions are crucial, for the push toward unionization has seriously challenged professional patterns of personnel decision making.

The major negative consequence of faculty unionism may be a protectionist, job-security orientation that could thwart personnel policies so that incompetency is protected and seniority, not merit, becomes the main decision-making criterion. We would view this outcome as very unfortunate, of course, and strongly support traditional notions of academic professionalism. We believe that subjective performance criteria can be successfully used for peer evaluation of faculty members; that merit can be judged and should replace seniority as the basis of tenure and promotion; that incompetence can be identified and dealt with; that students as the principal clients should be involved in personnel decisions; and that our institutions, students, and publics deserve the best, quality-oriented faculties. We fear that in their quest for job security, faculty unions do not always share these basic beliefs and may undercut them.

In their efforts to expand due process, unions seek to protect their members by insisting that employment evaluation be based on detailed, specific criteria. Unfortunately, specific criteria are difficult to establish in education. Traditionally, the profession has compensated for this difficulty by depending on a complex, subtle, peer evaluation process much akin to a jury system. Furthermore, because such criteria are not easily developed, the ones that are suggested and used are often challenged if they actually result in a faculty member's dismissal—student evaluation of teaching being a case in point.

An evaluation system this is based on overly specific criteria could result in a process we call "tenure by default." The logic of tenure by default produces this pattern: (1) The union maintains that it is the burden of the institution to prove incompetency—not the burden of the faculty member to prove competency. (2) The union rejects the subtle, subjective peer evaluation process and demands concrete, specific criteria. (3) When specific criteria and evidence relating to them are presented, the union challenges them as irrelevant, inaccurate, or biased. (4) When specific criteria and evidence are unavailable or challenged, then the faculty member goes unevaluated by default and the institution is unable to make a substantial case for dismissal. The union has, by default, ensured job security.

If the default option were reversed so that the individual had to prove competence, then we believe the demand of the union for hard, specific criteria would be dropped, and that the traditional peer evaluation process would be more readily accepted. For example, as long as the default option favors the individual, faculty members will resist student evaluation and colleague observation of classroom teaching. If, on the other hand, the failure to prove competence resulted in dismissal, we suspect unions would favor more evaluation by students and faculty colleagues rather than less.

So far, tenure by default has not become a serious problem, particularly at the four-year and graduate levels. Peer review is still strongly defended by many unions in higher education. In fact, it is possible that faculty power over personnel decision making will be compromised to a greater degree by unilateral administrative action than by union contracts. However, at some two-year and some four-year colleges, there is much less commitment to the discretionary power of peers to render what is, in effect, a decision about job security. Thus, tenure by default provisions are increasingly likely to appear in union contracts at these institutions.

In discussing this controversial issue, we must emphasize both sides of the coin, for evaluation procedures in the past have been unclear, arbitrary, and in many cases indefensible. In short, the older unprofessional procedure of "nonrenewals by default" and by administrative arbitrariness was all too common. Unions have every right, even an obligation, to fight against such processes. Nevertheless, the opposite extreme of "promotion and tenure by default" is equally unprofessional. Somewhere between the two extremes must be a compromise that protects the individual against unreasonable and arbitrary procedures while simultaneously protecting the institution and its students against personnel decisions that occur by default. Both responsible unions and administrators will have to build the framework for a workable compromise. This compromise must necessarily include tightening up procedures and creating specific criteria. The compromise must also allow for the unmeasurables and the nonquantifiables that are the essence of academic work and for which peer evaluation remains the major judging process.

In the midst of all this confusion it is not surprising to find many complaints and much turmoil. We anticipate that this issue is far from settled and will continue to be a major crisis on the academic work scene.

Institutional Control

We have been describing the working world of the faculty—their activities and the evaluation process under which they work. This working world varies substantially depending on the institutional setting. We will now try to understand more about these institutional settings, particularly the way institutions try to regulate work behavior.

All organizations develop rules and regulations to help control work activities. In some organizations, those rules and regulations are numerous, detailed, and have strong impact. In professional organizations, however, it is generally assumed that the professionals will manage themselves without much interference from the organizational administration. At the same time, since we found that work activities were radically different in different institutions, we suspected that rules and regulations would also vary substantially.

Our hypothesis was simple: in institutions where the faculty had strong expertise (high percentages of faculty members with doctorates), where graduate teaching and research was highly developed, and where most of the evaluation was done by faculty colleagues, we anticipated that the organization would have fewer rules and regulations. By contrast, we suspected that the less prestigious institutions would be run more like traditional bureaucracies: there would be more rules and regulations, and more administrative supervision.

We measured bureaucratic rules by three questions. These

questions do not cover all the possible rules in an institution, but at least they cover several important aspects of professional work and provide a hint of overall patterns. The questions were: (1) Is your contract extremely specific about work you are to perform, or is it more open-ended and like a "gentleman's agreement?" (2) Do you have a great deal of freedom in the courses you teach, or are your courses more or less specified by administrators? (3) Does your institution have very strict accounting procedures in travel regulations?

It might be argued, with some validity, that our measures of "bureaucracy" are not the same ones other people would have picked. Our questions do not cover the number of forms that have to be filled out to register a student or hire a faculty member. They do not deal with the frustrations of trying to change a grade, adjust a pension-fund mistake, change a course in the catalogue, or get a parking sticker. These are the common frustrations that most people think about when "bureaucracy" is mentioned. And these frustrations are probably universal, with little regard to specific institutions.

Our concern was with bureaucratic control of professional behavior—the bureaucracy and detailed regulation that strikes directly at the professional work environment. For that reason we ignored these relatively superficial symptoms of bureaucracy and focused on issues we believed were more at the heart of the professional task, such as faculty contracts, professional travel, and control of the curriculum. The validity of this approach seems confirmed by the responses portrayed in Table 8. On all three questions about bureaucratic rules, enormous differences appear between elite institutions and the less prestigious ones. And the difference is always generally in the same direction. In the public sector there are more rules and regulations in community colleges, less in prestigious institutions; in the private sector there are more in private junior colleges, less in the elite multiversities.

The literature on professionals suggests that faculties with high levels of expertise will be given enormous autonomy in managing their own professional affairs. Our results clearly agree with that literature. In elite institutions, contracts are more like gentlemen's agreements, while in the less prestigious institutions contracts are very specific about teaching loads, courses to be taught, and work

Table 8. Work Environment of Faculty.

	Bureaucratization: Rules and Regulations			Professional Autonomy				
	A. *Contracts:* Reporting rigid contract.	B. *Courses:* Reporting faculty has little control over courses they teach.	C. *Travel:* Reporting strict travel regulations.	D. *Peer Evaluation:* Evaluation done by faculty peers.	E. *Courses:* Reporting department has much control over its courses.	F. *Promotions:* Reporting department controls faculty promotions.	G. *Hiring:* Reporting department controls faculty selection and hiring.	H. *Budget:* Reporting department has much control over its budget.
Private Multiversity	14%	15%	25%	64%	84%	49%	76%	40%
Public Multiversity	17	27	62	43	69	44	82	38
Elite Liberal Arts	25	15	39	58	73	39	66	40
Private Liberal Arts	31	46	85	29	54	30	64	31
Public Comprehensives	34	34	78	38	55	23	52	27
Public Colleges	57	34	73	25	62	13	37	43
Community Colleges	48	52	92	23	48	18	44	29
Private Junior College	56	53	83	9	55	8	21	33

regulations. Only two types of institutions show up with few travel regulations: the Private Multiversities and the Elite Liberal Arts Colleges. Even the Public Multiversities have strong travel regulations. Finally, the more elite the institutions are, the more likely it is that the faculty will determine the courses they teach. By contrast, Community College faculty members seem to teach courses determined by department heads or deans.

The Autonomy of the Academic Department

As a professional group, college and university faculty members are splintered into various disciplines and departments. In fact, according to Burton R. Clark, "The college and university are fractured by expertness, not unified by it. . . . The campus is not a closely knit group of professionals who see the world from one perspective. As a collection of professionals, it is decentralized, loose, and flabby" (1963, p. 244).

In colleges and universities, departments are not merely bureaucratic arrangements made for the sake of coordination and management. They are centers of professional activities. They are where one interacts with his professional peers, establishing particular methodologies and theories, and furthering the accomplishments of one's intellectual specialization. Indeed, it is from these centers that professionals select new members to enter the field, train them, evaluate them, and grant the degrees necessary to permit full admission to the discipline. In short, it is within these departments that the professional milieu is generated and expanded throughout the field. Therefore, if we are to examine the decision structures and processes of colleges and universities, we must study the academic department and its procedures.

We assumed that institutions with higher levels of faculty expertise would have stronger departments with: (1) more peer evaluation, (2) more control over courses, (3) more autonomy in determining who got promoted, (4) more influence in selecting new faculty members and (5) more ability to determine how budgets were spent. The survey findings portrayed on the right-hand side of Table 8 support our assumptions. In the elite institutions, the academic departments are quite strong. For example, faculty members report strong peer evaluation, much control over courses, and considerable influence in the selection of new faculty members. In addition, departments in the prestigious institutions have much influence over faculty promotions, although the strength of their influence here is lower than on hiring. This was probably because deans and institutional promotion committees are also very important in this process. Finally, in elite institutions, there is a slightly greater ability to control budget allocations—although in all institutional categories there is much administrative control over this key activity.

At the opposite end of the scale, community colleges and the less prestigious public institutions show a marked weakness in the departments' power and influence. They have, for example, less autonomy in selecting faculty and determining courses. But their weakness particularly shows up in faculty promotions and peer evaluation; administrators rather than the departmental faculty seem to have most control over promotion and tenure issues. Furthermore, since most of the promotions in those institutions are probably made by seniority, it is likely that *nobody* has much influence. Seniority effectively removes the need for decisions, making the process automatic.

The results from our survey can be enriched with insights from our seven case studies. We frequently asked people on campus about institutional regulations and the departments' power to control professional work. The interviews brought out trends that did not show up in the survey.

First, people everywhere complained about the increase in outside pressure from trustees, community groups, and state boards. The institutions' response to these calls for accountability was to gradually increase rules and regulations. In some institutions we found that department chairmen were being required to keep class attendance records on faculty. In many situations, deans reported they were involved in the promotion and hiring process much more than they ever were before.

Second, our case studies showed that the recent financial crisis has brought a sharp increase in rules and regulations. We suspect that on all of our measures we would find stricter rules resulting from financial shortages if we repeated our survey today. We are reasonably sure that travel regulations are now tighter, that departmental control of budgets is more limited, and that contract language is more specific. This change probably holds true for all kinds of institutions. Nonetheless, the *relative* positions of the institutions would probably remain the same—with the more elite institutions having less regulation even now, in spite of the financial crisis.

Third, our interviews suggested that the union movement is having the effect of increasing the amount of rules and regulation. In those institutions where unions are now bargaining for the faculty, everyone—faculty and administrators alike—reported a rash of new rules, regulations, and bureaucratic systems. On the one hand, this is because the unions demand more rules to limit administrative discretion. On the other hand, the administrators were also demanding more rules to ensure that contract provisions were being observed. The result is a whipsawing motion toward increased bureaucratization.

All in all, our case study interviews suggest that even those institutions which previously have had a great deal of flexibility, autonomy, and freedom from bureaucracy, are joining the ranks of the bureaucratized. Academic work, unfortunately, seems to be getting more rule-bound all the time.

Major Differences in Bureaucracy and Autonomy

In the sections above we have *described* the great differences in bureaucracy, rules, and departmental control of work activities. In this section we want to attempt to *explain* why those differences exist. Three major themes guide our explanation. The first two we have often mentioned, but the third is new and will need elaboration.

1. External environmental controls increase institutional bureaucratization and reduce faculty autonomy.
2. Faculty expertise reduces bureaucracy and increases autonomy.
3. Institutional size and complexity reduce bureaucratization and increase the faculty's professional autonomy.

External Controls Increase Bureaucratization and Reduce Faculty Autonomy. Research in other fields suggests that the working autonomy of academic professionals is significantly changed under conditions of high environmental control (Clark, 1960; Baldridge, 1971). This includes research on such other complex organizations as the public school (Bidwell, 1968; Carlson, 1964), voluntary social service agencies (Rose, 1955), and police organizations (Bordua and Reiss, 1966). We can summarize their findings by saying that when professional organizations are well "insulated" from environmental influences, then professional values, professional norms, and professional work definitions dominate the processes of the organization. When external influences increase, the professionals within are frequently reduced to the role of hired employees doing the bidding of bureaucratic managers—and the level of bureaucratic regulations increases sharply.

If it is true that increased environmental penetration reduces the operating authority of the professional faculty, then we should expect to find in those colleges and universities with high environmental influence that (1) the faculty have less influence and fewer decision-making opportunities over professional issues, (2) organizational rules and regulations govern more decision outcomes than do the academic professionals within, and (3) administrators, not faculty colleagues, are the primary evaluators for promotion and tenure. Where this is true, it is the organization that maintains rules and regulations governing these professional matters, and many decision processes also are centralized in the hands of the administrators.

Do the figures from our national survey support our hypothesis about environmental interference? Clearly they do. Table 9 contains a number of items from the survey, the first three of which deal with the external environment: formal control, affluence, and faculty's perception of outside interference. Three statements summarize our findings:

First, *the degree of formal control over an institution does not necessarily predict the levels of bureaucratization or professional autonomy within it.* It is commonly assumed that state institutions are much more highly regulated than private ones. In addition, it is normally assumed that faculty in private institutions have much more autonomy. Our data do not support those conceptions; the results are quite mixed. In some situations it is clear that private

institutions have an advantage: faculties report more control themselves over their *courses* and fewer regulations over *travel* (Table 9,
Item 1, "Formal Control"). But state institutions report less rigid
contracts than do private ones. On the issues of professional
autonomy, such as peer evaluation and faculty personnel policies,
government-controlled institutions are often more likely to have
autonomy than private ones.

The obvious exceptional cases are the "local" government
institutions, the community colleges. They clearly have more
bureaucracy in such things as travel regulations and the courses that
professors teach. In addition, they are typically lower in the areas of
professional autonomy. Their rates of peer evaluation are much
lower, departments have less control over budgets, and faculty
influence over personnel decisions is quite weak.

With the exception of the community colleges, however,
expected large variations between public and private institutions do
not show up. The reason is obvious but often overlooked. The
variations on bureaucratic rules and professional autonomy seem to
have to do more with institutional quality than with whether they
are state or private. Among the public institutions are some of the
very best, and among the private institutions are some of the very
worst. And the higher quality public institutions have far more
professional autonomy than the lower quality private ones.

*Second, the more wealthy the institution the less bureau-
cratization and the more professional autonomy there is.* The differences shown in Item 2, Table 9, are striking. There is nearly double
the amount of bureaucratic regulation in poor institutions as there is
in rich ones. And the levels of professional autonomy are much
higher in rich institutions. Again the reason is probably more related
to quality than anything else; rich institutions hire better faculty,
who in turn receive more autonomy.

*Third, where the faculty perceive external interference,
bureaucratization is high and faculty autonomy is low.* The two
measures discussed above—formal control and affluence—are fairly
"objective" factors; they exist apart from anyone's opinions. We
decided we would ask a "subjective" question as well. "Do you
believe that outside groups such as trustees and state officials inter-
fere significantly with policies and curriculum of this institution?"

Faculty members were asked to express their opinions rather than any kind of objective fact.

We found that when the faculty *feel* threatened by outside influences, the objective conditions in the institution seem to match their feelings. Each measure of bureaucratization is higher in institutions where faculty feel external interference. And when the faculty feel high outside interference they report that their autonomy is considerably lower. The relationship is strong: on *every* measure, faculty autonomy is felt to be significantly higher in institutions where the faculty do not feel as much outside interference.

In general, then, the data support our hypothesis about external influence and pressure. The greater the outside influence, the greater the bureaucratization and the lower the faculty professional autonomy. This finding is related to those in Table 7 on bureaucratization and professional autonomy by type of institution. It is clear that the differences by type of institution are partly tied in with this external relations issue. The more prestigious institutions have managed to build greater insulation from the external environment. The lowest professional autonomy and the highest bureaucratization are found in the community colleges, those institutions most open to environmental influences of various kinds.

Faculty Expertise Reduces Bureaucracy and Increases Autonomy. Logically, then, professional autonomy should be greatest in colleges and universities with high faculty expertise and advanced graduate studies. Expertise buys power in any organization. Hospitals depend on doctors, legal firms depend on lawyers, research organizations depend on scientists, and military organizations depend on weapons specialists. Like other kinds of professional organizations, colleges and universities have experts who handle the complex tasks of teaching and research. And those professionals always demand control over working conditions in their organizations. Thus, other things being equal, the greater the knowledge required in an organization, the greater the power of the experts. They will have fewer bureaucratic rules and greater professional autonomy.

We measured the degree of expertise in colleges and universities in a rather straightforward fashion. First, we examined the percent of the faculty with doctorates. In itself, this is not a par-

Table 9. Factors Influencing Bureaucratization and Departmental Autonomy.

	Bureaucratization: Rules and Regulations				Professional Autonomy			
	A. *Contracts:* Reporting rigid contract.	B. *Courses:* Reporting faculty has little control over courses they teach.	C. *Travel:* Reporting strict travel regulations.	D. *Peer Evaluation:* Evaluation done by faculty peers.	E. *Courses:* Reporting department has much control over its courses.	F. *Promotions:* Reporting department controls faculty promotions.	G. *Hiring:* Reporting department controls faculty selection and hiring.	H. *Budget:* Reporting department has much control over its budget.
1. Formal Control								
State (N = 109)	37%	43%	82%	32%	52%	26%	58%	32%
Local Government (N = 56)	45	51	94	22	55	18	46	24
Private (N = 135)	48	33	66	30	61	15	42	41
2. Affluence ($ per student)								
High (N = 79)	34	25	59	43	66	24	58	38
Medium (N = 84)	43	41	79	27	60	20	47	38
Low (N = 78)	59	51	88	19	54	18	44	35
3. Faculty Perception of External Influence								
Low External Influence (N = 101)	42	31	65	35	62	19	50	41

Medium External Influence (N = 102)	44	42	79	29	61	21	49	34
High External Influence (N = 97)	46	46	87	25	49	19	46	30
4. Percent Faculty Ph.D.								
High (64%+) (N = 60)	25	23	56	49	71	31	70	40
Medium (41–63) (N = 83)	46	37	73	30	61	20	51	39
Low (0–40) (N = 157)	50	48	87	21	50	16	38	31
5. Highest Degree Offered								
Ph.D. (N = 32)	24	26	53	48	72	39	76	38
M.A. (N = 56)	34	36	71	42	64	22	57	36
B.A. (N = 94)	49	35	72	26	58	16	44	39
A.A. (N = 118)	49	50	90	20	59	16	40	30
6. Size (Faculty)								
Large (301+) (N = 48)	26	36	66	45	68	39	76	34
Medium (76–300) (N = 118)	41	41	76	33	57	22	55	35
Small (1–75) (N = 134)	53	41	82	21	54	11	33	35

ticularly significant fact. But with more doctorates comes more research, more graduate teaching, and more technical training. The percent of doctoral degrees on the faculty, therefore, is a good indicator of the complexity and sophistication of tasks on that campus. In addition, we examined the highest degree that the institution offered, making the simple assumption that an institution offering a doctoral program had a much more complex and demanding task than ones that offered only an associate in arts or bachelor's degree.

With a few minor exceptions, there is a relentless tendency for institutions with more doctorates and offering higher degrees to have lower levels of bureaucracy and higher faculty autonomy (see Table 9, items 4 and 5). Moreover, the pattern is not only regular, it is extremely *strong*. In short, expertise does buy power—it reduces the level of bureaucratization and increases the level of autonomy.

The Impact of Size and Complexity on Bureaucratization and Autonomy. Where, we wondered, can an individual professor best protect his or her specialized academic interests and retain the freedom to teach, write, and conduct research without interference? Under what organizational conditions can academic departments control their own destinies by determining curriculum, hiring and promoting faculty, and managing their own budgets?

The common academic conception is that a "community of scholars" is found only in small colleges. It is on the smaller campuses many think, where individual faculty members and departments are able to pursue their own intellectual interests and control their own destinies. Writers like Paul Goodman (1962) and John Millett (1962), for instance, argue that small colleges have escaped the creeping bureaucratization infecting the multiversities, and that professional autonomy is greater on small campuses. The common theme warns us against the dangers of complicated bureaucracies in the large universities.

But is this conception accurate? Does size and structural complexity negatively affect the work activities of professors? Does the large, complex university restrict academic autonomy by burying people in bureaucratic red tape? Does the large institution restrict professional decision making in academic departments? Will young professors entering the profession be wise to avoid the complex schools and head for the community of scholars on a small campus?

Our research strongly suggests that small colleges do not necessarily promote professional autonomy and that large institutions do not necessarily impose more bureaucratic regulations. In fact, the astonishing result is exactly the contrary. The size breakdown (item 6 in Table 9) shows surprising figures.

First, twice as many professors in small institutions (53 percent) report that their contracts are very detailed and rigid than in large institutions (26 percent). There is only a small difference between large and small institutions on course offerings, with larger institutions giving the professor a little more freedom. But there is sharp variation in travel regulations, with smaller institutions being significantly more rigid and rule-bound than large institutions.

When we consider professional autonomy we find the advantage of large institutions still holds. Twice as many professors in those institutions report that faculty peers are the primary evaluators for promotion and tenure. Additionally, more departmental autonomy is found there, and more faculty control and influence over courses, promotions, and the selection and hiring of faculty. There is not much difference between large and small institutions in their ability to control budgets. But, in summary, it appears that large institutions are significantly less bureaucratic than small ones, and give much more autonomy to faculty members and their departments.

We have been discussing several different types of bureaucratization and professional autonomy. To simplify our analysis of the data, we used factor analysis to construct a simple index from several measures which conceptually fit together. The scores were averaged for each institution on (1) contract specification, (2) travel, (3) courses taught, (4) peer evaluation, (5) faculty selection, and (6) tenure decisions. This gave a *single overall measure:* the higher the index number the less bureaucratization and the more professional autonomy.

Table 10 shows the index scores when we break down our 300 sample institutions into groups according to size and other factors. No matter how we break it down, the advantage always lies with the larger institutions.

What are the reasons for this positive relationship between size and many aspects of professional autonomy? Numbers alone do not explain the dynamics, the actual processes by which size affects

Table 10. Bureaucracy and Autonomy Index.

		Small (0–75) Mean	Medium (76–300) Mean	Large (over 300) Mean	Total Mean	N
I.	All Schools Combined	32.6	41.5	54.4	39.6	300
II.	Highest Degree Offered:					
	A.A.	27.4	36.8	40.6	30.9	118
	B.A.	37.8	41.3	44.2	39.6	94
	M.A.	48.0	44.5	50.3	46.5	56
	Ph.D.	45.3	56.1	60.6	59.4	32
III.	Student Selectivity:					
	Open Door	28.7	36.7	42.3	33.0	142
	Selective	35.1	37.2	52.0	38.0	80
	Highly Selective	42.7	52.3	62.1	53.1	78
IV.	Formal Governance and Control:					
	State and Local	26.1	28.5	44.0	29.5	12
	Local Goverment	26.3	40.5	28.0	32.8	44
	State Government	30.5	37.5	53.4	40.6	109
	Private	36.0	45.9	65.4	41.9	135
V.	Major Fund Sources:					
	State	27.9	37.7	48.1	35.4	138
	Church and Tuition	31.1	46.1	0	32.9	26
	Tuition	37.0	43.1	55.2	40.5	88
	Dispersed Funding	40.8	51.8	60.7	53.3	48
VI.	Faculty Perception of Control by Outside Groups:					
	High Interference	27.6	35.3	50.4	34.3	101
	Medium Interference	32.8	39.5	54.0	39.1	102
	Low Interference	38.0	47.9	63.5	44.9	97

Note: The higher the index number, the less bureaucracy and the more professional autonomy. The index is a combined measure of the bureaucracy and professional autonomy variables used in Tables 11 and 12. It was produced by factor analysis, a statistical technique that allows combining of many factors into a single combined measure.

the work setting of a professional. Size must be associated with *organizational processes* which directly affect autonomy. Not only that, we must consider whether factors such as the financial base or the "quality" of a school, and not size, are affecting professional autonomy. The following paragraphs offer some interpretations, and show that size has major impact even when other important factors are taken into account.

First, *increased size is almost always related to more complex tasks,* such as conducting sophisticated research, teaching graduate students, and consulting on outside projects. In turn, more complex tasks require more highly *trained experts* who demand and receive more autonomy. It is reasonable to expect this last, and that administrators would be more willing to relinquish decisions to those experts. So the equation is not surprising: larger schools have more complex tasks and employ more highly trained experts, therefore the degree of professional autonomy in those institutions is higher and the level of bureaucracy is lower. The expertise of the faculty is probably the critical link between size and autonomy. Section III of Table 10 also suggests that higher quality students are also related to more professional autonomy.

A *second dynamic process that helps explain the positive influence of size is "differentiation," the division of complex organizations into subunits.* Large organizations tend to fragment into specialized departments concentrating on unique tasks. Sociologists have found high correlations between size and specialization regardless of the kind of organization: the larger the size, the more specialized the units (see Blau, 1973).

Why does this increased differentiation result in more professional autonomy? In effect, larger size means that the individual professors deal primarily with subunits, not with the whole organization, and they can more effectively influence decision processes. In addition, the subunits tend to be specialized, and they become powerful because they have faculty with the necessary expertise to deal with special knowledge and special tasks. In short, increased complexity promotes the growth of strong *professional enclaves,* islands of autonomy within the larger institution. The reverse side of this equation is that administrators in larger institutions simply cannot, because of size, meddle in every department's activities. The situation is simply too complex for careful, over-the-shoulder scrutiny. By contrast, in small institutions, deans, vice-presidents, and presidents can—and do—impose more direct supervision and inter-fere more often in departmental affairs. The small institutions may have more opportunities for developing a "community of scholars," but they also are small enough to allow "mother hen" interference by top administrators.

Third, size is connected to the "environmental relations" issue. Earlier in this chapter we suggested that *control over vital institutional resources* by outside groups (legislatures, church groups, special interest groups) decreases autonomy and increases bureau-cracy. In fact, when "environmental pressure" factors were correlated with professional autonomy, a strong negative correlation ($r = .50$) resulted. The impact of environmental pressure is definitely affected by size considerations.

Increased size apparently acts as a buffer against environ-mental pressure, since faculties in the smaller schools lost more au-tonomy from environmental pressure than those in larger schools (Section VI of Table 10). Again, the big institutions seem to offer places to hide. The professors and their departments seem to be more insulated from environmental demands. Does the state legislature demand cost-accounting for faculty time? By the time the regulation finally reaches the individual faculty member in a larger institution, layers of sympathetic administrators have undermined the regula-tion's effectiveness and protected the faculty against intrusion. Does a conservative benefactor want fewer radical professors on campus? In the large institution, radicals can hide more easily within the shelter of their departments, attracting less attention and surrounded by allies. In short, greater size increases the number of sheltered professional enclaves where faculty can escape the harsh scrutiny of outside groups. Sections IV and V of Table 10 deal with other en-vironmental aspects that reveal the same basic pattern: outside pressures do affect autonomy, but they always negatively affect smaller schools more than larger.

Summary

Faculty members belong to one of the largest major profes-sional groups. They share many of the attitudes and problems of other professionals—teachers, lawyers, doctors, social workers—who work in large organizations. Professors, like other professionals, demand autonomy, freedom from bureaucratic control, and control over their professional tasks. There are many similarities between professors and other professionals.

There also are many similarities within higher education, but there are many significant differences, as well. In many ways higher education has a collection of mini-professions gathered under the umbrella of "professor." A community college instructor may have more in common with the local high school teacher than with a professor in a major graduate center. And the graduate professor may feel more at home with a colleague in a private "think-tank" like RAND Corporation than with the community college instructor. Furthermore, the variation in *academic tasks*—teaching, research, community service—at any level is enormous.

There are also substantial differences in the way institutions support professional values and autonomy—or tie them down with bureaucratic regulations and control. Some institutions are tight bureaucracies, while others seem to be loosely confederated collections of departments that have much autonomy. The following are some of our conclusions.

First, professionals in the large, more prestigious colleges and universities engage in a greater degree of *peer evaluation* than their colleagues in smaller, less research-oriented institutions. When work is assessed, it is often faculty peers who do so in larger schools, while it tends to be administrators in small institutions.

Second, larger, more prestigious institutions support higher levels of *departmental autonomy*. Professors identify strongly with their disciplines in these institutions, and authority is lodged in academic departments. In larger, research-oriented institutions characterized by a high degree of faculty expertise and task complexity, more discretion is accorded the department to select its faculty, control its courses, and arrange for promotions and tenure. However, budgets are administratively controlled in all schools.

Third, there is less *bureaucracy and regulation* in large, more prestigious schools. Having special knowledge at their command, most academic professionals seek and get independence from organizational controls and routinization. Complex schools with highly trained faculty afforded the professionals greater freedom from bureaucratic regulations and "standard operating procedures." Such institutions have fewer travel regulations, are less likely to specify the courses faculty are required to teach, and have more flexible, open-ended, personnel contracts.

This study suggests that the large college or university may provide faculty members with more opportunities to preserve autonomy and avoid bureaucratization. Our research undermines the conception that small colleges best enhance academic autonomy. On the contrary, we find that larger schools provide the most autonomous work environment for the professional. The multiversity may yet prove to be a threat to cherished values, and the small college may still be an enclave of professional opportunity. As we have measured it, however, professional autonomy has a better chance in the multiversity than in the legendary small college environment. People may argue that we measured the wrong factors, that if we had measured X or Y our conclusions would be different. But we believe our measures were indeed central to the professional task, and do indeed provide a realistic barometer of campus climates.

This does not mean of course, that all large universities are havens of autonomy. Many definitely are not. Petty tyrants often hang their hats in large as well as in small colleges. Our results do not imply that all small colleges have little professional autonomy, or that their administrations are constantly breathing down the professors' necks. To be sure, there are many examples of small, elite colleges that resemble the legendary "community of scholars." Professors at Amherst, Reed, Carlton, or Antioch would probably deny our picture of the small college as being less professionally autonomous. Nevertheless, in spite of the obvious exceptions, our data do show a strong trend toward greater autonomy in larger, more prestigious institutions.

Chapter 6

Institutional Climates
and Faculty Morale

This chapter investigates the morale of college and university faculty members by asking a number of questions: What attitudes do faculty hold toward the colleges and universities that employ them? Do they feel they are partners in the educational enterprise or merely hired hands? Do they think the administration is on their side, or do they lack confidence in it? Are they satisfied with their students, their offices, and their teaching loads? Would they choose to stay in their jobs or depart for greener academic pastures if presented with the opportunity? Do the orientations of the faculty towards the administration in private institutions differ from those in public institutions? Are junior college faculty members more, or less, content with their lot than are university professors? The responses to questions such as these can help us better understand the multifaceted aspects of faculty morale.

    The area of worker morale is not new to organizational

theory. Some of the earliest studies of complex organizations dealt at least partially with the morale of organization members. The attitude of workers towards the organization was an important element of the landmark studies by F. J. Roethlisberger and W. J. Dickson in the Western Electric Plant (1939). A later work by R. Blauner, *Alienation and Freedom* (1964) links the alienation of assembly line workers from their jobs to a loss of responsibility and craftsmanship that results from highly routinized labor.

The question of the morale of *professionals* poses a somewhat different problem. Professionals work on highly complex, wholistic tasks with which they strongly identify. It follows then, that the morale of professionals is not reducible to alienation from routinized, segmented tasks. Furthermore, the nature of professional organizations requires that authority be shared by the professionals responsible for accomplishing the goals of these organizations. Therefore, the core tasks of colleges and universities, teaching and research, are basically the responsibility of the faculty, and the *attitudes* of the individuals charged with these tasks certainly affect the manner in which they are accomplished. This impact of professional morale on the tasks of higher educational institutions is far-reaching but somewhat hard to measure. And morale has important effects on governance, as well. It is, in fact, crucial in its impact on the politics of academic decision making.

As usual, we find great diversity among faculties spread throughout higher education. In some segments, morale is high: faculty trust their administrators, are satisfied with their working conditions, and are closely identified with their local campuses. In other segments there is a troubled, almost hostile relation between the faculties and their institutions. Those feelings show up in low morale, distrust of administrators, dissatisfaction with working conditions. They also show up in action—such as joining unions. In the first half of the chapter we will *describe* these patterns of morale; in the second half we will offer theories to *explain* why these patterns emerge.

Patterns of Faculty Morale

What exactly do we mean by faculty morale? Obviously, a number of attitudes could be included in a definition of morale. For this study, four elements have been chosen: trust, satisfaction, institutional identification, and militancy.

Trust. By "trust" we mean the attitude of faculty toward administrators. The concept is borrowed from William Gamson (1968). According to Gamson, "partisans" (in this case faculty) express feelings of trust toward "authorities" (in this case administrators) in terms of two key elements: bias and efficiency. First, the faculty may perceive that the administrators are "biased," essentially a feeling that the administrators may or may not be "on their side." The second element of trust is the faculty's feeling that the administrators are "efficient," that they are capable of making fair intelligent decisions, and then backing them up with action. All the right motivations, intents, and policies of administrators are useless if they cannot get the job done. Inept administrators cannot be trusted to produce a favorable outcome if it is beyond their capabilities. Gamson's analysis refers to trust on a *specific* issue to be decided, but we use the term as a *generalized* attitude of confidence, or lack of it, that a faculty holds toward its administration. This concept of trust was measured by asking the faculty to agree or disagree with five statements:

1. In general, the top administration of this institution is competent, able, and energetic (67 percent agreed).
2. If faced with a major campus disturbance, the administration would be likely to give in to outside pressure (33 percent agreed).
3. In general, this administration has a very progressive attitude about faculty welfare, salary, and work conditions (58 percent agreed).
4. The administration generally understands the needs of academic professionals and works to make this a place where the faculty can work productively (61 percent agreed).
5. Communication between the faculty and administration is usually open, easy, and effective (58 percent agreed).

In every case a majority of the faculty indicated fairly high confidence in its administration, although agreement with the item on communication between faculty and administration was lower than the other indicators. (Note that agreement expressed confidence for every question except number two, where *disagreeing* that the administration would give in to outside pressure was an expression of confidence.)

Because working with five separate items of trust was awkward, a single measure was constructed by scoring each respondent on the number of expressions of confidence. That is, if the person answered three questions showing confidence in his administration, he received a score of three. Every individual was scored from zero, extremely low trust, to five, extremely high trust. To devise an even simpler measure, respondents were then divided into high and low groups; three or more positive evaluations was rated high trust, and two or fewer low trust. When all respondents were divided into high or low trust, 59.5 percent were rated high on the scale and 40.5 percent were rated low.

Satisfaction. Our definition of the second component of faculty morale is "satisfaction with working conditions." This component's definition is more specific than the broader definitions used by other researchers. For example, Likert and Willits (1940) define "job morale" as "an individual's mental attitude toward all features of his work and toward all the people with whom he works." Guion (1958) defines satisfaction as "the extent to which the individual's needs are satisfied and the extent to which the individual perceives that satisfaction as stemming from his total job situation." Studies focusing on "satisfaction" by those definitions are usually concerned with the impact of supervision, the work group, job content, wages, promotional opportunities, and work. (Vroom, 1964).

In this study, satisfaction specifically means the degree to which participants are content with their *work situation:* their salary, their teaching load, the competence of their students, and the adequacy of their office facility. Satisfaction was measured by asking faculty members to agree or disagree with four statements:

1. My office facility is adequate as a comfortable efficient work place (75 percent agreed).
2. The typical student at this school is academically competent (72 percent agreed).
3. My present annual salary is reasonably good in light of my qualifications and experience (66 percent agreed).

4. My teaching load is too heavy; it is unreasonable in light of my other responsibilities (24 percent agreed).

For the most part, faculty members seem content, at least according to these measures. Although most think their salaries, teaching loads, offices, and students are acceptable, in each item there is a substantial proportion—26 to 33 percent—who are dissatisfied.

As with the trust dimension, we constructed a single satisfaction measure for each individual based on the number of positive evaluation items marked. A respondent with three or more positive evaluations was ranked as high satisfaction. When the sample was divided, 66.2 percent were characterized as high in satisfaction, and 33.8 percent ranked low in satisfaction.

Institutional Identification. The third dimension of faculty morale with which we were concerned was "institutional identification." Gouldner (1957–1958) discusses the professional's dilemma of split loyalties. He argues that in the process of professional socialization an individual develops loyalty to and identification with his profession. When he accepts a position in an organization, long-established and deep-seated loyalties to his discipline will detract from his identification with the employing organization; the "cosmopolitan" may conflict with the "local" feelings. In this study, institutional identification reflects the loyalty of the faculty member to the college or university where he is employed. To measure institutional identification, we asked for a response to the following statements:

Your identification with the institution as related to employment possibilities elsewhere: (Check one)

1. My identification with this institution is very strong. I probably would not leave except under very unusual circumstances.
2. My identification with this institution is moderate. I probably would leave for a better job.
3. My identification with this institution is fairly weak. I probably would leave for a better job and perhaps even for a comparable job.

Forty-nine percent of the faculty respondents are strong (high) in institutional identification. They answered "I probably would not leave except under very unusual circumstances."

Militancy. We suspected that prounion sentiments are likely to reflect low morale among faculty. Dissatisfaction with working conditions and institutional policies, we reasoned, would move the faculty to express attitudes favoring collective negotiations (35 percent did), supporting strikes (15 percent did), and desiring more "militant" stands in regard to administrations (23 percent did).

In our 1971 survey the responses were rather low, although a solid third of the faculty favored collective bargaining. By 1977 we have additional surveys (for example, the Ladd and Lipsett series in the *Chronicle of Higher Education,* 1975–1976) that show the number of faculty favoring prounion, militant attitudes has almost doubled from the 1971 levels. In this analysis we will use the 1971 figures. We know the *absolute* numbers will have increased, but we are confident that the *relative* distribution (say between community colleges and universities) of people holding these attitudes is about the same as it was in 1971.

Individual Characteristics and Faculty Morale

Let us break those gross national averages down, starting with some *individual characteristics.* It is possible to get a feeling for faculty morale across the country by examining several distinct individual characteristics (see Table 11).

Trust, satisfaction, and international identification all seem to *increase with academic rank and publication rate* (Table 11, items 1 and 2). This is easily understood. Those individuals who are rewarded by the system with rank and security are most likely to have a greater confidence in the system. That confidence level also seems related to the faculty member's degree: the higher the degree, the higher the level of satisfaction with working conditions (item 3). Essentially, we have a "fat cat" phenomenon. The people who are well-off are also more satisfied.

What are the differences in morale between *faculty members and administrators* (Table 11, item 4)? It is clear that administrators are more satisfied, more trusting, and have greater identification with the institution than with the faculty. Among administrators, it is also apparent that members of the central administration have higher morale than college or school administrators, who in turn, have higher morale than departmental administrators. Of course, given the way the questions in the scales were phrased, that pattern would be expected. The items on the trust scale, in particular, reflect confidence (or lack of) in the administration. It would be a sorry group of administrators indeed who registered low confidence in themselves. But the increase of morale with proximity to the center of things might also reflect the man-in-the-middle role of departmental administrators. Their scores place them right between faculty and major administrators. They are Janus-like looking both ways at once, and holding morale levels right between the groups.

Turning to *sex differences,* men are higher in trust and satisfaction than women, but men express a lower institutional identification. Since women are still discriminated against in higher education as well as in other segments of our society, the lower trust and satisfaction level of women seems logical. But if so, why should their institutional identification be higher than that of men? Perhaps Gouldner's (1957–1958) arguments on split loyalties apply here. The longer the period of professional socialization and training, the greater the professional's orientation to a discipline, at the expense of his loyalty to the employing institution. Highly trained individuals whose primary loyalty is to the discipline are characterized as "cosmopolitans." Less highly trained individuals are more likely to be "locals," loyal to their employers. We know that women in higher education are overrepresented in the junior colleges and under-represented in the four-year colleges and universities. Fewer women hold doctorates than men, and women are, on the average, less highly trained. Therefore, women are more apt to be "locals" than are men, and their higher institutional identification reflects this orientation. The male/female differences will be further discussed in Chapter Eight.

The *subject matter* split is very interesting. Humanities and social sciences rank lowest in trust; natural sciences are medium; professional and vocational are highest. What explains these differences?

During the post-Sputnik boom in funding for the sciences,

Table 11. Faculty Morale and Individual Characteristics.

	High Trust	High Work Satisfaction	High Institutional Identification	Want Unions[a]	Favor Strike[a]	Favor More Militancy[a]
National Average	60%	66%	53%	35%	15%	23%
1. Rank						
Professor	70	79	69	27	10	20
Associate	62	68	49	33	15	24
Assistant	52	62	34	37	17	27
Lecturer/Instructor	55	57	34	43	10	23
2-year Vocational/Technical	46	57	59	52	11	14
2-year Academic	52	56	57	55	20	26
2. Number Articles in Last 4 Years						
1–10	57	60	52			
11–20	60	70	46			
21–30	65	79	50			
Over 30	71	79	55			
3. Degree Earned						
Bachelors	65	64	55	41	10	14
Masters	56	60	50	43	16	23
Professional	66	62	49	29	14	25
Doctorate	57	71	47	30	14	25

4. Administrative					
Position					
None	57	65	44		
Department Chair	71	72	66		
Dean	77	74	72		
Central Administration	86	82	71		
5. Sex					
Male	61	68	48	35	16	25
Female	57	59	54	37	11	16
6. Discipline					
Humanities	53	62	46	40	19	32
Natural Science	62	70	50	31	10	33
Social Science	55	69	42	36	23	17
Professional	65	68	61	30	10	13
Vocational/Technical	67	62	56	44	11	17

[a] Blank spaces indicate data not available.

humanists and social scientists ground their teeth with envy as labs and cyclotrons blossomed on the face of the land. Poets groaned of imbalance in academic priorities. Small wonder that "hard" scientists are higher in trust—confident that they will continue to prosper—while humanists and social scientists do not see their positions as being so favored. The financial crisis of the seventies has continued these trends. At the opposite end, there is an element of marginality to vocational education in many academic circles that may serve those teachers grateful for their status within the system. The alternative for vocational education teachers in colleges is, in many cases, high school teaching. In any event, the differences in morale between subject areas are not huge; about fourteen percentage points separate the high morale people from the low.

In summary, what have we learned about the relation between morale and individual characteristics? The data say that those closer to the center of power and who have more advantages have higher morale. They are more established: they are professors more than assistant professors, publishers more than nonpublishers, men more than women, administrators more than nonadministrators. The results are consistent with objective advantages.

Institutional Characteristics and Faculty Morale

Now let us shift gears, moving from *individual* to *institutional* characteristics. If we compare the range of scores on trust, satisfaction, and institutional identification according to institutional types, a trend becomes obvious (see Table 12). In general, trust and satisfaction in Multiversities and the Elite Liberal Arts Colleges are high, and institutional identification is low. In the Community Colleges and Private Junior Colleges, on the other hand, trust and satisfaction are low, while institutional identification and militancy are high.

The Private and Public Multiversities. Large in size, with high-prestige faculties, these institutions are buffered from environmental onslaughts by their reputations and by institutional size itself. Because academics in these institutions are influential, in general they are confident of their positions, and their high morale reflects their confidence. Their *trust in administrators* is above average, but not markedly so. The slightly higher trust evidenced by faculties in private multiversities reflects their slightly greater influence, since their administrators are accountable to broadly-based boards of trustees rather than to regents or legislatures.

Table 12. Faculty Morale Levels in Different Types of Institutions.

	Measures of Morale					
	High Trust	High Satisfaction	High Institutional Identification	Want Unions	Favor Strikes	Favor More Militancy
National Average						
All Institutions	60%	59%	53%	35%	15%	23%
Private Multiversity	66	80	46	27	11	21
Public Multiversity	62	76	48	28	13	21
Elite Liberal Arts	73	80	47	24	9	18
Public Comprehensives	54	56	47	36	15	25
Public Colleges	59	59	45	33	13	28
Private Liberal Arts	63	60	56	29	9	21
Community Colleges	56	54	56	56	18	23
Private Junior Colleges	53	48	62	32	6	23

Note: Numbers are the average percent of faculty in each institutional group who expressed the attitude.

In these Multiversities, *work satisfaction* is extremely high—twenty to thirty percentage points above most institutions. By almost any measure, these faculty are at the very top of the academic totem pole—and they know it! However, they have a lower level of *institutional identification*. This is a reflection of their "cosmopolitan" outlook, their loyalty to their disciplines. If a better opportunity exists elsewhere, these faculty members will weigh the advantages seriously. Their publications create a professional visibility that encourages offers, but institutional reputation acts as a constraint. Although sought after and mobile, individuals usually shift from positions in one multiversity to a similar appointment in another. They may move, but they do it within the same tier.

The Elite Liberal Arts Colleges. Behold, the bastions of collegiality. In these institutions highly expert academicians emphasize general education in the arts and sciences for top quality students. These are the "name-brand" Liberal Arts Colleges: Reed, Smith, or Dartmouth. The smaller scale of these colleges reduces complexity and increases faculty allegiance to the whole institution, instead of merely to one's own disciplinary department. The administration is visible without being overwhelming, and may join the faculty in being caught up in the saga of the school's mission; faculty members in these colleges have the nation's highest level of *trust* in their administrations (73 percent). Burton R. Clark (1970, p. 262) suggests that institutions with a deep, rich heritage develop in faculty members strong attachments and high morale; these in turn help overcome cosmopolitan detachment and engage the faculty with institutional ideals. "Careerist motives are not enough; an embodied idea is the institutional chariot to which individual motive becomes chained. When the idea is in command, men are indifferent to personal cost. They often are not even aware of how much they have risked, and how much they sometimes have sacrificed. As ideologues, as believers, they do not care. They are proud of what they have been through, what they have done, and what they stand for. They feel highly involved in the worthwhile collective effort and wish to remain with it. For the organization, the richly embellished institutional definition that we call a saga, can then be invaluable in maintaining viability in a competitive market. It is also invaluable as a foundation for trust within the institutional group, easing communication and cooperation."

In the Elite Liberal Arts Colleges, the working conditions are among the best—pay is high, students are good, colleagues are excellent, prestige is high. And faculty *satisfaction* matches the plush conditions, with 80 percent reporting high satisfaction. Their levels of *militant attitudes* are quite low. But like other cosmopolitans in other elite institutions, the faculty in these elite liberal arts colleges still keep a wary eye open for a better job elsewhere—their *institutional* identification is not extremely high. Even in academic paradise the faculty are fickle professionals.

Public Comprehensives. These are the solid middle-quality state institutions that comprise a fairly large portion of the American academic scene. The typical faculty at these schools is slightly above the middle range in expertise, with about 55 percent holding doctoral degrees. Faculty morale, as measured by trust (54 percent, tied for lowest place), and satisfaction (56 percent, one of the lowest), is much lower in these institutions than in the Elite Liberal Arts Colleges, the Multiversities, and even the Public Colleges. What is operating here may be invidious comparisons by faculty who look upon their colleagues in the Multiversities with envy. Their own professional lives seem relatively unsatisfactory because they do not carry out the amount of graduate teaching and research that is done in those other institutions. Research is the key to publication, and thus to prestige, influence, and the chance for mobility. In addition, their students are not so highly selected, there are more of them, and teaching loads are heavier as a consequence. As highly trained professionals, they are acquainted with conditions in the Multiversities, but they stand just outside the elite circle and their morale suffers by comparison.

Public Colleges. This is the least prestigious group among the state institutions. Their faculties have fewer doctorates, teach undergraduates almost exclusively, and do little research. Many were former "normal schools" or teachers' colleges. In many ways, their "objective" situation is worse than that of most other four-year institutions.

The surprise, however, is that in spite of their relatively disadvantaged positions, the morale of faculty at public colleges is really not lower than the better-off Public Comprehensives, and by some measures it is slightly higher. In general, it is fair to say these public colleges are in the middle on *trust* and *work satisfaction*. However, there is a hint of uneasiness, for they have the highest level of "favoring more militancy," and among the highest levels of those who "want unions." Also surprising is their level of *institutional identification*; their 45 percent is the lowest score of all institutions. In the elite institutions we see low identification as simply a sign of personal marketability, but since faculty in the Public Colleges have little visibility and fewer opportunities to move, we suspect their low identification is really a morale factor—they really want to escape their situations in spite of their low marketability.

Private Liberal Arts Colleges. Of small to moderate size, these institutions are similar, professionally, to the Public Colleges.

Whereas the public colleges face problems of accountability to the legislature or regents, the private institutions' environmental concern is securing enough tuition to keep the ship afloat. Given the similarity to public colleges in terms of *trust* and *satisfaction,* the much higher *institutional identification* of these private college faculties stands out remarkably. One factor may be relative pro-fessionalism—about 30 to 40 percent of the faculty have doctorates. Chances for mobility are limited, both by lack of visibility in the professional market and by individual aspirations. A number of these schools have ties to a particular religious community, and religious loyalty coupled with dedication to the college's mission may act as a self-imposed restraint.

Community Colleges. These are characterized by low *trust* and *satisfaction* and high *institutional identification.* Because teach-ing, not research, is the professional activity here, there are fewer faculty doctorates. Relative newcomers to the scene, these colleges are not buffered from the environment. They are subject to strong budget control from state and local governments, "accountability" demands that leave much of the decision making in the hands of the administration or the board of trustees. Research grants bring no lush facilities, and most of these colleges have open admissions from a given locale. Faculty members, mere employees, reflect their lack of influence and power in their low trust and satisfaction. Moreover, they have the highest prounion attitudes, and express strong militancy.

A lower degree of professionalism probably accounts for the high *institutional identification* of these faculties. Faculty members not known through research or publications are not eagerly sought after by other institutions. On the other hand, their "relative" situa-tion may not be all that bad in their own eyes. By comparison to similarly credentialed colleagues in high schools, these faculty mem-bers are well off and they evidently feel they should stay where they are.

The Private Junior Colleges. These institutions are the lowest in trust and satisfaction, and highest in institutional identification. They are struggling to stay alive. Money is tight and budgets are slim. These factors keep power in the hands of the administration, and the limited expertise of the faculty provides little basis for influence or options for other teaching positions elsewhere. A number of these colleges, as sectarian schools, raise institutional identification levels even higher than in the community colleges.

Factors that Explain Morale Differences

Up to this point, this chapter has *described* the patterns of faculty morale at different institutions. In the remainder we will try to *explain* why these differences occur. Four general propositions guide our explanation: (1) Increased environmental pressure reduces morale; (2) Higher levels of faculty professionalism increase morale; (3) Size has a mixed, complicated impact on morale; and (4) Higher bureaucratization reduces morale, while greater professional autonomy increases it.

Environmental Arguments. Earlier, we pictured the relationship between an educational institution and its environment as a two-way street. The impacts on bureaucratization and professional autonomy were clear at institutions with high environmental pressure: authority became centralized, the discretionary leeway of departments was reduced, standardization and regulation by bureaucrats proliferated. When an institution was buffered from the environment, these tendencies were less obvious. For example, despite legislative pressure, the traditional prestige of many large, well-known institutions protects them from environmental demands.

What differences do these environmental relationships make to the trust, satisfaction, and institutional identification of college and university faculty members? Does faculty morale in institutions that are largely dependent on one financial source differ from morale at institutions where funds are drawn from many sources? Will trust be greater in institutions that are assured a reliable and select supply of students than in schools struggling to stay alive? We argue that strong pressure from environmental factors causes faculty influence to suffer. Further, the perceived threat of interference in the running of the institution by politicians, groups of citizens, funding agencies, and so forth has real consequences for faculty morale. A faculty that is powerless against environmental influences can expect that professional benefits will be reduced, and lowered confidence in a work situation should result in lower trust. Accordingly, we hypothesize that as environmental pressure increases, trust and satisfaction decrease. Let us see if the data support this proposition.

There is no easily interpreted relationship between morale and the type of formal control (see item 1 in Table 13). Trust and satisfaction are highest in private institutions and lowest in locally-controlled institutions. Institutional identification is found to be highest in local colleges and lowest in state institutions. Remember, in Chapter 5 we did not find any significant relationship between formal control and bureaucracy—between professional autonomy in private versus public institutions. Again, the public/private division—that old standby of entirely too many studies in higher education—does not seem to be particularly valuable. Too many other factors are at work, and the public/private distinction is simply too crude to be meaningful. The only real difference is in the "local" community colleges, and we doubt that their public control is the real factor at work.

The data showing reliance on a particular pattern of *financial relations and funding* sheds a little more light on the scene (Table 13, item 2). The major differences are between institutions with "dispersed" sources of income, compared to all the others. We have stated earlier that institutions with dispersed, as opposed to concentrated, funding have maximum professional autonomy. When the finances come from a variety of sources, the issue of accountability to a specific interest group is not paramount. Power is decentralized and more of it is shared by the faculty. These dispersed-funding institutions are characterized by the pick of the student crop, the most renowned faculties, and—not coincidentally—the best salaries and working conditions. That combination of factors leads naturally to more satisfied faculties. Accordingly, trust and satisfaction are highest in these "dispersed-funding" institutions, which include some of the most distinguished American universities.

On the bottom of the *work satisfaction* totem pole are institutions heavily dependent upon church funds. Because their faculties are low in satisfaction it seems somewhat incongruous that these same church-funded institutions are highest in *institutional identification,* have few militant attitudes, and are reasonably high in *trust* of administrators. A plausible interpretation is the religious dedication of a large percentage of faculty—ordained teaching members of churches and dedicated laymen. Usually, administrators at these institutions are also religion-affiliated, binding faculty to administration in the struggle to make the best of things. In other words, man does not live by bread alone—nor apparently by salaries, offices, students, and teaching loads alone. This represents a version of "organizational saga" far removed from the elite, "distinctive" colleges that Burton R. Clark wrote about.

A few other institutional characteristics should be briefly mentioned. Institutions rate *high* in trust and satisfaction when they are (1) wealthy, (2) older, (3) selective in student admissions, and (4) low in the amount of external influence the faculty perceive (item 3, Table 13). By contrast, institutions have lower morale when those conditions are reversed.

Let us now shift for a moment from institutional back to certain *individual* attitudes. The individual differences in morale that were shown earlier in Table 11 make sense in the light of environmental relationships. The discipline group lowest in trust and satisfaction was humanists. Perhaps this dissatisfaction and mistrust is based on actual environmental threats. Millions of dollars poured into science and engineering in the fifties and sixties in response to the Sputnik has left the humanists at a relative disadvantage. Even today, it is easy to see a cost-conscious board economizing by cutting the "frilly" humanists rather than the "practical" sciences. In other words the financial crisis of the seventies has continued the threats to the humanists that started two decades ago.

By rank, it is the assistant professors, not the tenured ones, who are low in trust and satisfaction. It is they, not the older, tenured faculty members, who are let go when cutbacks are made. Since the young assistant professor knows he will be sacrificed first, his faith in the institution is shaky, especially in financially troubled times. The lower ranked professors also get heavier teaching loads, the least desirable offices, and lower salaries.

In short, as we might expect, the individuals who feel least protected are those who feel most threatened by the environment. Their low trust and satisfaction reflect their status as pawns. This is not to say, however, that trust and satisfaction respond to environmental pressure for the same reasons. Trust is subtle and sensitive to

Table 13. Institutional Characteristics and Faculty Morale.

	High Trust	High Satisfaction	High Identification	Want Unions	Favor Strikes	Favor Militancy
1. Formal Control						
State	57%	59%	47%	38%	15%	23%
Local	56	53	59	59	19	24
Private	64	63	55	30	9	21
2. Financial Relations						
Public	56	56	52	49	17	24
Church	61	48	66	29	3	18
Tuition	62	63	52	30	9	23
Dispersed	67	69	49	29	12	19
3. Perceived External Influence						
High	47	56	51	48	17	28
Medium	64	66	54	36	13	20
Low	69	67	54	31	9	18
4. Highest Degree Offered						
Associate in Arts	56	54	47	50	15	23
Bachelors	62	61	51	31	10	22
Masters	65	62	51	31	13	21
Doctorate	60	72	47	31	14	24
5. Doctorates on Faculty						
Low (0–40%)	57	53	57	46	14	23
Medium (41–64%)	63	61	50	30	11	22
High (65% +)	63	73	47	30	13	22

6. Size

Small	60	55	56	40	10	21
Medium	61	62	51	37	14	22
Large	57	66	49	37	16	25

7. Autonomy Index (Higher Score = less bureaucracy, more faculty autonomy)

Low	51	51	54	47	13	24
Medium	64	60	56	36	11	20
High	64	67	49	33	15	22

both real and perceived threats. Satisfaction, on the other hand, is a direct reflection of objective differences in faculty working conditions.

Professional Impact on Morale. We have argued that the basis of a faculty's influence and power is its expertise—the knowledge and skills required to teach and conduct research. The more complex and esoteric the tasks of the institution, the higher the degree of expertise exhibited by the faculty. This increased expertise, translated into faculty power, leads to more professional autonomy and influence. Now we turn to the impact of task and expertise on faculty morale and attitudes.

Task (highest degree offered) and expertise (percent of faculty holding a doctorate) are closely related. Therefore, we might expect morale to be affected similarly by them. And in fact *satisfaction* does clearly increase with the complexity of the tasks and the need for a greater level of expertise in their accomplishment (see Table 13 items 4 and 5). People who hold doctorates are more satisfied with their pay, facilities, students, and teaching load—the dividends accrued through expertise. Furthermore, their professionalism is closely related to their cosmopolitan orientation, and hence their low institutional identification. Interestingly enough, trust does not seem to be strongly related to professional expertise, with the exception that in institutions characterized by less sophisticated tasks and fewer doctorates (the junior colleges), trust is not high.

Structural Factors: The Impact of Size and Complexity. Our earlier conclusions that size and complexity enhance professional autonomy and faculty influence run counter to prevailing concepts. Nonetheless, the evidence clearly shows that faculty members in the larger institutions feel better off than their counterparts in smaller settings. Will faculty morale reflect these differences? The answer is "yes" on some factors, "no" on others (see item 6, Table 13). *Work* satisfaction clearly increases with larger size, while *institutional identification* decreases—a pattern we have learned to expect. The increased faculty autonomy in large schools appears to result in more satisfaction with pay, students, facilities, and teaching load. The positive association between size and expertise is also reflected in this decreased faculty identification (more cosmopolitanism).

However, a surprising finding is that there seems to be no relationship between trust and size. Perhaps Paul Goodman and other advocates of the small college get some support here. We have shown in the previous chapter that increased size enhances autonomy, and increased autonomy increases trust; smaller size diminishes autonomy, and diminished autonomy reduces trust. Why, then, does trust not increase with larger size and complexity? In large institutions, it may be that increased impersonality and alienation *offsets* the positive effects of high professional autonomy. In smaller institutions, a feeling of in-group cohesion serves to enhance trust, offsetting the negative effects of low professional autonomy. Thus the overall relation between size and morale is mixed. Large size increases satisfaction, but makes no difference one way or the other on trust of administrators.

Bureaucracy and Morale. The level of bureaucracy and autonomy, and the feeling that faculty can effectively participate in decision and policy making at their institutions, can also affect the morale patterns of colleges and universities. In general, we expect higher morale when bureaucratization is low and faculty autonomy high.

The reader will recall that we measured "bureaucratization" by asking about institutional control of courses, faculty contracts and travel. And we measured "faculty departmental autonomy" by looking at departmental control of hiring, promotions, curriculum, and budget. These numerous individual measures were combined into one index score, using factor analysis. The Autonomy Summary Index is shown in Table 13, item 7, divided into high, medium, and low autonomy.

The results are as expected. Institutions with low bureaucratization and high faculty autonomy have higher levels of trust in administrators, greater satisfaction in their working conditions, and lower levels of pro-union sentiment. In short, autonomy and freedom from bureaucracy *do* seem to increase morale.

Summary

Let us look back over this discussion and summarize the issues. The morale of college and university faculty members is a complex subject, but a number of salient points emerge. First, morale is not dependent on a single issue. Trust, satisfaction, institutional identification, and militancy are distinct and separate attitudes. Each taps a different area of morale and faculty attitude, and each in turn is responsive to different environmental, professional, and organizational factors. It is a mistake to talk about "faculty morale." The only meaningful discussion of morale is in terms of different aspects and different attitudes.

Second, different types of morale vary significantly within the range of colleges and universities represented in our typology of academic institutions. Trust and satisfaction tend to be higher in the Multiversities and Elite Liberal Arts Colleges and lower in the two-year colleges. By the same token, institutional identification and militancy are high in the two-year colleges and low in the Multiversities and Elite Liberal Arts Colleges. Why do these variations occur?

Trust in administrators has to do primarily with two factors: the level of bureaucracy relative to autonomy, and environmental pressures. In general, when bureaucracy is low and faculty autonomy high, trust is high. And when environmental influence is high, trust is low. Academics are conscious of the environmental *milieux* of their colleges and universities. When the balance of power swings toward outside influences at the expense of faculty interests, trust is reduced and militancy is increased.

Larger *size* and higher levels of *expertise* seem to act as "buffers" against bureaucracy and environmental pressures. Even when environmental pressures are strong, large size and high expertise seem to protect the faculty, giving them professional enclaves in which to hide—keeping their trust levels high in spite of environmental pressure. By contrast, smaller institutions with less professional prestige are strongly influenced by environmental pressure and create more bureaucracy—so trust levels are lower.

Satisfaction with working conditions is a straightforward factor. The benefits which faculty members derive from their work vary considerably among kinds of institutions. Salaries, facilities, time off from teaching for research, and the quality of students—all are factors tied to a school's prestige and security, and its place in the higher education marketplace. Older, more affluent, more prestigious, larger schools can pay higher salaries and provide better working conditions—producing higher satisfaction.

Institutional identification depends on a syndrome of related factors. Whether or not faculty members identify strongly with their colleges and universities depends heavily on their expertise and training. Those who are more highly trained tend to be cosmopolitan rather than local in their orientations. They base their careers on their broadly based disciplines rather than on the particular schools where they are teaching. The less highly trained know that their horizons are limited, and as a consequence are more interested in maintaining or improving their positions where they are. "Reference group theory" plays a useful role in interpretating these facts. For many of the less highly trained faculty members, the relevant reference group is not the universities' elite corps of research-oriented Ph.D.s, but their equally less highly trained peers in the community colleges and high schools.

Thus, there are a number of factors that might account for the levels of trust and satisfaction displayed by a particular faculty:

1. *Objective working conditions.* The better the actual conditions in terms of salary, student, and teaching load, the greater the satisfaction reported by the faculty.
2. *External pressure.* The more the faculty felt threatened by powerful outside groups (trustees, church officials, legislators), the lower the morale evidenced.
3. *Reference groups.* The level of morale partly depended on a faculty's "reference group." Some objectively disadvantaged groups (such as community college faculty) compared themselves favorably with even more disadvantaged groups (such as high school teachers) and consequently had higher morale than might be expected. On the other hand, some priviliged groups did not have particularly high morale: they had many advantages, but they had learned to expect even more!
4. *Professional autonomy and freedom from bureaucracy.* Faculty groups with a direct role in decision making had higher morale; those tangled in bureaucracy felt helpless and had lower morale. This was true even when factors such as institutional quality and size were taken into account.
5. *Size and professionalism.* These factors seem to act as "buffers," providing professional enclaves, and protecting against the intrusion of environmental pressures and administrative bureaucracy.

Chapter 7

Impact of Bargaining on Campus Management

@@@@@@@@@@@@@@@@@@@@@

Faculty unions have achieved a prominent place in American higher education. Faculty unionization began only in the late 1960's, but by 1976 over 400 campuses in the United States had unionized faculties, and about 100,000 faculty members (about one sixth of the total) were members of unions. A few facts will be helpful:

- About 90 percent of unionized faculty members are on public campuses.
- Nearly two thirds of the unions are on two-year community college campuses.
- Most private institutions, and most of the "prestige" institutions have not unionized.

The authors extend a special thank-you to Frank R. Kemerer for his help in preparing this chapter.

154

- *Private* institutions are all under Federal government law, the National Labor Relations Act. All *public* institutions are under individual state laws, and recent Supreme Court rulings indicate that the federal government has no role in controlling state employee relations. Consequently, laws controlling public institutions develop on a state-by-state basis.
- Only about half the states allow faculties at public institutions to unionize—mostly industrial northeast and midwest states. When other major states pass appropriate legislation, unions are likely to expand further.

Much has been written about the causes and progress of faculty unionization. Few studies, however, have focused on the *consequences* arising from collective bargaining in higher education. The Stanford Project staff decided to commission a special study of this critical issue. That special study resulted in a book, *Unions on Campus,* co-authored by Frank R. Kemerer and J. Victor Baldridge (1975). In this chapter we summarize some of the crucial themes from that collective bargaining special study—themes that are related to other aspects of this book.

We have divided our discussion into two parts, the first looking at the effect collective bargaining has on components within administrative ranks and the second assessing the way management processes change when collective bargaining occurs.

The Power Game: Who Gains, Who Loses?

Many administrators perceive collective bargaining as threatening their management power. They fear that campus polarization will make effective decision making virtually impossible. On the other hand, many faculty members are hopeful that unions will serve as a counterbalance to what they feel is excessive administrative power. What does the research show concerning the effects of collective bargaining?

The picture is certainly mixed. On one hand, 46 percent of the presidents of unionized colleges indicate that collective bargaining has decreased their power, compared to 16 percent who say their power was increased. An almost equal percentage feels their power has not been affected (46 percent). Only presidents at private liberal arts institutions said they have either maintained or actually gained power. Union chairpersons, however, more often report that administrative power has decreased (56 percent). And when we questioned what might happen in the future, almost no union officials and only about one fifth of all presidents held that *"Where it occurs, faculty collective bargaining will increase the power of the administration at the expense of the faculty."* Administrators at two-year institutions perceived less hope for administrative gains than presidents of other institutions. This is not surprising, since the stated union goal at two-year colleges is to enfranchise the faculty at the expense of the administrators who previously dominated institutional decision making.

The Stanford project questionnaire also asked, *"Has collective bargaining increased faculty influence over issues that were previously the domain of administrators?"* Roughly one third of the campus presidents indicated that the influence of the faculty has increased, with the highest level of agreement—42 percent—in two-year institutions. About twice as many union chairpersons said faculty influence had increased (62 percent). While many in both groups reported no significant change in faculty influence, only a handful said collective bargaining had decreased it (13 percent of presidents, 9 percent of chairpersons).

How realistic are these fears—or hopes, depending on one's perspective— of administrative impotence? Our observations show a complex, multi-faceted picture.

First, unionism can weaken the administrative dominance of many two-year institutions, and those administrators can expect major changes. Second, we do not believe that unions have thus far jeopardized administrative authority on most four-year campuses. Most of the evidence seems to point to union, not administrative, weakness. Faculty contracts lack union security agreements, the scope of bargaining is limited, controversy often ranges within faculty ranks about the idea of unionism, and faculty unions often lack effective sanctions to apply against the administration.

Of course, the picture may change as unions gain tactical experience and wider legislative support. At the same time, administrators may also gain some of the same political advantages. In short, our general conclusion is that although collective bargaining does complicate the administrative process, administrators do not appear to have lost power, and may potentially have more—as we will explain next.

Outside Power Groups Seem to Gain Power

A union adapts to the organization it wants to influence; "parallel power pyramids" are constructed. If the campus is organized locally, the union organizes locally. If the campus is part of a system, the union organizes systemwide; and system-level influence is growing. Although the drive toward coordination of public higher education occurred before unions appeared, collective bargaining and centralization are ready-made stimulants for each other. In order to be effective, unions must deal directly with the power centers. It would come as no surprise, then, that systems of education tend to have systemwide bargaining. There has to be a union power center equivalent to the central administrative offices—and vice versa. The result is that centralized bargaining stimulates the trend toward centralized control. Moreover, unions must move to where the financial power lies, to the governor's office or the legislature. Our survey asked presidents of non-unionized and unionized campuses their reaction to the statement, *"System management is increasing all the time."* About 75 percent of both two-year and four-year college presidents agreed with the statement.

Interestingly, the movement toward collective bargaining in the first place partly reflects faculty anxiety over the erosion of local autonomy by statewide boards and coordinating agencies. Many faculty have embraced collective bargaining as a weapon to use against economy-minded legislators and trustees who insist upon cost reductions and improved accountability. Yet, ironically, collective bargaining promotes centralization through large bargaining unit determinations and by focusing on economic issues that must be settled off campus. Thus, the circle is complete: anxiety about system control stimulates unionism, and unionism accelerates system control.

Forces contributing to centralization include: (1) large bargaining units; (2) a limited choice of bargaining agents; (3)

common problems that provoke common responses, such as desires for greater economic benefits and job security; (4) the centralizing and standardizing effect of master contracts; and (5) the decision making of legislatures, public employees relations boards and courts that rarely grant higher education separate treatment. Forces safeguarding diversity include: (1) the voluntary nature of collective bargaining (it is not imposed from outside the campus, with the important exception of the multicampus bargaining unit); (2) the restriction of unionization largely to the less prestigious faculties and institutions; (3) variations within the legal framework, such as management rights clauses and arbitration procedures, that produce different styles of campus bargaining; and (4) the professionalism and tradition of academia that helps confine bargaining largely to economic rather than governance issues at many campuses. In short, there are many contradictory pressures that make it difficult to say positively what the impact of unionization will be. The danger of increased centralization as a result of unionization, however, is very real.

The pattern of increased outside control is echoed in our survey. One question asked, *"How has faculty collective bargaining affected the power of off-campus central agencies on your campus?"* On public campuses, few felt that central power has decreased and 57 percent said it had *increased* as a result of collective bargaining. The results were fairly consistent for all types of public institutions. Union officials were less pessimistic than presidents.

Our respondents also agreed that *"Wherever it occurs, faculty collective bargaining will result in greater influence on campus decision making by outside agencies (such as arbitrators, courts, or state agencies)."* Eighty-four percent of the presidents and 53 percent of the union officials agreed. Many also felt that collective bargaining in public institutions *"Will stimulate greater faculty concern about state and local politics."* About one third of the presidents at *non*union schools agreed, 55 percent of presidents at unionized colleges agreed, and 84 percent of union chairpersons agreed.

In short, these responses indicate that collective bargaining is one more factor promoting centralized decision making. Up to now, collective bargaining has been a relatively weak force; it is still in its infancy. Yet, the reciprocal circle feeds on itself: power moves off campus to systemwide boards, the union organizes on a system basis to gain influence, and this in turn drives even more issues from the local campus into the hands of the system board.

Presidents as Middle Managers

Campus presidents are not usually considered middle management. But in large state systems the twin forces of system-level centralization and collective bargaining may make them so. Our survey data clearly show that presidents of public unionized campuses see their power being divided between faculty unions and system management. In addition, they are becoming more accountable to an enlarging circle of evaluators: local union officials, system officers, and legislators with political ambitions. Will campus presidents fall between the cracks?

Centralized bargaining may cut both ways, sometimes helping the local presidents, sometimes hurting. A local campus president may sigh with relief that most of the conflict between administrators and union officials occurs at central headquarters rather than in his office. Off-campus decisions leave more time for local presidents to strengthen their academic and intellectual leadership.

Not all the results are positive, however, and the costs can be high. By shifting power upward and off campus, centralized collective bargaining lessens the decision-making autonomy of local administrators. In addition, the fragmentation of union groups leads to a "multiple adversary system." Many of the adversaries may make end runs around the local administrators, appealing directly to elected officials and government bureaucrats who function with little coordination and, frequently, with much contradiction of effort. For both the union and the campus president, this proliferation of "bosses" poses complex problems, if only because it is an intricate situation that invites a round-robin of buck passing.

In short, the complexities of power sharing may eventually reduce local campus presidents to middle managers who execute policy but have little influence on decisions. And although faculties have viewed their presidents as bargaining adversaries, they may regret losing their academic spokesmen.

Unionization Complicates Role of Department Chairpersons

Department chairpersons have traditionally performed at least some administrative tasks on most campuses. This fact has created a serious problem when collective bargaining arrives. Should department chairpersons be included in the bargaining unit? It is unclear whether department chairpersons are "supervisors" or "employees." Yet there is no middle ground in collective bargaining—they must be classified as one or the other.

Excluding chairpersons from the bargaining unit has obvious consequences for shared governance: influential faculty leaders would be on the opposite side of the managerial fence from their colleagues, and peer decision making in the departments would undoubtedly be affected. The implications are greatest at institutions with a history of strong faculty influence over departmental policies, because excluded chairpersons might become more management-oriented. That division could paralyze the department, thereby encouraging school deans to usurp critical decision making.

But department chairpersons *included* in the unit may be subject to pressures from all sides. Under most collective bargaining agreements, they are required to administer *procedural* aspects of the contract such as faculty evaluation, workload adjustments, and grievance processing. At the same time, they must retain their functions in *substantive* decision making such as tenure conferral, dismissals, and appointments. A new collective bargaining contract often produces a "shirt-pocket contract mentality," with faculty members acting as quasi-lawyers, checking their ever-ready contracts against possible administrative violations. This relentless and defensive faculty behavior can frustrate department chairpersons from imposing sanctions or making hard decisions. A reprimand or tenure denial may produce an instant confrontation with the union and the possible filing of a grievance.

In the four-year institutions of the City University of New York (CUNY), the departments have been instrumental in hiring, promoting, and tenuring faculty, and the department chairpersons have always played a key role in the process. Under collective bargaining, the unit determination includes department chairpersons with the faculty. As a result, chairpersons wear three hats: (1) *Supervisor:* Management expects department chairpersons to be accountable for careful decision making at a time of declining growth and "tenuring in"; (2) *Faculty Spokesman:* Faculty expect their elected department chairpersons to be their advocates; and (3) *Shop Steward:* The union, after battling with the administration to secure procedural guarantees in personnel decision making, expect department chairpersons to scrupulously oversee contract provisions.

Nevertheless, the CUNY union has often lodged grievances *against* department chairpersons. (While grievances are formally filed against the university, department chairpersons are usually called as administrative witnesses in hearings.) And yet the union does not want department chairpersons to be considered management, although the administration has defended department chairpersons against union attack. In short, the chairperson becomes the mediator, subjected to all kinds of cross-pressures.

While the chairperson's behavior may change through inclusion in faculty bargaining units, the administration's attitude toward departmental effectiveness also may be altered. As one CUNY dean noted, the department chairpersons more and more "waffle and buck-pass where hard decisions are needed." The power of chairpersons diminishes as higher administrators begin to distrust the decisions being forwarded, and as they shift administrative functions to higher-level administrators. Under such circumstances, the first line of objective, serious decision making will be not at the department but at the school dean's level or in school-wide faculty review committees.

Middle-Level Managers and Collective Bargaining

The most likely trend for campus administration is to add associate deans and other specialists to fill the administrative functions not effectively served by department chairpersons who, as members of faculty bargaining units, are partly under union control. The growth of *middle management* seems inevitable, but at the same time our case studies reveal that frustration, isolation, and insecurity are particularly prevalent within the ranks of deans, assistant deans, budget officers, and others within the middle-management category. In most instances, middle-level administrators are not included in either faculty bargaining units or at the bargaining table as part of the employer contingent. Yet the decisions reached through bargaining affect their salaries and fringe benefits, their professional roles, and their managerial responsibilities. Middle-level administrators consequently fear being squeezed between the opposing forces of collective bargaining and economic retrenchment.

With only a slight involvement in faculty unions and a tenuous identification with the top administration, middle-level administrators may evidence a half hearted commitment to effective decision making. Even deans may join department chairpersons in refusing to handle decisions if the benefits they receive do not outweigh the costs of increasing antagonism and conflict with co-workers. And this is particularly true as they become aware that the trend toward administrative centralization has removed their ability to make effective decisions. As one dean said, "I'm damn sick of the vice-president holding me accountable, yelling that I pass the buck, when everybody knows he long ago took away most of the deans' real power." Collective bargaining, then, reinforces already existing trends that have long been undermining middle management.

Specialists Replace Generalists

There is an influx of specialists into administrative ranks. Faculty generalists, long the source of most administrators, usually lack the experience and skills needed to cope with negotiating and administering a collective bargaining contract. One specialist important to successful bargaining is the *institutional researcher*. A research team is often necessary to (1) prepare for negotiations by gathering background data on the institution and its faculty; (2) provide detailed and specific information to administrators engaged in negotiations (such as costing out a union retirement proposal); and (3) record grievances, questions, contract violations, and unexpected costs occurring during the administration of the contract.

Lawyers are considered essential to successful negotiation and are becoming more vital to contract administration, particularly in relation to personnel policy and practices. In addition, labor relations experts and budget officers are playing a larger role in educational administration. While it may seem anomolous to be enlarging the administration when deficits demand cost-cutting, hiring specialists may be a shrewd management technique that actually cuts long run costs such as fringe benefits, which "pyramid" far into the future.

Our survey asked respondents how collective bargaining has affected the need for specialized administrative manpower on their campus. Over 85 percent of the presidents responded that *"The need for specialists has increased."* Not a single president reported a *decrease.* Sixty percent of the union chairpersons agreed that the need for specialists had increased; and like the presidents, the consensus was uniform across institutional types. Not only do presidents feel that more specialists will be needed, but about three fourths of them expect that *"Experts eventually will replace the generalists."* On this issue, however, the union officials disagreed—only 32 percent felt specialists would replace generalists.

The Changing Processes in Campus Administration

In the sections above we have been examining the impacts of faculty collective bargaining on the actors, the various administrators. Now we will shift to a different, but related, issue: How does collective bargaining affect the processes of administration? Does unionism change faculty/administrative interaction, cause conflict, or complicate decision making? In the next sections we will examine these issues.

Collective Bargaining Separates Faculty from Administration. Administrators have traditionally been identified with the faculty with whom they share certain kinds of academic accountability. For their part, faculty generally have accepted administrators as faculty members engaged in the mundane task of seeing that the wheels of the academic red wagon turn. Presidents and other administrative officers have often been included in the faculty senate. They normally hold professorial appointments and occasionally they teach classes. Collegiality has often been the accepted pattern of faculty/

administration interaction. Even with exceptions to these general patterns, it is not too idealistic to say that faculty and administration have held similar academic values.

Recent events, however, have made it increasingly clear that the administrative and faculty roles are not always interchangeable. Beginning with the student rebellion of the 1960s and continuing with the economic crisis of the 1970s, administrators have been forced to make decisions frequently in opposition to faculty interests. Such events have, to some extent, placed the faculty and administration in conflict. Collegiality has been breaking down, and contributing to this breakdown has been centralization in the public sector—a process that siphons power off campus to central authorities and prevents informal relationships from developing between central authorities and those affected by their decisions.

Like centralization, collective bargaining helps to formalize relationships; it fosters a "we-they" mentality inherent in the bilateral legal framework. The Stanford survey showed most respondents agree with the statement: *"Where it occurs, collective bargaining will formalize relations between faculty and administration."* The agreement was consistent for both union officials (89 percent agreed) and campus presidents (87 and 96 percent, respectively, for presidents at nonunion and unionized institutions).

Collective bargaining clearly separates employer from employee at the bargaining table, and there is growing evidence the dichotomy continues during contract administration. The more that faculty performance criteria are written into a contract, the greater the monitoring responsibilities of administrators. A recent study of unionized community colleges shows many presidents take a "watchdog" role over faculty under a contract, thereby perpetuating tension between the faculty and the administration. As an example, one trustee cites the president's responsibility to supervise faculty sick leave and make certain it is not abused. The same community college study shows that when things get tough during bargaining, board members view the faculty as the opposition and the president as the ally. This differentiation continues beyond the bargaining sessions. "It was interesting to note that the majority of trustees indicated that while their understanding of the president's role has increased in a positive sense, the 'status' of the faculty has diminished. . . . They certainly are not as likely to be influenced by them as they were in the past" (Channing, Steiner, Timmerman, 1973, p. 70).

The aggressive administration usually faces an aggressive union that cannot afford to allow its membership to be co-opted. To maintain visibility, the union leadership must constantly seek out and publicize points of contention between administrators and faculty. Coupled with a worsening financial climate and tough bargaining, the constant repetition of the "we-they" theme may force the two constituencies into entrenched positions. Should bargaining turn into an impasse, the resulting polarization could have disastrous consequences for collegiality. Prolonged conflict between the parties, particularly where a strike is used, calls public attention to internal problems and may seriously damage the reputation of the institution.

Collective Bargaining Helps Regulate Conflict. We believe that conflict is normal in academic organizations; it grows out of the very real, divergent desires of various interest groups. We do not subscribe to the widely held "communication gap" theory of conflict that assumes most conflict could be eliminated if only everyone had the same information, could reason together, and could be sensible. This position ignores the very real diversity of goals and values among campus constituents.

To the extent that the faculty, the administration, and the students have different goals, they are engaged in a political struggle to determine the course of their lives at the university. The result is persistent conflict on campus, varying in degree from place to place and time to time. Certainly the confrontations of the 1960s demonstrated that conflict existed and that existing mechanisms were inadequate to channel and resolve it. Now, in the 1970s, the growth of collective bargaining indicates that administrations and faculties on many campuses have very different interests.

Many observers of higher education have come to believe that if a high level of conflict continues to characterize faculty-administrative relations, collective bargaining will be one means of controlling it. For example, one Carnegie Commission report concludes: "We may be involved in a long-term period of greater social conflict in society and greater tension on campus. If so, it may be better to institutionalize this conflict through collective bargaining than to have it manifest itself with less restraint. Collective bargaining does provide agreed-upon rules of behavior, contractual understandings, and mechanisms for dispute settlement and grievance handling that help to manage conflict. . . . Collective bargaining, thus, is one aspect of the rule of law, if and when a rule of law is required" (Carnegie Commission, 1973, p. 51).

Unfortunately, that "rule of law" can be very disruptive in early stages of faculty collective bargaining. As in the early days of industrial unionism, faculty grievances proliferate, threatening to overwhelm the fragile grievance/arbitration machinery. The contracts themselves are often limited in scope, leaving matters to be handled in traditional ways. Sometimes contracts are poorly worded and generate conflict by their very existence. Nevertheless, these beginnings probably will lead to a more mature relationship between administration and union; the early conflict-stimulating experiences will give way to a conflict-managing process.

In its mature stages, collective bargaining manages conflict in three ways. First, the fixed-term contract stabilizes the responsibilities of the parties and limits their freedom of action regarding the substance of the agreement. Second, the grievance/arbitration provisions channel and resolve conflicts over the negotiation and administration of the agreement. Finally, over time, the developing relationship between the parties lessens the adversarial character of collective bargaining. In these ways, unionization can help channel and resolve the conflict that it initially helped to generate.

In some institutions studied in the Stanford Project, the conflict-managing process is well under way. Collective bargaining has continued longest at the City Colleges of Chicago, and Chancellor Oscar E. Shabat believes conflict at these colleges has finally been reduced by the mechanisms established through collective bargaining. He argues, "The key to conflict management is learning to work out what is unclear. In a sense, the contract becomes a living document." The Chicago administration, notes Shabat, finally has started to work out a stable relationship with the union after years of deep division and hostility.

Although we have been suggesting ways in which collective bargaining might reduce conflict, remember that collective bargaining is an intrinsically adversarial process. We do not wish to minimize the problem. Certainly our Stanford questionnaire shows that presidents and union chairpersons have mixed views about the conflict-managing properties of collective bargaining. About 70 percent of all presidents agree that *"Faculty collective bargaining will result in more conflict in the governance process."* There is no consensus among union chairpersons, with 42 percent agreeing and 58 percent disagreeing.

Collective Bargaining Helps Regularize Decision Processes. We believe that collective bargaining helps to encourage the elaboration and codification of campus governance procedures. Even when the contract itself does not spell out the jurisdiction of campus groups in governance, the administration is likely to take the lead in demanding that governance responsibilities—such as senate jurisdiction, the role of student government, and the role of the faculty union—be clarified to prevent a chaotic situation from becoming even worse. The complexity is greatest in large state systems because the relationship between campus administrators and system officials must also be taken into account.

Administration activities are likely to become more consistent and predictable, for collective bargaining forces administrators to avoid ad hoc decision making. Decision makers must consider union response at the bargaining table and the costs of potential grievance suits. One by-product is improved communication and understanding within administrative ranks. For example, a study of several unionized community colleges reveals that trustees have a better understanding of the problems presidents face and are more willing to listen to their recommendations, especially those concerning bargaining and contract interpretation (Channing, Steiner, Timmerman, 1973). In many large systems, bargaining has forced a better understanding of the relationship between central offices and local campuses.

Contractual provisions, court decisions, and the rulings of arbitrators help rationalize and regulate campus decision making because they increase awareness of how decisions are reached; they contribute to the legitimacy of decisions by reducing the likelihood of arbitrariness; and they force administrators to be more accountable for their decisions by pinpointing responsibility. In short, collective bargaining may be a strong internal factor promoting the regularization of decision-making procedures.

Collective Bargaining Can Widen the Amount of Faculty

Participation. Collective bargaining can give the faculty greater access to decision-making channels, for two reasons. First, it compels the *sharing of information* with the union, something administrators have been hesitant to do with faculty groups in the past. Administrators' control of information has often curtailed effective faculty participation in campus decision making. The laws and the rulings of collective bargaining boards have made information exchange a mandatory part of the bargaining process. This is one reason the faculty, frustrated by administrative reluctance to share needed information with governing bodies, turn to unionization in the first place. If administrators want traditional senates and committees to coexist with unions, information must be presented to both union and senate. At unionized campuses this has resulted in an increased faculty impact on administrative decision making.

Second, collective bargaining has a *democratizing effect.* Gains in faculty power are not restricted to a few, but are spread among a range of faculty members. Because bargaining units in higher education are broadly comprised of many different kinds of academic employees, often from disparate institutional types, a "leveling" action has occurred. Large unionized units can democratize decision processes—sometimes at the expense of previous power holders. Judging whether this outcome is good or bad depends on one's values, the local institution's history, and one's beliefs about professionalism. At unionized schools, about 25 percent of presidents and 72 percent of faculty chairpersons agreed that *"Faculty collective bargaining will democratize decision making by allowing junior faculty to play a greater role."*

Bureaucratization May Increase. Collective bargaining introduces new bureaucratic factors to campus governance. First, there are the complexities of the union itself; union policies must be established by internal operating procedures. Second, bargaining is a slow process, for both union and administration must consider their constituents. Third, after a contract is ratified, grievances and changes in administrative policies usually involve the union and require its consultation. For all of these reasons, the union becomes yet another bureaucratic feature of campus governance.

After the bargaining phase, the contract contributes to bureaucratization because it sets forth rules and regulations for personnel decisions and other organizational processes. Since a contract often requires that other documents, such as board bylaws and senate constitutions, be reworked completely, it contributes to burgeoning bureaucratization throughout the institution. As the contract grows more detailed, more red tape is produced to complicate the routine of campus administration.

The consequences of increased bureaucratization can be very serious. First, the proliferation of rules and regulations now makes it much easier for unions to challenge negative personnel decisions through the grievance process. The obvious danger is that personnel decisions that depend on subjective, subtle, and nonquantifiable academic judgment will be harder and harder to make. This means that merit may be sacrificed to egalitarianism. Where the discretion of peer judgment is curtailed by increased bureaucratization, status differences among faculty related to rank, publication, degrees, and experience will be reduced.

As more groups become involved in decision making, some people fear that campus processes may grind to a halt because decision making committees will be trapped by the competing claims of interest groups. David Reisman in *The Lonely Crowd* popularized the term "veto groups." These are groups in a complex society that cancel each other out, that can *stop* action, and that rarely cooperate enough to accomplish anything. Is it possible that veto groups are now expanding on our complex campuses? Are the environmental stresses and the economic problems generating so many conflicting demands and so many hostile interest groups that creative action may be stifled?

Unionism will probably contribute to this complex environment. Certainly the respondents to our questionnaire had divided opinions on this issue. We asked for agreement or disagreement with the statement *"Collective bargaining will increase the effectiveness of campus governance."* The answers were sharply different between presidents and union officials: between 10 and 20 percent of the presidents agreed, but an overwhelming 77 percent of union chairpersons agreed.

Collective bargaining forces administrators to be more efficient in management. In order to conduct negotiations, the administration must analyze the cost of various proposals advanced by union bargainers, and must project future impacts on the institution. Since most union demands concern economic issues and personnel decision making, it is especially crucial that administrators consider the long-range consequences of accepting proposals such as a new fringe benefit plan or shortening the probationary period for tenure. Once these matters are settled, it is unlikely that the administration can successfully regain what it has bargained away.

A contract signed and ratified by the union membership restrains the exercise of administrative authority. Faculty have turned to bargaining primarily to protect their jobs from arbitrary administrative action. The specific wording of employment rules in collective bargaining contracts provides concise guidelines for an insecure faculty. In addition, everyone from the president on down who discharges administrative duties must understand not only the implications of contractual provisions, but also the explicit details. At the Cortland campus of the State University of New York (SUNY), for example, the first contract was quickly followed by related policy changes from the board of trustees and an additional "twenty-one typed, single-spaced pages of memoranda of understanding at the local level which have the force of the agreement" (Hedgepeth, 1974, pp. 11–12).

Administering-by-the-book can dramatically affect administration. From department chairpersons to campus president, people may simply be overwhelmed by paper work and complex procedural requirements. For example, one study suggests that an increasing amount of a community college president's work day is committed to contract-related noneducational matters. Chief among them is grievance processing, advising lower-level administrators, and planning for new bargaining sessions (Channing, Steiner, and Timmerman, 1973).

To summarize, on the one hand, procedural regulations will help rationalize the administration and protect the faculty from arbitrariness; on the other hand, the proliferation of organizational rules could create a situation best termed "the paralysis of the nitty gritty."

Summary

We have explored the impact of bargaining on campus management and governance. Our conclusions are summarized as follows:

1. *Presidents on unionized campuses feel they have lost power to unionized faculty* and foresee a steady erosion of administrative capacity by faculty unions. Presidents of campuses in state systems believe they are particularly vulnerable to a two-directional power loss—to unionized groups and to central headquarters.

2. *Despite the presidents' feelings of vulnerability, evidence indicates that there is actually a shift toward greater administrative power.* Internally, more and more decisions are forced upward, away from departments to the central administration. Governing boards are certainly gaining power at individual campuses. In addition, system-wide collective bargaining means that power accrues to the system administrators.

3. *The nature and composition of administrations will gradually change in response to collective bargaining.* In order to negotiate and administer contracts successfully, traditional faculty-related administrators are likely to be replaced with specialists such as lawyers, labor relations experts, and institutional researchers—a situation that will further widen the gap between administrators and faculty members.

4. *The burdens of negotiating and administering the complex provisions of contracts compound the difficulties of administration.* Campuses are increasingly balkanized into "veto groups," and administrative discretion to respond to campus problems is increasingly circumscribed by contractual provisions, particularly in personnel areas.

5. *A majority of both campus presidents and union chairpersons foresee outside arbitrators and courts playing a greater role in campus decision making.*

6. *Collective bargaining will realign many of the major power blocks in the traditional academic setting.* Traditionally, senior professors and administrators have dominated the decision-making practices of most colleges and universities. Faculty collective bargaining will seriously challenge that pattern of governance, because it is the junior faculty and part-time faculty who most frequently join unions to make their voices heard. If the "most aggrieved" members of the faculty are successful in their unionization efforts, they will upset the past political processes of academic governance. Further, students—who until now have been gaining

more voice in governance practices at most institutions—will be adversely affected. One of the most interesting aspects of this shifting political scene is the position of administrators. It is clear that their lives will be enormously complicated and more harried when faculty members unionize. But it is also clear that many decisions that formerly were made in faculty committees will now be pressed upward into the controlling hands of the administrators. In short, it seems likely that administrators will have more power because of faculty unionization but will have a harder time using it.

7. *A number of positive consequences stem from unionization.* Because this is a time of financial stress for the academic profession, one of the major objectives of unionization is to preserve and extend economic benefits as well as achieve job security. We anticipate that faculties across the nation will benefit economically from unionization.

8. *Greater procedural protection for faculty promotions and tenure, less arbitrariness about administrative decisions, more job security and protection for nonteaching professionals, and greater economic security in general—all are more likely with unions than without.* These benefits would even apply to those faculties that do not unionize, for trustees and administrations are inclined to make concessions to ward off unionization just as much as to appease an already existing union.

9. *Faculties will use unions to establish stronger faculty participation in decision making in institutions that have never had a strong tradition of faculty governance, and to preserve their role in governance where it is being challenged.* The administrative dominance that is so characteristic of many community colleges and small liberal arts colleges will undoubtedly be tempered by healthy faculty unions. Another possible advantage is that unions will work to eradicate discrimination against women and minority groups. However, this outcome is somewhat questionable because it is not clear whether minorities and women will be any more successful in mounting the necessary pressure within unions than they have been within institutions.

10. *Senates are unlikely to convert to unions successfully.* Collective bargaining laws hinder such a change, and senates lack the support of national union affiliations.

11. *Senates and unions have different responsibilities, with*

unions addressing economic issues and working conditions, and senates dealing with curriculum, degree requirements, and admissions. Areas of joint responsibility include such personnel issues as hiring, promotion, and tenure. Neither senates nor unions have much control over budgets, selection of administrators, overall staffing arrangements, physical plant, and long-range planning. In these areas, administrators are in command.

12. *Senates will not collapse with the arrival of collective bargaining, but, as union influence continues to expand into areas of traditional senate responsibility, the current pattern of union and senate influence may not remain stable.* Where senates and unions presently coexist, unions curtail senate influence on economically related issues. Although unions and senates today share concurrent jurisdiction in relation to personnel decision making, how long this dual influence continues will depend on many factors, of which unionism is only one. Most senates are susceptible to problems of faculty apathy, administrative interference, and changing legal conditions. These realities will help determine the future viability of senates in the face of union challenges.

13. *One critical element in how unionization will affect senates is the relationship of an institution to larger systems.* For example, at Central Michigan University, the campus senate and union have a reasonable though uneasy chance of coexistence, because the issues and major actors are confined to the local situation. In contrast, at Hunter College within the City University of New York, the senate has been seriously undermined by the twin threats of an off-campus central union contract and a powerful system administration. Local senates may find themselves with little authority to oppose such potent competition. Senates and other mechanisms of faculty governance are fragile, and, if not protected and supported, they will be destroyed by the political winds sweeping the campus.

14. *Faculty unionization will add one more strong interest group to campus politics, further complicating the decision-making process and constituting a potential veto to beneficial organizational change.* Unions, formed to fight administrative bureaucratization and the centralization of power, will themselves generate substantial amounts of red tape and concentrated control. Procedural regularity

will often be balanced by endless procedural restrictions. The concentration of power in the hands of union executives will unquestionably undermine some traditional faculty governance processes. Moreover, off-campus administrative power will burgeon as state systems become unionized and state governments respond by building ever greater off-campus educational bureaucracies. All of these factors are serious ones that can be expected to accompany and complicate unionization.

In sum, academic unionism is on the threshold of becoming a major force in higher education, and it is difficult to predict its long-term impact on academic governance. Decades of traditional governance patterns are now confronted with the relatively new phenomenon of collective bargaining. In some respects, collective bargaining is a natural outgrowth of trends that have long existed in higher education, but in other ways it strongly contradicts some time-tested governance traditions. Whether the benefits outweigh the costs is a delicate question. Although its long-range effect is still largely unpredictable, the impact it has already had means that, for better or worse, academic governance will certainly never be the same.

Chapter 8

Women Faculty in Higher Education

Up to this point, the various chapters have covered a variety of issues, taking *all* faculty as the focus. This chapter looks at some of the same issues, but reanalyzes the data by separating males and females. As our data will clearly show, men and women faculty members have radically different types of activity, career patterns, institutional involvement, and morale levels. In a real sense, men and women often live in different worlds within higher education.

Other writers and researchers have, of course, examined these differences, but we believe our survey has unearthed new insights into the subjects. First, the Stanford survey covered a *greater variety of issues* than most studies on sex differences. We have data

This chapter draws on work by Sharon Renee Tolbert, "Women Faculty in American Higher Education: A Study by Institutional Type," an unpublished dissertation, Stanford University, 1975. Ms. Tolbert was a staff member of the Stanford Project on Academic Governance.

on the standard topics: publication rates, rank, and professional activities. But we also have information on women in governance and decision making, on their attitudes toward their institutions, and on their satisfaction rates—items not generally covered in studies of sex differences.

Second, we will study how women and men differ *in particular types of institutions.* Not only do faculty as a whole act differently in different types of institutions but women and men faculty within their sex group differ according to type of institution. The problem in past studies was a lack of specificity. All studies show that women faculty are quite different from men in publication rates, rank, salary, influence, and so forth. But is that difference because women in *similar* institutions are so much different— because women at Yale are so much different from men at Yale? Or do these national statistical differences show up because women are *located* in different settings. For example, do women have different profiles, on the whole, from men because women are concentrated in community colleges and men are not?

We believe the differences are traceable to both factors: sex *and* location. Many studies seem to emphasize sex differences; we wish to balance that perspective by stressing that much of this difference is caused by the distribution of women within the system. Within institutions, women are similar to men to a much greater degree than most studies would have us believe. Women in community colleges think and work about the same way as men in community colleges. Women at Yale are very similar to men at Yale. We have shown that community colleges and nonprestigious public institutions produce faculty attitudes and work situations that are quite different from those at other institutions. It is not surprising to find that women (like men) in those settings act differently from faculty (largely men) in other institutions—or that, since women are concentrated in these two environments, the statistics for women overall are skewed in that direction.

In this chapter, we will examine five issues:
1. The *distribution* of women within higher education (*where* are they located?)

2. The *career activities* of women as contrasted with men (publications, teaching activities, research).

3. The *academic reward* system as it applies to men and women (rank, tenure, salaries).

4. Role of women in *governance* (committees, influence activities, union preferences, role in administration).

5. *Satisfaction* and *morale* of women in higher education.

As we discuss each issue, we will try to show how the differences are explained by both style of *activity* and *location*.

Distribution of Women in Higher Education

Higher education in America has undergone an unprecedented growth over the past fifty years. College enrollment just in the past twenty-six years has tripled from 2.3 million students in 1950 to 7.5 million in 1976. In absolute terms, women have shared in this educational boom. Yet, in relative terms, women have lost ground in academia over the past fifty years as they have failed to benefit in the same ways and in the same proportion as their male counterparts.

One factor which might account for a part of the difference between men and women in higher education is the earning of doctorates. In the 1920s, women earned 15 percent of all doctorates. Except for the war years, there was a steady decline in the proportion of degrees earned by women until, in 1963, the proportion dropped to a low of 9 percent. Since 1963, this proportion has gradually increased. By 1971 women were receiving 13 percent of the doctorates awarded. Of course, this is still less than the percentage reported in 1920.

For our purposes, the important question is whether women are well represented in academic positions. Overall, we observe, the number of women holding faculty positions has steadily increased. During the academic year of 1939–40, there were 40,000 women employed in faculty positions; in 1950, there were over 71,000; by 1971, there were over 109,000. Thus, since 1939 the number of women had almost tripled by 1971. Yet, in relative terms, the proportion of women in academic positions has declined. In 1939 women constituted 28 percent of the faculty; by 1963 this percentage had dropped to 22 percent; and by 1971 women comprised only 20 percent of the nation's faculty.

However interesting, national averages tell only a small part of the story. Our study was concerned with the distribution of women within various types of colleges and universities. As shown in Table 14, faculty representation by sex differs markedly according to institutional type. Column B of Table 14 answers this question: "Within each institutional type, what percent of the faculty are men and what percent are women?" The pattern is clear. The more prestigious the institution, the fewer the women on the faculty. Among the elite, research-oriented multiversities, only 13 percent of the faculty are women. In the middle group of institutions, the percentage of women jumps to 21 to 25 percent. In the private

Table 14. Where Are Men and Women Faculty Located?

Institutional Type	A. Of all men and women, where are they located?		B. Within each institutional type, what percent are men and women?		
	Men	Women	Men	Women	
Public Multiversity	14%	8%	87%	13%	100% (N = 7376)
Private Multiversity	27	17	87	13	100 (14,310)
Elite Liberal Arts	6	7	79	21	100 (3,527)
Public Comprehensives	18	20	79	21	100 (10,708)
Public Colleges	6	6	78	22	100 (3,207)
Private Liberal Arts	11	15	76	24	100 (721)
Community Colleges	17	24	75	25	100 (10,516)
Private Junior Colleges	1	3	58	42	100 (6,876)
	100% (N = 46,218) (80%)	100% (N = 11,005) (20%)			

junior colleges the percentage of women faculty is a very high 42 percent.

Let us turn the question around. Column A of Table 14 answers the question "Of *all* women, where are they located in terms of institutional types?" We see in Table 14 that only 8 percent of the women faculty in higher education are employed in *Private Multiversities* compared with 14 percent for males in these institutions. Similarly, only 17 percent of the women faculty in the nation are employed in *Public Multiversities,* while 27 percent of the nation's men are located in that sector.

In the prestigious *Elite Liberal Arts Colleges* such as Vassar, Smith, Dartmouth, and Swarthmore, women's distribution of 7 percent seems proportionate to men's of 6 percent. This is partly because there are many women's colleges in this category, and they have a far greater proportion of women on their faculties—from 23 to 58 percent. On the other hand, the number of women on the faculties of men's colleges is quite restricted; there, they have the lowest participation rate—fewer than 4 percent (Robinson, 1971).

The proportion of all of the women faculty versus all of the men faculty found on *Public Comprehensive and Public College* campuses is not particularly notable—20 percent of the women, 18 percent of the men; the percentages for public colleges alone are 6 percent for both sexes. These colleges, you will recall, include former teachers colleges and normal schools which have broadened their curriculums by adding male-oriented programs such as business administration or engineering and some female-oriented programs such as nursing. As teachers colleges, they attract more women than men. The addition of both traditionally female and traditionally male fields has not significantly changed the proportions of each sex in terms of students or faculty.

In the less exclusive private liberal arts colleges, there is an interesting phenomenon in the representation of women on faculties. The higher proportion of all women (15 percent) as compared with all men (11 percent) found on those campuses can be partly accounted for by two particular categories of colleges: Catholic women's colleges and black colleges, both of which have comparatively large proportions of women.

Public Community and *Private Junior Colleges* have the

largest proportion of women on their faculties in both absolute and relative terms. Of all women faculty members one out of four is on the staff of a two-year college. In the Private Junior Colleges, 1 percent of all men but 3 percent of all women make up the faculty, where four out of every ten faculty members are women.

Current literature offers several explanations for the over-representation of women faculty in two-year colleges (Carnegie, 1974; American Council on Education, 1971). An important reason is the rapid growth of two-year colleges, and the recruitment of many women out of high schools. In 1920, there were 207 two-year colleges in existence—137 private and 70 public; by 1940, there were 258, of which 217 were private; in 1969, there were 694, of which 272 were private and 422 were public. Students in these colleges today account for nearly 30 percent of all undergraduates in higher education. This growth represents a striking change in higher education, not the least important aspect of which is the rapid increase of faculty in two-year institutions. It is important to note that, up to 1963, the percentage of women faculty in all institutions was decreasing; as community college enrollments rose, the percentage of women faculty began to climb again. One might speculate that without this growth in community colleges women would still—in spite of affirmative action programs—make up a decreasing proportion of faculty nationally.

Profiles of Work and Career Activities

The previous section showed *where* men and women faculty are located. This section deals with *what they do* there. Sex differences in academic career patterns analyzed by Jessie Bernard (1964) have recently caught the attention of many scholars whose subsequent works have revealed striking differences in academic work and career patterns.

First, women tend to be in traditionally "women's" disciplines. The stereotyped imagery of the masculinity or femity of a discipline is very strongly related to the percentage of women within the disciplines. An examination of subject areas shows that women teach mainly in the humanities, in the lower paid areas of education and nursing, and in vocational areas in two-year college terminal programs. Male faculty are much more heavily concentrated in the sciences, the social sciences, and the higher paid professions such as law, medicine, engineering, and business administration.

A second major difference is that women college faculty are only about half as likely to hold earned doctorates as their male counterparts. Only about 32 percent of women faculty members hold doctorates, as compared to about 61 percent for male faculty members. Moreover, the master's degree predominates among women faculty members, with 59 percent of all female academics reporting that the master's is the highest degree earned. For males, this figure drops to 32 percent. This pattern is broken only in Public and Private Multiversities where women and men hold doctorates in approximately the same proportion. Of course, in these senior research-oriented institutions an earned doctorate is basic to job entry requirements.

Clearly, if the doctorate is considered to be essential to academic life, women are significantly less advantaged than men in most colleges and universities. Probably the earned doctorate is not yet critical to professional advancement in the public, two-year college where men and women, alike, hold only the master's degree. But in all other sectors of higher education the doctorate represents a badge of expertise. To the extent that this badge is necessary for favorable consideration in promotions and high-status institutional assignments, only half as many women as men are properly "credentialed."

The third major difference is that women are mainly involved in teaching whereas men are more often involved in research as well. Robinson (1971) sampled 140 colleges and universities to obtain current institutional data about the activities of women faculty members. Her report shows that a higher percentage of women, 39 percent compared to 29 percent of men, spend thirteen hours or more per week in teaching. Kreps (1971), Bayer (1970), and Bernard (1964) offer additional data suggesting that women are more likely than men to carry heavy responsibilities for teaching, especially at the undergraduate level. Bernard, in fact, goes so far as to describe academic women as a "statistically different population" from academic men because their "career preferences emphasize different functions than their male counterpart." Nationwide studies of faculty members have found that women spend considerably more time teaching than do their male colleagues, who are more likely to combine teaching duties with research. In a recent Carnegie Commission Report Feldman (1974) indicates that "even now" women graduate students and women faculty express a greater interest in teaching than do their male counterparts.

Our Stanford Project data agree with these other studies in showing that women spend proportionately more time than men in teaching. We asked faculty members what percentage of their time was spent in: (1) undergraduate teaching, (2) graduate teaching, (3) research and scholarship, (4) community service outside the institution, and (5) committee work, institutional service, and administration. The response nationally shows that the mean percentage of time that women spend teaching is 71, while for men it is 63. For this same activity according to undergraduate/graduate levels, women reported 64 percent of their time in *undergraduate teaching,* men only 47 percent. For *graduate teaching,* the mean for women was 7 percent, about half that of the men's 13 percent. Thus, our national estimates and other studies conclusively demonstrate that women spend considerably more time in teaching than men—and that their teaching responsibility is mainly confined to the undergraduate level. Women fare poorly and are significantly underrepresented in graduate teaching, which is usually considered a higher-status responsibility.

What happens if we break these overall national figures into separate institutional types? The figures in Figure 2 indicate that in all types except Private Junior Colleges, women faculty invest a greater proportion of their time teaching undergraduates than do their male counterparts. Within all types having graduate programs, men spend a greater proportion of their time than do women in graduate teaching.

Continuing with this analysis, we see that Private Multiversities, Public Multiversities, and Public Comprehensives emerge as the three institutional types emphasizing graduate programs. These three types also clearly show the greatest sex differences in terms of proportion of time spent in undergraduate and graduate teaching. The teaching proportion difference between women and men engaged in undergraduate teaching is particularly pronounced in

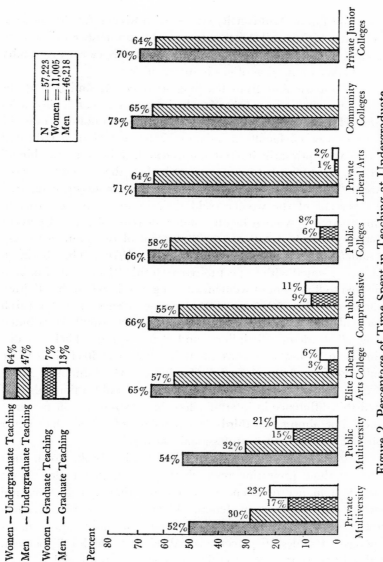

Figure 2. Percentage of Time Spent in Teaching at Undergraduate and Graduate Levels by Sex and Institutional Type.

Private and Public Multiversity types—with women faculty showing significantly higher. Likewise, a comparable pronounced difference also emerges for graduate teaching—but in this case men faculty show a higher proportion of graduate teaching.

When we shift from teaching to *research,* similar patterns emerge. It is often asserted that faculty interest in research also varies by sex. H. Astin and Bayer (1975, p. 103) maintain: "only 11 percent of women faculty as against 27 percent of men indicated that they were primarily interested in research rather than teaching." In 1976, Ladd and Lipsett reported that their faculty survey showed: "Twenty-eight percent of the men in our survey, compared to 17 percent of the women, said their interests lay primarily in research. Among women faculty under 35 years of age, 23 percent preferred research, compared to 38 percent of the younger males" (*Chronicle of Higher Education,* May 10, 1976). The Robinson 1971 report stated with respect to research that 21 percent of men as compared to 8 percent of women were engaged in research activities. Feldman's study (1974, p. 60) likewise argues that "research activity like strong teaching orientation" is not equally distributed among all academic disciplines, and that the more likely "a discipline is to be low in research activity, the more likely it is to be female dominated or viewed as feminine." H. Astin and Bayer (1975, p. 103) also said, incidentally, that "publications also reflected this difference in interests: less than two-fifths (39 percent) of men, but almost two-thirds (63 percent) of women had never published an article in a professional journal."

When Ladd and Lipsett (1976) further broke down their figures on those preferring research they found that males almost always had higher preferences for research than females: natural sciences—males 37 percent, females 15 percent; professional school faculties—males 21 percent, females 8 percent; humanities—males 24 percent, females 16 percent; social sciences—males 32 percent, females 42 percent. The exception, of course, is the social sciences.

Before we can offer an interpretation of these data, we must point out that certain subtle differences between male and female faculty preferences might be masked somewhat by reporting national averages. For example, Bernard (1964) suggested that if enough variables are controlled, sex differences in productivity may be reduced almost to insignificance and that a college or university position might be a better predictor of research and scholarly publication rates than sex. Similarly, Henderson's (1970) comparison of men and women faculty members with doctorates shows minimal difference by sex in preferences for teaching and research. Astin (1974) also found that women doctorates were similar to men doctorates in teaching assignments and published works. Thus, it seems essential to accurate interpretations of data on sex differences to control on other factors that might influence variations among faculty.

Overall, our research shows that the national average of women's mean percent of academic time spent in research and related scholarly activity is 8 percent, while for men the national average is 15 percent. This finding is consistent with other national studies where control variables were not used. Table 15 has the complete set of findings related to this issue.

However, our analysis *by type of institution sheds more light on the issue*. Nationally, men report nearly *twice* as much time on research as women. But when we break these figures down by type of institution we come to a startling development: *within* each type, women are much nearer to men in their research efforts (with one major exception).

Table 15 shows that in every institutional type except Public Multiversities women average almost as much time on research as men do. Except for the Public Multiversities, the difference between men and women is no where near double—double being what we might expect according to our national research data. Why? Obviously, women by and large are located within nonresearch faculties, and perform much like their male colleagues in those institutions. Location within the system, not merely work habits, helps explain the time spent on research.

Two cases stand out as special. The Public Multiversities have quite high levels of research, but here is the one case where men still spend twice as much time as women on research (24 percent for men, 12 percent for women). Why this clear exception? From our data we find that, compared to men, women in these institutions

Table 15. Research and Publication.

	Average percent of time on research		Average number of articles in last 4 years		Average number of books in last 4 years	
	Men	Women	Men	Women	Men	Women
Private Multiversity	26%	21%	7.4%	3.5%	.9%	.6%
Public Multiversity	24	12	6.8	2.1	.8	.4
Elite Liberal Arts	15	11	3.2	1.4	.5	.3
Public Comprehensives	11	6	2.5	2.0	.5	.5
Public Colleges	10	7	2.7	1.3	.6	.4
Private Liberal Arts	9	6	2.3	1.0	.3	.2
Community Colleges	6	5	2.0	.7	.3	.0
Private Junior Colleges	4	5	1.9	.7	.3	.1
National Average	15%	8%	4.3%	1.4%	.6%	.3%

are (1) younger than men, (2) have fewer doctorates, (3) teach more undergraduate and fewer graduate students, (4) have more committeee assignments, and (5) are in lower ranks. All these factors add up to less *opportunity* to do research. Of course, we cannot know whether all these activities hindered women's research or whether women's lack of interest in research lead them into these nonresearch activities.

The high productivity of women in Private Multiversities (21 percent of time spent in research) compared to women in all other types (12 percent) is the second unusual pattern. Their scholarship may to some extent be explained by their having come, many of them, from distinguished institutions, and are therefore likely to model themselves after distinguished faculty. Secondly, women who are attracted to and hired by Private Multiversities may be more motivated to perform research to begin with, and thus more research oriented in their careers. However, these women also suffer some of the problems faced by their less research-oriented women colleagues in public institutions—lower rank, less graduate teaching, and so forth. Nevertheless, they have proved quite interested in research in spite of the disadvantages.

The Reward System—Rank and Salary

Rossi (1973) asserts that the number of women in the academic world decreases dramatically as the importance of the position increases. If we take academic rank as one indicator, the percentage of women who hold positions at every rank is much lower than men. Women are below the national average in the top two ranks (full and associate professor), quasi-equal at the assistant professor level, and well above the national average in the instructor/lecturer category. Nearly two thirds of all men faculty are in the top two ranks compared to approximately one third of all women faculty.

The fact that women more frequently than men are found at the lower academic levels may in part be a function of differences in types of institutions. Table 16 shows that within every type of institution except the two-year colleges, women's ranks are extremely disproportionate when compared to men's ranks. In most four-year institutions, the ranks of *professor* and *associate professor* (usually the tenure ranks) appear to be a male domain. This particularly holds true in the Private and Public Multiversities, where the relative frequency of nearly 4 to 1 for men to women in the full professor rank is striking. The male/female difference in ranks is greater in the elite multiversities than in most other institutions, but the overall pattern is that men hold higher ranks, women lower.

Let us now turn our attention to the matter of *tenure*. Rank and tenure are closely related, and tenure patterns are similar to rank patterns. Overall, 61 percent of all faculty men and 50 percent of all faculty women have full-time tenured positions. Within all institutions (except two-year types), women are more likely than men to be in marginal, irregular, nonladder, part-time, exceptional, or fringe positions. In the two-year colleges, women have more secure positions, with tenure patterns similar to men's.

The concentration of women in nontenure positions, particularly their concentration in lecturer/instructor ranks, has important implications for their academic careers. Although the number of women faculty in higher education is increasing, their status

Table 16. Distribution of Faculty by Rank, Sex and Type of Institution.

	Professor			Associate Professor			Assistant Professor			Lecturer/Instructor		
	Women	Men	Difference	Women	Men	Difference	Women	Men	Difference	Women	Men	Difference
Private Multiversities	13	47	−34	19	27	−8	39	22	+17	29	2	+25
Public Multiversity	10	40	−30	25	29	−4	34	24	+10	25	6	+24
Elite Liberal Arts	20	30	−10	21	26	−4	35	32	+3	20	8	+11
Public Comprehensives	18	29	−11	20	28	−8	36	31	+5	25	10	+14
Public Colleges	21	24	−3	23	35	−12	37	31	+6	18	8	+10
Private Liberal Arts	14	25	−11	20	24	−4	35	32	+3	28	8	+20
Community Colleges	8	13	−4	11	12	−1	13	13	0	16	12	+4
Private Junior Colleges	5	5	0	10	12	+2	21	12	+9	16	9	+7
National Average	14	31	−17	18	25	−7	30	25	+5	38	19	+19

Note: + greater proportion of women, −lesser proportion of women.

or career profile is not improving as much as expected because their positions rarely offer comparable salaries, fringe benefits, access to tenure, and access to other university resources.

Salary is a reflection of faculty rank and tenure. A wide variety of studies show that in the aggregate, academic women are paid less than their male colleagues (Bayer, 1970). Salary differences persist even among women and men with equal educational attainment. Among doctorates who have always worked in academia, the mean of single women's salaries is about $500 per year less than for men, while the differential for married women is about $700 less a year. Salway (1971) found that among more recent doctoral recipients employed in academic settings that cross academic fields, there ranged a difference of more than $1,000 per year in education, $800 in the natural sciences, and about $400 in the humanities. Thus, even when the amount of professional experience is added to degree and productivity, the salary differentials between women and men remain fairly substantial.

Let us summarize this section on academic rewards. The profile of women faculty compared to their male counterparts suggests that women indeed differ from men in the area of academic rewards. This is particularly obvious in women's teaching loads: they are more likely than men to carry heavy responsibilities for undergraduate teaching, while men spend more time teaching graduate students and doing research. But if we control for type of institution, many of the differences appear less dramatic.

The huge apparent differences shown in the literature are often a result of aggregating all faculty women instead of analyzing them by type of institution. Most studies produce a distorted research picture by comparing the universe of men to the universe of women. In reality, women in the top institutions not only outproduce men in most other types, but emerge as extremely high achievers. Thus, the work pattern for women, as for men, is definitely related to the institutional setting.

Ironically, although academic research is more highly regarded and appears to earn men faculty higher rank and tenure status, this pattern does not appear to hold true for comparable women. Regardless of the institutional setting, men tend to occupy the highest ranks. Women are most often instructors and assistant

professors. Additionally, the biases operating against women concerning rank and tenure are reflected in salary differences. Obviously,
academic rewards are not evenly distributed. They vary substantially from one institution to another, and even within similar
institutional types women's profiles differ from men's.

Participation in Institutional Decision Making

Faculty participation in institutional decision making is an
intrinsic aspect of academic life. Some people serve on senates and
institutional committees. Some busy themselves working through
unions, through accrediting agencies, or involving themselves in
strikes. Most people, however, are simply apathetic.

Although there is a voluminous literature dealing with decision making and governance, there is little research on women
faculty's involvement. The few existing studies indicate that there are
sex differences in governance just as there are in most other areas of
campus life. Henderson (1970) found that women faculty served on
fewer and less prestigious committees than men. A sampling of
national institutional reports revealed that women faculty participation rates are very low. For example, from 1960 to 1970 at the
University of Chicago, only two women appeared on the list of
university boards, committees, and council appointments—of which
there are between 100 and 110 per year. At the University of
California, Berkeley, the percentage of women appointed to selected
senate committees in the last 50 years ranges from 0 to 1 percent.
When the low participation rate of women in the standing committees of the University Senate was noted at the University of
Pittsburgh in 1974, the Chancellor urged the inclusion of more
qualified women. In the next year, the number of women increased
by only one!

Oltman's (1970) research asserts that: "Women are often
found in positions which have minor relationship to policy making
and which involve sex stereotypes. . . . The mean number of
women department heads in all schools is less than 3 per institution.
Women holding department chairmanships are found mostly in
home economics, physical education, English, languages, nursing,
and education. . . . Women are less likely to be represented on

committees for scholarships, judicial problems, educational or advisory policy, or to be advisers to campus organizations."

Women, of course, make up less than a fourth of all faculty. Men dominate policy and decision making by sheer weight of numbers. However, a question still remains: Do women participate *proportionately,* relative to their absolute numbers, in decision-making positions in colleges? The results of our investigation are summarized in the following.

First, women are badly underrepresented in administrative ranks.

Where does the power lie on college and university campuses? Obviously, power accrues to some people by virtue of their occupying an administrative position. Administrators make decisions and formulate policy recommendations, and they exercise a great deal of operational power. Our data agree with most other national studies in that they show few women in such positions. One survey (Oltman 1970) showed that 88 percent of presidents are men (and the 12 percent that are women are largely confined to women's colleges), 93 percent of vice-presidents are men, 95 percent of development directors are men, and even 57 percent of head librarians (where one might expect many women) are men. When women are in the administrative ranks, "they are working at jobs . . . without much relationship to policy making or influence. Generally they are in positions at middle-management level or in jobs which involve sex stereotypes, such as Dean of Nursing." (Oltman, 1970, p. 14).

Our second conclusion is that women are less likely than men to participate in policy-making activities such as committees and senates. One question on our questionnaire asked whether the respondents consider themselves "inactive"—that is, rarely participating in policy-making activities. In the national sample, about 46 percent of both sexes together characterized themselves as inactive. Women, much more than men, were likely to report inactivity. About 40 percent of the men said they are inactive compared with 60 percent of the women. This varies substantially by type of institution, however. The larger the institution, the more people report they are inactive. This is fairly logical, since the larger the institution, the smaller the percentage of people needed to serve on institutional committees.

Our survey also found that women serve on significantly fewer committees than men. But if we take rank into account—comparing women and men only of equivalent ranks—the differences are not nearly so sharp. In fact with rank controlled, the surprising result is that women serve on almost as many committees as men. Obviously, however, because women are concentrated in the lower ranks, the overall result is that they serve on fewer committees. And our results show that even when women serve on these committees they are almost never in leadership positions.

Another interesting conclusion is that fully two thirds of all women in the sample, including those with administrative assignments, reported that their committee activities were trivial. By comparison, only 30 percent of their male colleagues report that their committee time was spent in nonessential matters. Not only do women serve on fewer committees, but they also report that the committees they do serve on are trivial!

Another interesting question in our survey was: "Compared to other people in your department, do you think that you have greater or less influence on important policy matters?" The percentage of men who reported that they had significant influence over departmental matters was 80 percent. By contrast, only 38 percent of the women reported that they had significant departmental influence.

All these observations suggest that women not only are underrepresented in the decision-making process but are engaged in what they consider less important activities, serve on "trivial" committees, and have very little influence over activities even within their home department. Part of the reason for this general powerlessness of women is obviously related to the other factors we have talked about. They are younger, lower in rank, frequently do not have a doctorate, are less well paid, and are located in disciplines which are stereotyped as "women's fields." All of this in itself suggests that women faculty members as a group are going to be low in status and consequently low in power.

Our third conclusion is that the attitude of women toward unions presents a mixed picture. In the face of mounting problems, faculty members regardless of sex are looking for outside help such as unions to articulate their interests in university affairs. The movement toward unionization in recent years has been steady. Currently there are about 500 campuses unionized, two thirds of which are two-year colleges.

Given their powerless, disadvantaged condition, it seems logical to expect women particularly to seek help through unionization. As Croman puts it: "Several social forces are converging at present to make collective bargaining a new and powerful vehicle for remedying sex discrimination within faculties. The growing acceptance of collective bargaining in higher education, the increasing strength of feminist organizations on and off campus, and the recent spate of federal antidiscrimination laws—three independent, but mutually reinforcing phenomena—make this the best time in history for women at the bargaining table" (1975, p. 61).

Do women, given their disadvantaged position in the power structure, use unions to help them break down the barriers? The indications are quite mixed.

First, women are less likely to voice support for unions, or to join them. In our 1971 data, 38 percent of men and 31 percent of women favored unions. By early 1977 the percentage who favored unions had almost exactly doubled! Interestingly enough, however, women still were less inclined than men toward unions, by about the same relative margin.

As a remedy against discrimination, collective bargaining presents both an opportunity and a challenge for women. For one thing, administrators often agree to bargain over issues of concern to women: equal pay and fringe benefits; appropriate medical insurance and care; maternity and parental leaves; day-care facilities; and clear and equitable standards for such things as access to grants, supportive services, extra earning opportunities, promotion, and tenure. Administrators do not want to be seen as unwilling to help eradicate discrimination, and they may be able to bargain toward a solution directly tailored to the particular needs of a campus. Yet, gaining enough clout *within* the union to force bargaining on these issues presents a distinct political challenge to women. Unions work primarily for the interests of the majority, and, without tight organization and concerted effort, women and minorities will be as powerless vis-à-vis the union as they have been vis-à-vis the institution. In order to use the union effectively as a political weapon, women must first develop tactics for influencing them.

The key tactic, of course, is involvement. One woman member of the CUNY union attributes contract provisions promoting equality for women to "the hard work of a small group of women within the union who formed an ad hoc committee on the status of women, which later became a standing committee" (Croman, 1975, p. 29). Such involvement might promote debilitating strife within the union, but it is probably the only way for women and minorities to be effective.

So far, women and minority groups have had some success. Most contracts contain an affirmative commitment by unions to admit all eligible persons without regard to race, color, creed, national origin, sex, age, or marital status, and to represent all members equally regardless of whether they are union members. Groups in several institutions have worked hard to erase past discrimination against women. For example, a determined effort by women at Rutgers University succeeded in obtaining provisions in the 1972 contract that remedied salary inequities. At Oakland University in Michigan, women used collective bargaining to adjust salary inequities, promote a fairer sabbatical leave policy for them, achieve salary parity of the library faculty (mostly women) with other faculties, and secure a paid maternity leave. A woman union member at Oakland argues that the union offers an avenue to leadership positions that is more accessible and democratic than the traditional governance structures within the institution (Schwartz, 1975, p. 11).

In summary, women and minority groups may find the union an effective political tool to help alleviate persistent discrimination. But making use of that tool will not be easy. Other competing interest groups will be trying to capture the union for their own goals. Internal conflict over union priorities will be fierce, and without persistent, organized pressure, discriminated groups will once again find themselves outside the power structure. Unions are no more likely to respond to demands merely because they are "just" or "right" than are other social institutions. The name of the game is politics.

Attitudes, Morale, and Satisfaction Rates of Women Faculty

What attitudes do women faculty have toward the colleges and universities in which they work? Do they view themselves as valued members of the academic community? Do they think the administration is on their side, or do they lack confidence in it? Are they satisfied with their academic participation, with the way they are evaluated, with their students, offices, and general work conditions? Would they choose to stay at their respective institutions or would they prefer to move to another type of institution?

In general, it would be reasonable to guess that women, given their disadvantaged status as shown throughout this chapter, would be very unhappy, dissatisfied, and restless. Actually the picture is much more complex than that. In some ways women *are* unhappy, but in other ways they report higher levels of satisfaction and morale than men. Let us examine the different aspects of this mixed picture.

The first test of morale and satisfaction in our questionnaire was the series of questions about *trust in administration* mentioned in an earlier chapter. Faculty were asked to agree or disagree with the following:

- In general, the top administration of this institution is competent, able, and energetic.
- If faced with a major campus disturbance, the administration would be likely to give in to outside pressures even if the actions were unpopular with the faculty.
- In general, the administration has a very progressive attitude about faculty welfare in terms of salary and working conditions.
- Generally, the administration understands the needs of academic professionals and works hard to make this a place where academics can work productively.
- Communication between the faculty and administration at this institution is usually open, easy, and effective.

It was difficult to work with five separate items of trust, so a simple measure was constructed by scoring each respondent on the number of expressions of confidence (High Trust = 3 or more, Low

Trust = 2 or less). When everyone is divided into high or low trust our national estimates indicate that 60% of all faculty express trust in the administration. They believe their administrators are competent, share their professional values, and work to enhance the academic programs on the campus. The general trend is for *both* men and women to trust administrators more in elite, high-prestige institutions, and less in community colleges and big nonprestige public institutions.

As Table 17 shows, women were somewhat less likely to express "trust" in the administration than men were, and were significantly less likely to do so in the Private Multiversities and Elite Liberal Arts Colleges. This is particularly interesting because we showed earlier that women in these two elite institutions were the most productive and did the most graduate teaching of any group of women. Presumably, these women, the elite in many ways, were more critical of their situations. This is a fairly common finding in social science: progress in overcoming discrimination, coupled with the emergence of an elite group of people, usually produces *more* dissatisfaction and *more* pressure for change.

The second measure of morale concerned *satisfaction with working conditions,* as measured by these statements: (1) my office facility is adequate as a comfortable, efficient work place, (2) the typical student at this school is academically competent, (3) my present annual salary is reasonably good in light of my qualifications and experience, (4) my teaching load is appropriate.

As with the trust dimension, we constructed a single satisfaction measure for each individual based on the number of positive evaluations marked (High = 3 or more, Low = 2 or less). Naturally, most faculty members seem content with their general status and academic workload. However, a substantial minority—between 23 percent to 31 percent depending on the type of institution—expressed dissatisfaction. Again, the same institutions that reflected high trust reflect high satisfaction—the more prestigious on our institutional typology, the greater the satisfaction rate.

But there were differences between women and men. There is a persistent tendency for men to be more satisfied with their working conditions than women—an attitude that corresponds to our earlier argument that men really *do* have more advantages. In some

Table 17. Faculty Morale and Satisfaction: by Sex and Type of Institution.

	Average Percent Expressing *Trust* in Administrators		Average Percent Expressing *Satisfaction* in Working Conditions		Average Percent Expressing Strong *Institutional Identification*	
	Women	Men	Women	Men	Women	Men
Private Multiversity	39%	60%	56%	81%	34%	45%
Public Multiversity	60	57	59	79	56	48
Elite Liberal Arts	58	71	80	80	50	51
Public Comprehensives	49	49	55	57	54	48
Public Colleges	62	57	57	65	47	49
Private Liberal Arts	49	62	60	66	63	53
Community Colleges	41	55	60	62	61	56
Private Junior Colleges	41	45	55	59	62	49
National Average	50%	61%	59%	73%	58%	51%

cases, however, the small differences between men and women took enormous jumps. Three types of institutions stand out: the Private Multiversities (men satisfied = 81%, women = 56%), the Public Multiversities (men = 79%, women = 59%), and the Public Colleges (men = 65%, women = 57%).

You will remember from Chapter Six that the third dimension of faculty attitude, *institutional identification,* reflects the loyalty of the faculty members to the college or university where they are employed, whether they would leave for another job. Nationally, 53 percent of the faculty respondents are strong in institutional identification (Answer 1). As the prestige of the institution increases, institutional identification *decreases.* Elite faculties have the *least* local identification; two-year colleges have the strongest institutional identification. This leads us to suggest that this attitude reflects a syndrome of related factors: whether or not faculty members identify strongly with their colleges and universities may be dependent in large part on their marketability, their training, and their expertise. Those who are more highly trained tend to be "cosmopolitan" rather than "local" in institutional loyalty, identification and commitment. Moreover, the elite faculties have stronger identification with their *disciplines* than with their local campus.

The overall figures hide a great deal of variation between women and men. First, women generally report somewhat *greater* institutional identification: 59 percent of women, 51 percent of men. On the whole, women seem less likely to want to move—in spite of their obvious dissatisfactions. When we designed our questionnaire we assumed the question about "willingness to stay" would be an overall measure of morale and satisfaction. Our logic was simple— perhaps too simple: if people were unhappy they would want to move elsewhere. Ladd and Lipsett, in their 1975 survey of faculty, made a similar assumption. They comment: "Academic women are not doing as well as academic men by a host of criteria, but they are no more dissatisfied. If anything, the reverse is true. . . . Thirty- one percent of the men feel they would be better off at some other college, compared with 28 percent of the women. While younger women are, on the whole, much more dissatisfied than older women, they are not as unhappy as younger men. Forty-five percent of the men under 35 years of age would rather be at some other institution, compared to 39 percent of the women" (*Chronicle of Higher Education*, January 29, 1975, p. 2).

Ladd and Lipsett, their findings similar to ours, interpret the results as showing satisfaction among women—just as we had planned to interpret our similar question. However, all our *other* measures of satisfaction (the specific measures about salaries, working conditions, colleagues, students, and trust in administrators) showed women were *less* satisfied than men. Our so-called "general" measure of satisfaction (willingness to stay put) conflicted with our "specific" measures of satisfaction. Why is this?

We now believe that we, as well as Ladd and Lipsett, incorrectly judged the meaning behind the women's response. All our other measures showed more dissatisfaction among women than men. The lack of inclination to move to a new institution was not so much a measure of *satisfaction* as it was of limited *opportunity*.

Their own backgrounds—often high school teaching careers and without doctorates—persuaded the women, rather realistically, that they did not have the *chance* to move. Moreover, since many of the women *were* former high school teachers who moved into community colleges, they compare themselves favorably with their former high school reference group. Looking back at that reference group, looking at their personal qualifications, looking at the tight market conditions, looking at their family situations, and looking at the competition in other institutions—these women have realistically resigned themselves to staying where they are.

This "opportunity" theory is supported by the fact that the women—and men too—most likely to report they would not move are in 2-year colleges (62 percent for staying) and in less prestigious liberal arts colleges (63 percent). The women *most* likely to indicate an interest in moving are in the elite Private Multiversities, where only 34 percent say they would not move—the lowest for any group, male or female, in the entire nation. Obviously these women, with higher degrees and more publications, have much greater opportunity to move to better positions.

In short, the women's greater willingness to stay where they are does not necessarily mean they are happy. It may simply mean they are realistic enough not to desire a move. In fact, our other satisfaction measures show women to be significantly more dissatisfied than men. And, as both Ladd and Lipsett's survey and our own data show, the younger women are more dissatisfied and obviously have higher aspirations.

Let us stop for a moment and summarize our findings on morale and satisfaction. What does the evidence show? First, women are slightly more inclined than men to feel that administrators are not competent, and women more than men feel that administrators are biased against the faculty. In short, women have lower levels of trust—but the differences are not pronounced.

Second, women do report pronounced lower levels of *satisfaction* with their working conditions—with salaries, offices, students, and colleagues. These feelings can be explained by *objective facts:* their position really is disadvantaged; their attitudes toward administrators probably *should* be less trustful.

Third, there are substantial variations among women at different types of institutions. The more elite the institution, the *less* satisfied the women are. This is an interesting fact, because we might assume that these women, at the top of the status ladder, might be more satisfied. Their dissatisfaction probably is due to a number of factors.

First, although women in elite institutions are at the top of the ladder relative to other women, relative to their male colleagues (with whom they have more direct contact) they are in less advantaged positions. They carry heavier teaching loads, they have fewer graduate students, they have fewer research grants.

Second, the *competition* in the elite institutions is fierce, especially in these days of tight money and declining enrollments. With fewer publications and fewer doctorates, women in elite institutions may feel uniquely threatened.

Third, women in the elite institutions seem less satisfied because men in those settings report *extremely high* levels of satisfaction—absolutely the highest of any group of institutions, and fully 20 percent higher than women in those same institutions. In elite multiversities, both public and private, about 80 percent of the men report high satisfaction compared to about 57 percent of the women. It is not so much that the women are unusually low, but that the men are so high.

Finally, both men and women show fairly high levels of *institutional identification,* a willingness to remain in their institutions. But there is a persistent tendency for women to be *more* willing to stay than men (overall average: men 50.8 percent, women 58.3 percent). This "stay-put" attitude is most pronounced for women in the two-year colleges and less prestigious liberal arts colleges. One might suspect that women in those settings often compare themselves to high school teachers where many had their career origins. By comparison they are satisfied with where they are. Also, women in the two-year colleges and liberal arts colleges rarely have doctorates, rarely publish, and almost never teach graduate students. Thus, their mobility is sharply limited and their "stay-put" attitude is clearly reinforced by market pressures, by their inability to get jobs elsewhere.

Summary

In this chapter we have explored some of the differences—and similarities—between men and women faculty. Most of the conclusions support well-known facts in the literature. But several key findings go beyond what is commonly known. Let us summarize the issues.

First, women are distributed very differently than men within the higher education system:

- Women are overrepresented in community colleges, in less prestigious private liberal arts colleges, and in large nonprestigious public institutions.
- Women are underrepresented in the major graduate centers and the elite multiversities.
- Women are concentrated in the humanities and traditional women's professions. They are underrepresented in physical sciences, social sciences, engineering, and high-paid professional schools.

Second, on the national average, women have different styles of professional activity:

- Women are much less likely to have doctorates.
- They teach more undergraduate and fewer graduate students.
- They do less research, and they publish significantly less often than men.

Third, in all the different aspects of academic rewards, women are far behind men:

- Women start in lower ranks and rise less slowly than men.
- Women are much more likely than men to have nontenured part-time or temporary appointments.
- Women are paid lower salaries.

Fourth, women are basically powerless; they are not as heavily involved in institutional governance:

- Women are drastically underrepresented in administrative positions, and when they are administrators they are in very traditional "women's" areas (such as nursing and home economics).
- Women serve on proportionately fewer committees, report their committee work to be "trivial" (two thirds of the time, compared to one third for men), and rarely take leadership roles on committees.
- Even within their departments, women feel powerless compared to their male colleagues.
- Women have some hopes that unions may redress their problems—but join less than men. And male dominance of unions may be just as great as male dominance of administrations.

Finally, in light of these dismal conclusions, it is no great surprise to find that women have lower morale and trust levels:

- Women are slightly more inclined to distrust administrators, although both men and women have fairly high trust levels.
- Women were much more inclined to be unhappy with their working conditions—offices, students, salaries, colleagues, teaching loads.
- Women are, however, less likely to want to move out of their current situation. This is probably a reflection of their inability to move in a tight market, and family constraints.

When we lay out all these facts it appears that women are quite different from men in higher education. However, these gross national differences between men and women mask an important fact: *within* institutional groups the gap narrows substantially. That is, women act quite similarly to men in similar settings. Women in elite institutions act more like men in elite institutions, women at community colleges act more like men at community colleges. To be sure, even within types there are still significant differences—but nowhere near the huge differences that show up on gross national figures.

In short, the explanation for the difference is due to two factors: (1) some differences are simply because women have different activity styles *within* the same settings; (2) but even more of the gross national difference is due to the *concentration* of women in less prestigious institutions—where they act quite similar to the men in those same institutions.

Men, by comparison, are more evenly spread throughout higher education. Thus, we have a situation in which women, concentrated in less prestigious institutions, are compared to men who are more evenly spread around. Too many studies on women show gross national differences without taking this distribution into account.

Our argument, then, is that women are different from men in higher education when gross national statistics are used. But those differences are not so pronounced within institutional types. The policy implications are clear. Instead of blaming women for not "catching up," we must work on public policy to more evenly *distribute* women in the higher education system. Of course, this is exactly what the affirmative action laws are attempting to do. These research findings strongly support and undergird that effort.

And needed most of all is an increase in *absolute numbers* of women in higher education. Without more women in the system, the professorate will continue to be male-dominated even if women are helped to succeed and are distributed better. Unless doctorate-granting institutions and academic departments take it upon themselves to recruit and to award doctorates to increasing numbers of qualified women, there is little that can be expected of employing colleges and universities beyond that which they are currently doing. The degree—the academic "badge"—is essential to women's achievement in academia, just as it traditionally has been essential to males.

Chapter 9

Current Trends and
Future Projections

≋≋≋≋≋≋≋≋≋≋≋≋≋≋≋≋≋

The institutional patterns we have painted thus far in the book are primarily static pictures of how things currently exist. However, as any reader knows, the times are changing rapidly. Academic governance is being reshaped rather significantly in the late 1970s. Where are things going? Will academic management be taken over by an army of state bureaucrats? Will some vestige of "collegial" management survive? Will faculty lose power to administrators, or students, or state authorities? How will the picture look in ten years?

Of course, we were on safer ground up to this point. We can say how things *are* with some confidence; but people who gaze into crystal balls are wrong about as often as they are right. Nevertheless, here are our best guesses about where current trends are leading us. The picture is not, we fear, very rosy.

This chapter was prepared with the able assistance of Patricia Miller.

Both decreased enrollments and lowered public support have caused a drastic change in the resources available to higher education. It is apparent that we are in the middle of a financial crisis in education. Enrollments, finances connected with enrollments, and federal monies are declining or levelling out. And inflation means this money purchases less than before in goods and services. What impact will tightened resources have on decision processes, morale and satisfaction, and political participation by faculty members? We can forecast with some confidence what will happen to governance as institutions move from financial feast to famine. There will be shifts in power, a decline in collegiality, greater bureaucratization, less power for faculty and more for outsiders and administrators, decreases in student power, and the formalization of conflict via unions. Let us examine these trends more closely.

Reduction of Faculty Power on Many Campuses

From the 1940s through the early 1960s, college and university faculties obtained a high degree of influence in the governance of their institutions. They enhanced their professional status, reserved for themselves many critical decisions over curriculum, faculty, and student affairs, and gained power over many of the academic policymaking networks. The "Academic Revolution" described by Jencks and Riesman (1968) propelled the professor to the forefront of academic decision making. The growth of faculty power was selective—it happened in the elite institutions more than in the nonelite, and in the private institutions more than in the public ones. Nevertheless, the thrust of faculty control, power, and autonomy was felt to varying degrees in all areas of the academic professions.

Faculty autonomy and power developed when certain forces in the society converged: expanding enrollments; a public belief in education's ability to solve social problems; increased financial support; the growth of large-scale research requiring more faculty experts; and a shortage of qualified personnel that bolstered a faculty's bargaining position. These forces boosted higher education's governmental priority, and strengthened the academic disciplines' role. Faculty influence then became institutionalized, both within departments and disciplinary associations as well as through the growing force of academic senates and the American Association of University Professors.

Although many social forces acted to enhance both faculty power and the general status of higher education, recent events have begun to undermine and threaten that situation. Lower enrollments and oversupplies of faculty with doctorates have caused the public to question its support of higher education and have lessened the bargaining power of professors. Changes have also occurred in the belief system of a society that once accepted the legitimacy of higher education's claim for public support. The backlash against student revolts of the 1960s, the disbelief in the ideology that education could solve most social problems, the rising skepticism about education's contribution to occupational success, and the strident attacks on faculties by politicians have produced a crisis of confidence. The impact of these factors is now commonly recognized: lower financial support, more state control of educational policy, and less research money.

These changes have resulted in more controls, restricted budgets, frozen faculty salaries, and the elimination of "unproductive" departments. The execution of major decisions often occurs over the strong objections of faculties that feel professionally and politically impotent. This is particularly true of faculty members in local community college systems, in some weaker liberal arts colleges, and in stringently regulated state college networks. Of course, not all faculties feel threatened. But it seems probable that many people sense a growing personal and professional threat.

The environmental factors listed above have quite different impacts on different colleges and universities. Some institutions have relative independence from their environment, based on a self-perpetuating board of trustees, wealth derived from endowments and research money, and a continuously high student application rate that insures abundant tuition money. On the other hand, there are many institutions virtually captured by their environmental setting. Such institutions are closely supervised by local community agencies and almost exclusively dependent on one source of money, such as church, school district, taxpayers, or legislature. In addition, their supply of tuition money is sometimes precarious due to fluctuations in student demand. Whether an institution is highly independent or highly dependent is an extremely important factor that influences internal governance patterns.

As we have often argued, institutions that are virtually captives to strong environmental pressures have faculties that are very weak in the governance process. Academic departments in such institutions have very little control over selection and promotion of faculty, courses offered, and other academic issues. Faculty members have little autonomy about the courses they teach and are highly regulated by strict rules and regulations. Faculty participation in the determination of institutional policy is very limited. At the other end of the continuum, however, among institutions that are insulated and relatively free from environmental control, faculties are central in policy-making processes, are lodged in strong departments, and are relatively free of bureaucratic rules and regulations.

Heavy environmental dependency also results in a strong "dominant coalition" of administrators. The more dependent a college is on its environment, the more likely the administrators are to have power. When the legislature demands "accountability" from the faculty, the administration is given the power to enforce it. When resources are short and a few powerful financial barons are controlling the purse strings, the administrators translate that dependency into power over educational policy. Is the client pool drying up, resources growing scarce, or a few outside agencies maintaining a stranglehold over programs? Then the administrators consistently have more power to determine educational policy, to allocate resources, to make critical policy decisions. In short, dependency on the outside world increases the power of administrators, and concentrates power in a few hands; a "dominant coalition" of administrative elite emerges. Moreover, this dominant group of administrators is very likely to be in some central headquarters off the campus, in a state system office.

If the faculty are now losing power after decades of gains, who are the groups most likely to gain influence?

Shift of Power Relations Within the Institution

A number of changes are undermining the traditional power distributions in colleges and universities. Let us examine some of those changes.

The "technocrats" are gaining influence. Various specialists seem to be gaining power. At present, the administrators are most often the people who hold true power. They have power not just to initiate but to implement decisions within the university. However, much of their power for initiating new ideas and activities is shared with the central core professionals, the faculty. The faculty can influence the administrators in matters such as setting up new programs or changing the curriculum, because of their expert knowledge of the field.

But the unquestioned authority of the faculty to be the chief advisors is now challenged. With these days of limited finances, administrators are hard pressed to take the projections and desires of the faculty as the only basis for implementing changes. A new group of professionals is obtaining power at the expense of the faculty. This group is made up of "financial technocrats": cost controllers, financial specialists, budget forecasters, fund raisers, and—last but certainly not least—lawyers. The new technocrats are flourishing everywhere.

With information provided by these cost controllers and budget forecasters, the administrators are now able to determine whether a new program is financially feasible. The faculty argument may be true that a class which happens to be expensive to run adds to the prestige of the department and increases the quality of student applicants. But if these faculty suggestions are not "revenue generating," or at least self-sufficient, they may receive extra scrutiny by the sharp eyes of the budget hawks.

The administrators usually come from the faculty ranks themselves. In times of greater resources they are very much attuned to faculty interests. They understand the effects of building a department and increasing its stature with the addition of new courses, new professors, new equipment. But the financial specialists have the facts and figures to show whether the institution can afford to take the risk or has the time to reap the pay off. And increasingly the financial people have the attention of the administrators. The "cut, squeeze, trim, and reduce" experts have gained enormous influence as the financial crisis deepens.

The institutional *fund raisers* also command the attention of the administrators. These fund raisers have a sense of which programs will generate gift giving, and they advise the administrators and trustees which programs to implement. The outcome is often that these programs are activated while others, though recognized as valuable, may be left for another time.

The list of other technical specialists who are gaining influence is really impressive. *Lawyers* have seized much authority in this age of federal regulations, affirmative action policies, and constant lawsuits. *Personnel managers* are increasingly in demand as more personnel disputes arise. *Labor negotiators* are needed for both faculty and nonfaculty unions, which are proliferating at an unbelievable rate. *Management information specialists* are necessary to handle sophisticated management data banks. In short, the specialists are becoming a significant element in the power equation on campuses.

Power will move to areas of new strength based on student enrollment shifts. Students with liberal arts degrees are finding it more and more difficult to get jobs when they graduate. Consequently there is a shift in enrollments toward professional areas: law, business, engineering, and other vocational training fields. The strength of the faculty will increase in these areas, usually at the same time the liberal arts faculty is cutting back its members. Traditionally the liberal arts have been active participants in academic senates, sitting on decision-making committees and helping shape the direction of the institution. As their numbers dwindle and the number of scientists increases there will be a shift of power. For example, there may be changes in requirements for graduation. Or the field internship aspects of program requirements may be emphasized over the classroom lecture and seminar. At any rate, there will undoubtedly be significant shifts in the stated outlook and direction of the institution.

Extension services and nontraditional programming will gain power. In our present period of steady-state enrollments, campuses are vying with each other for students. A prime example of this is the proliferation of extension and nontraditional programs. High schools and community colleges used to dominate adult education classes. Now these courses are also offered through university extension divisions or local four-year colleges. The institutions now acknowledge that there is a limited number of "traditional" students.

So, to support their faculties, their committed capital expenses, fixed costs, and possibly some changes, the institutions are attempting to increase revenues by attracting new students. And they are succeeding. As the number of students in extension and nontraditional classes grows, the faculty and administrators of these programs will grow in numbers, increase their governance power, and gain positions on the institution's decision-making committees. They will have some influence over how their revenue and that of the institution is spent. This creates another group with input in the institution's academic governance system. As an additional factor in the governance process, they will probably dilute the impact of the more traditional faculty.

A limitation on this projected change in academic governance may be that in some institutions the revenues generated by the nontraditional programs might not "cross over" for general usage. If separate budgets for the two areas are maintained, with neither benefitting nor drawing from the resources of the other, a parallel governing structure in the special programs will develop. In this case, the people exerting influence and power within the special programs area will not reduce the influence of the more traditional faculty.

The faculty who are to obtain external money will have increased power within their departments and schools. Of course, this has *always* been true, but as money gets harder to obtain the influence of grants-specialists will go up even more. The professor who is able to obtain a grant supporting the studies of his fellow professors has considerable influence. Such influence may range from how to allocate the budget—should the institution purchase new laboratory equipment, increase the library, or add support staff?—to affecting curriculum decisions. Votes of the "wealthy" may carry more weight than those of others in the department or school.

Increased Conflict Within the Institution

In light of the developments listed above, and in the face of the financial crisis, conflict inside the institution will increase. We have often argued that academic decision making is a "political" process, and that conflict is normal. As present trends develop, the conflict level in the political process may increase even more. Some of these conflicts will develop on an individual basis: the grievance processes that pit the individual against the institution. Other conflicts take a more global form, such as arguments over future institutional goals.

Grievance procedures will proliferate. Almost all institutions now have a formal grievance procedure. These procedures are methods for resolving individual grievances. There is an increasing number of grievances around personnel decisions. As the "financial crunch" grows, the treatment of the individuals within an institution probably deteriorates. Faculty are asked to take on a heavier work load, such as teaching more students per class, or adding another class to their schedule. They are asked to expand their efforts in counseling and advising the students at the same time they are encouraged to maintain a "high" level in publishing and in writing proposals for research money. Even more importantly, there is increased pressure on tenure decisions, and many capable people are finding their careers threatened in ways that were unthinkable in earlier, more financially secure times. Naturally, all this leads to unhappiness and a resultant increase in grievances when people feel they are being treated unfairly and that too much is being asked of them. So, administrators and faculty move into adversarial roles. The goals of the institution become different from the more immediate goals of each professor, and grievances proliferate.

Arguments over goals are increasing. Administrators try to lower the costs of current programs, and to increase the proportion of "cheaper" programs. For example, proposals for new courses that draw many students to attend lectures, and that do not require laboratory periods of workshop sessions, might get a more favorable hearing from administrators. The cost per student hour is very much less than for more concentrated and elaborate courses. The faculty and the administration will disagree over what are the "best" courses and programs, over which values are to be considered.

But administration/faculty splits will often seem like minor battles compared to the wars over goals that will rage *within* the faculty ranks. Should the scarce resources go to liberal arts, or to direct vocational programs, or to student services and counseling? The conflict is sharp, and never seems to end. The political dynamics are indeed real between various groups of faculty.

Concentration of Power

All the trends listed above push in the same basic direction. Power within the institution—the "real" power of allocating money and personnel positions—is increasingly concentrated in fewer hands.

Operational control over decisions will move higher. Decisions once made by department faculty will now be made by deans; decisions once made by deans will now be made by a vice-president; presidents will become directly involved in matters they never concerned themselves with before; trustees will have a bigger voice. In the past, when the coffers were full, a department was given its annual budget with fairly standard increases. Within this budget, the department had much freedom to add a faculty member, increase the size of a laboratory, or shift office space. Now, the department may not have many choices at all. With most operating costs fixed, the department may get few increases, may indeed have to take cuts, and the plan for using the money may be specified by the "higher-ups." When there was ample money to go around, the deans could determine which of their schools' departments would have additional faculty. Now this decision is usually in the hands of a vice-president, and sometimes even the president. Now the deans must sell the administrators on the needs of the departments and schools—and often the administrators must convince the boards of trustees or legislators!

Administrators will have greater influence in governance. Faculty committees were often assigned the task of helping to allocate resources by setting priorities. These committees were good at determining how and where to get optimal results from each new input. These same faculty committees are *not* good at making cutback decisions. The politics and feelings surrounding reductions run high. Obviously these committees find it easier to bring on new faculty or new programs than to cut back. Putting it bluntly, the faculty members like to distribute the goodies, but want the administrators (who are a little more removed) to be the ones stuck with the job of cutting back their colleagues' jobs and programs. This is one realm of governance that the administrators have required by default.

Presidential power is complicated. We suspect that presidential power on many campuses is substantial, but it is being threatened by many new developments. Many presidents appear to be hemmed in by new controversies and crises. Although they still have substantial power, in our interviews with them they expressed strong worry about the erosion of their influence. As powerful state systems have developed, many presidents are now in the awkward position of middle managers. They are held responsible by everybody—the faculty below them and the state above. Even in private colleges and universities there are strong outside pressure groups and enormous financial crises that have restrained the president's ability to act. In fact, David Cohen and James March in their book *The American College President* (1974) suggested that growing institutional complexity and increased outside pressures have produced a generation of presidents who are largely ceremonial figures in no position to provide real leadership. Although we doubt that American college presidents are as impotent as Cohen and March suggest, it is nevertheless true that environmental, financial, and institutional forces have combined to make presidential power more complicated than it ever was before. This is particularly true as state systems pull power off the campus, and faculty collective bargaining complicates power on it.

Incidentally, it may seem contradictory for us to say at one point—as we did above—that power is being centralized, and at another point that presidential power is being complicated and undermined. But those seemingly contradictory statements illustrate just how complex things are becoming, for we indeed do believe both are occurring simultaneously. In fact, it is just *because* more decisions are being centralized while central offices and unions are undermining presidential power that governance has become so complex and filled with conflict. Though *demands* and *expectations* are greater, the *ability to perform* and make things happen may be less.

There is a proliferation of centralized information systems. The growth of management information systems provides administrators with huge volumes of information on faculty curriculum, student enrollments, and capital expenditures. With mountains of data at their fingertips on which to base their decisions, administrators are much less dependent on the opinions and expertise of their faculties. In fact, because of these management information systems, the administration may have more knowledge on any specific subject than does the faculty. All this undermines faculty influence.

These new management information systems may be another significant force promoting centralization, for at least three reasons. First, the bulk of the information provided by information systems is in the hands of campus administrators. This information is required if administrators are effectively to allocate resources such as faculty positions. The increased use of data-based decisions constitutes a fundamental change in college management practices.

Second, administrators can devote a considerable amount of time to studying this information. Academic organizations have been characterized as institutions in which time is a scarce resource (Cohen and March, 1974). For the most part, faculty members have little time to study the operation of various academic departments. Consequently, administrators are able to develop substantial and unopposed expertise in important areas of these operations.

Third, the new information produced by predictive information systems may bring changes of "high leverage" but "low salience" for the campus community. These changes have high impact but are not of directly political concern. For example, the provost of one prestigious university indicated that the most important thing he had done in ten years was to change the "indirect cost" charge on federal and foundation grants, a measure which caused little controversy but which produced substantially greater income for the university.

When a resource scarcity is coupled with powerful information systems in the hands of the central administration, there is double pressure for centralization. Under these conditions, the principle that decisions in academic organizations should be based on a joint effort between academic departments and college administration becomes little more than a formality.

Incidentally, unions may counterbalance the administrations' control of management information systems. Until recently, faculty had no right to the information held by administration. Unions, however, do have rights by law to much information administrators have withheld. As unions gain access to information on which faculty and budget decisions are based, the faculty gains access to it through the unions. This gives the faculty the opportunity to develop arguments in defense of their perceived needs.

Students in Academic Governance: Is Student Power Dead?

Student participation in the governance of American higher education is a fairly recent phenomenon. Historically, the extent to which students have been involved in decision-making processes has usually been limited to matters related to the "quality of student life." Undergraduates seemed content to confine their involvement in decision making to selecting homecoming queens, electing prom committees and cheerleaders, and writing school songs. Thus, when the 1960s began, very few colleges and universities involved students in decision-making processes of the faculty and the administration. But by the end of the period of student activism, student participation in campuswide decision-making bodies had become generally accepted throughout the nation. For the first time, student government was not merely thought of as a form of developmental student activity. Rather, it became recognized as a political force stimulated by motives and behaviors typical of other types of political interest groups working to achieve access, recognition, and efficacy in matters of policy formulation and governance. More specifically, we can see that one consequence of the student activism of the 1960s is that students have "formalized" their access to academic governance. During the 1960s, student influence over matters of policy was expressed through ad hoc associations of interest groups whose behaviors were labelled "alienated," "radical," and "extra-legal." But, in contrast to the late 1960s and early 1970s, student influence today over academic decisions is predominantly exercised through formal participation in committees and other academic decision-making bodies. Indeed, such participation is generally considered to be common to the routine governance procedure of many colleges and universities today. While the exact pattern of student membership and participation on administrative and faculty committees varies significantly from campus to campus, the extra-legal activities typical of the sixties have today become routinized, formalized, and to some degree bureaucratized.

Thus, the student revolutions of the sixties affected institutional decision making in a number of ways. On the one hand, they drew the wrath and fire from the environment in an almost unprecedented fashion. On the other hand, they increased student influence by providing a means for voicing student concerns and demands. In the late 1960s and early 1970s, it appeared that student influence in governance would indeed be significant. Students joined academic senates at hundreds of institutions, students were placed on departmental and institutional committees in great numbers, and student lobbies were formed around the legislatures of many states. It seemed that students would finally have a major voice in academic governance.

Then the roof fell in. The same pressures that reduced *faculty* influence have also reduced *student* influence—the economic crunch, the centralization of power, the growth of state regulations. In addition, the very steps that the faculty has taken to protect its sphere, especially the formation of unions, have undercut the students. In another book (Kemerer and Baldridge, 1975) we have discussed extensively the impact of unions on students. It is enough to say here that faculty unions—with rare exceptions—have not been favorable to student influence, and have effectively cut students out of the decision-making process on many unionized campuses.

As money has become tighter, faculty members have become fearful for their jobs and promotions. Although people once thought student evaluations "can contribute to the development and growth of the faculty," their evaluations are now unwanted. Anxiety levels running high, faculty members feel that including students in the process just raises another obstacle in making personnel decisions. Not only do the faculty not want the students' help in this critical job situation, the unions do not want them either. The unions have a vested interest in improving faculty working conditions—wages, hours, and work load. Student goals, wanting more from the faculty with no commensurate increase in costs, are more likely to be aligned with those of the administration than with the union or the faculty.

Several other factors contributed to the reduction of student influence in academic governance. First, the general apathy follow-ing the hot times of the 1960s sent students back to the study halls, beer parlors, and football games—away from the barricades, senate committees, and political rallies. Second, a rising concern with careers stimulated partly by the economic recession, propelled stu-dents back to their books and to worrying about jobs. Third, increased state control removed many decisions from the campus, the arena where students had their meager influence.

Finally, the promises of formal participation on committees and boards of trustees have not resulted in much student influence. Contemporary forms of student government involved a sharing of decision-making power among students and traditional authorities—namely, trustees, administrators, and the faculty. But students often find that routinized participation in decision making has a con-straining rather than liberating effect. Students have learned that formalized participation often means that others control the decision agenda; that the principles of democracy and majority rule can work to their disadvantage; that committee work is, essentially, a bureaucratic process requiring much time and perseverance; and, that professionalism and academic expertise usually outweigh the student appeal for academic reforms, no matter how well they are presented. In short, students have found that even the formal par-ticipation for which they worked so hard did not bring them any significant influence. For all practical purposes, student power is a dead horse—at least for the moment.

Increased Control by External Agencies and Actors

Outside forces grasp control in different ways. For example, state agencies attempt to eliminate program duplication among campuses. Decisions become formularized so that all campuses, schools, and departments are treated equally. Strong emphasis is placed on equalizing expenditures among campuses, schools and departments—bringing the more expensive in line with the less expensive. External agencies exercise their authority to a greater degree in times of financial pressure. Trustees, law courts, state central offices, the federal government, and legislatures are only a few of the actors who get involved.

Interagency rivalry is an unlikely but possible intervening

factor in this increased exercise of authority by outside agents. With each agency and actor trying so hard to gain control over the campuses and their budgets, they may find themselves competing with each other. A natural outcome would be a proliferation of paperwork for each agency to justify its decisions—with the possible result that the campuses may be left a few shreds of autonomy and self-determination as off-campus agencies fight among themselves. Let us examine a few of these external trends.

Boards of trustees become more involved when finances are tight. When the flow of incoming students and money is increasing, boards of trustees concern themselves with policy decisions about the operation of the institution. When money is tight, they tend to move from policy decisions to operational decisions. An example is a board becoming concerned with duplication of course offerings or duplication of expertise on one campus. What was formerly considered to be building strength in a specialty area, the board may now consider merely redundant, and ask the president to take appropriate action.

Of all the issues that have been studied about higher education, the activities of boards of trustees is probably the least understood—and one of the most important. There is a great need for training programs to help trustees learn about critical educational issues, and about ways to improve their management of the institution.

Central state offices become more involved in academic governance. They become more involved in the same way as boards of trustees move into the institutions' day-to-day activities. When the financial situation is comfortable, these agencies merely oversee the decisions and functions of academic institutions in a very general way and from a distance. Usually they do not exercise their role of final authority; they let the institutional leaders make the decisions, then merely approve them. With the financial crunch, these offices not only look more closely at the decisions being made but question who has the authority to make them—often determining that they themselves are the rightful authority. They withdraw the "unofficial authority" from the campus and exercise it themselves.

Politicians generally were displeased with higher education in the late sixties and early seventies. And they had a means in addition to control of the purse strings to bring the institutions "into line." That means was the coordinating agency which had come into existence in the fifties and early sixties but had not, except in isolated cases, exerted much control over the campuses. The seventies saw a much different picture—power and influence flowed outward from the institution to the coordinating agency.

Different states have established coordinating boards and agencies with varying amounts of control, and in three distinct patterns: (1) voluntary organizations; (2) the single board system for the coordination of all higher education institutions in the state; and (3) the coordinating board superimposed over any existing boards supervising the various institutions or systems. In their early days, the state agencies had emphasized cooperation and coordination; but as we moved farther into the seventies, the emphasis shifted more and more to direct coordination and control.

The amount of power in an institution is finite, and the influence that has gone to the board had to be lost from someplace within the institution. Generally it is the president who has given up power and influence. The areas controlled by the president and central administration were exactly the areas the states desired to "coordinate"—building programs, capital expenditures, and the introduction, expansion, or contraction of new programs. Regarding admissions standards, an area of responsibility generally shared by the administration and faculty, the boards have also taken an interest. And in a number of instances a special concern has been shown for minority enrollment programs, which are often mandated from the boards. The coordinating boards are less content to let the institution—in effect the faculty—control who is hired, who is fired, who is tenured, what specific class is offered, when it is offered, who gets a salary increase and what the graduation requirements are.

Legislators and governors also have become more involved. When there are sufficient funds to handle the plans for most institutions, the institutions themselves determine how to allocate their budgets. Both legislators and institutions tend to consider each campus as a separate entity serving a separate community. When finances are tight, however, this changes. The campuses are viewed by the legislators as part of a larger system; and the legislature and state boards try to eliminate duplication among programs in the system, cut costs, and generally exercise closer scrutiny.

Governmental regulation and legal action has significantly increased. In a landmark case, a student from the University of California, Davis, took a question of admissions to the medical school to the United States Supreme Court. The student claimed that because of reverse discrimination—alleged admissions priorities for blacks—he had not been accepted for medical school while others less qualified had been. The student won the case at the district court level, and the Supreme Court is, at this writing, reviewing the case. The important thing for us to note is that a question regarding the admission of a student to medical school was decided in a court of law, not on the campus. These days, appeals to the courts are standard procedure. Suits are instituted over almost any issue: personnel grievances, failure to gain tenure, failure to be admitted as a student, allegations of discrimination, or a thousand other issues. The lawyer is now a major actor in the governance process!

Government regulations are another illustration of off-campus control. For example, the affirmative action program of the federal government affected, to a certain extent, faculty autonomy over hiring, firing, and promotions. The government mandated that affirmative action be taken in the recruiting process to make job opportunities available to minorities and women. The government also required that once these people were hired, the institutions do as they should have done all along—promote and fire without regard to race or sex. Government personnel were assigned to investigate complaints of discrimination, and the absence of blacks or females on a faculty could, without evidence to the contrary, be taken as apparent evidence of discrimination. While some faculty were in total agreement with the goverment program, others saw it as a quota system and an infringement upon academia's autonomy and academic freedom. For a good end or not, the affirmative action program did represent yet another example of loss of institutional autonomy.

Increase in Bureaucratization and Regulation

The erosion of local autonomy, the centralization of power, and the increase in conflict all work together to produce a bewilderingly complex set of rules, regulations, and formulas. This is a critical development. Issues that were once discretionary, for which *choices* could be made, are often now reduced to formulas, to pre-programmed decisions about which *there is no choice.*

At the individual personnel level, decisions are bureaucratized. Personnel policies became increasingly formalized and form-ularized because on one hand employees want rules to protect them, and on the other hand administrators want rules to blame for un-popular hard decisions. When a professor's anxiety runs high over the job suituation, he finds it comforting to know the objective criteria on which personnel decisions will be made. If he does not meet the formal criteria, there may be a formula for substituting experience or expertise in another area. Or, there may be a formula for petitioning or appealing to have a specialty area of effort and expertise recognized. Everyone wants things spelled out—"What do I have to do to survive in this job?" Grievance procedures help indi-vidual faculty members enforce the institution's policies.

The outcome of this standardization tends to be formulas for continuance or promotion based on length of service, with possibly some recognition given to outstanding production and research. But, because there is so much chance for a procedural slip-up, with consequent grievances and appeals, seniority often becomes the name of the game.

Rules and regulations proliferate to control costs. Faculty salaries, rank distributions within the departments, and capital budgets all have a myriad of memoranda, rules, and regulations tell-ing how to proceed in making decisions in these areas. Copies of these rules and regulations are distributed throughout the campus. Faculty members, department chairmen, deans, and administrators must put more time and effort into understanding and filling out all necessary forms to comply with these new rules. The bureaucratiza-tion increases; more levels are consulted in making decisions that used to involve only one or two levels; a chairman used to make decisions on hundred dollar expenditures; now deans do. As a result, decisions take longer. Both faculty and administration time is con-sumed in creating and standardizing cost controls.

Administrators increasingly try to impose cost control formulas to equalize departments. In the same way that external agencies try to use formulas to equalize *across* institutions, local administrators try to impose cost controls to equalize departments *within* the institution. Information is generated on student/faculty ratios, or on capital expenditures per student. Formulas are generated on how much it costs each department, per unit, per student. The obvious outcome of such studies is that the administration tries to bring the more expensive areas into line with the less expensive.

Effect of Unions on Centralization and Autonomy

We have already discussed the importance of the growing movement toward faculty collective bargaining—both in Chapter Seven and in the companion book from the Stanford Project entitled *Unions on Campus* (Kemerer and Baldridge, 1975). Consequently, we will not belabor the point about unions in this chapter. However, we cannot drop the issue without one important comment. Most of the trends we listed above, toward more off-campus centralization and less faculty influence, will be accelerated by unionization.

Although the drive toward centralization and coordination of public higher education started before that toward unionization, collective bargaining and centralization are natural stimulants for each other. Unions must deal directly with the power centers. And to be effective, the union must have a power center equivalent to the central administrative offices—and vice versa. The result is that systems of education tend to have systemwide bargaining. But another result is that centralized bargaining stimulates the trend toward centralized control. Moreover where the central administrative office is not the funding source, unions must move to where the financial power lies. There may be increased contact and conflict with, or lobbying against, noneducational agencies such as the governor's office or the legislature.

Interestingly, the movement toward collective bargaining in the first place partly reflects faculty anxiety over the erosion of local autonomy by statewide boards and coordinating agencies. Many faculty have embraced collective bargaining as a weapon to use against economy-minded legislators and trustees who insist upon cost reductions and improved accountability. Yet, ironically, collective bargaining promotes centralization through large bargaining unit determinations and by focusing on economic issues that must be settled off campus. Thus, the circle is complete: anxiety about system control stimulates unionism, and unionism accelerates system control.

Another threat to local autonomy is the standardization effect that collective bargaining agreements have on campus operations. Two examples come to mind. The evaluation scheme for junior faculty in the second CUNY contract is very difficult for large departments to carry out, yet all departments are forced into the same mold in evaluating personnel. Similarly, in the SUNY system, there is only one master contract despite the great geographical dispersion and divergent educational missions of the various campuses. A master contract covering a few systemwide matters such as salary and benefits, coupled with a secondary contract worked out at the local campus level, might ameliorate the trend toward standardization. However, such master-secondary arrangements have not been adopted, at least to date.

Although there are clear trends toward centralization, the long-term effect of unionization on institutional autonomy is certainly not settled. In concluding this discussion, we simply list the opposing forces that will probably determine the long-run patterns. Forces contributing to centralization include: (1) large bargaining units; (2) a limited choice of bargaining agents; (3) common problems, such as desires for greater economic benefits and job security, that provoke common responses; (4) the centralization and standardizing effect of master contracts; (5) the decision making of legislatures, employee relation boards, and courts that rarely grant higher education separate treatment.

Forces safeguarding diversity include: (1) the voluntary nature of collective bargaining (it is not imposed from outside the campus, with the important exception of the multicampus bargaining unit); (2) the restriction of unionization largely to the less prestigious faculties and institutions; (3) variations within the legal framework such as management rights clauses and arbitration procedures that produce different styles of campus bargaining; (4) the professionalism and tradition of academia that helps confine bargaining largely to economic rather than governance issues at many campuses. In short, there are many contradictory pressures that make it difficult to say definitely what the impact of unionization will be. The danger of increased centralization as a result of unionization, however, is very real.

Death of Collegial Governance?

In this chapter we have been guessing the future, outlining trends we believe will affect management and governance in higher education. In most ways these are depressing trends, movements which are likely to undermine the vestiges still existing in professional decision making and collegiality. Some observers are predicting even more bureaucratization, collective bargaining, state control, and centralization of power. There is widespread fear that the governance of higher education will be more like that of high schools, with strong centralized administrative power and very little student or faculty participation. We suspect that for a substantial part of higher education these predictions are correct. Collegiality, the ideal of so many, was probably never dominant in modern higher education, outside of a few departmental activities. But social trends will probably undermine even the limited collegial influence that existed. Frankly, it seems that collegial governance for the most part, is dead. We may not think it should be, but we definitely think it is.

In discussing these trends we do not mean to imply that all segments of higher education will be affected in the same way. We have said repeatedly that there is enormous diversity in American higher education. The strong forces reducing collegiality will not hurt all campuses alike. In the strong, high-quality institutions, faculty influence (and perhaps even student influence) will still be protected to some extent. There will still be strong enclaves within the large diverse systems where high-quality teaching occurs, where students have a voice in their educations, where faculty have influence over decisions. Higher education's immense size, complexity and diversity will mean that academic governance will continue to have many styles and patterns. The buzzing, booming confusion will probably increase, but flexibility and alternative styles of action will also remain—though probably in fewer and fewer places.

Changing Nature of Academic Management, Governance, and Leadership

For many chapters now we have tried to describe current and emerging features of academic organization, management, governance, and leadership in American higher education. In this chapter, we have painted a rather grim picture of the future. Increased centralization, increased unionization, reduced campus autonomy, financial hardships, declines in student enrollments, and loss of strong public support are but a few of the pessimistic factors that have led us to pessimistic conclusions. Many of our previous descriptions are riddled with implications for policy and administrative practices, but we have not yet made these implications explicit. We will now discuss several specific implications for policy and practice.

Responses to Environmental Change. First of all, we believe that college and university administrators will be required to devote increasingly greater attention, time, and energy to the management of *environmental pressures.* There is no longer any question as to whether academic organizations are affected by external forces. The only question is whether colleges and universities will be able to adapt to these strong and often conflicting environmental pressures. Will administrators learn to forecast revenues, enrollment trends, shifts in demands for particular kinds of education and credentialing, and fluctuations in public attitudes? Not all colleges will—or even should—respond to these pressures in the same way. Some institutions will modify their structures, programs, and practices to better accommodate new demands. Others, perhaps, will buffer themselves from outside influence. They will hold to particular beliefs and values, and strive to maintain their distinctiveness as liberal arts colleges, as major research centers, or as educational arms of particular religious organizations. In all cases, their ability to adapt and preserve their distinctiveness is dependent upon effective management of environmental pressures. This managment of pressures, in turn, depends on the institution's improved ability to understand change, quantify change, forecast change, and determine its implications. We offer the following recommendations.

Independently or through cooperative inter-campus agreements, colleges and universities should develop comprehensive institutional research programs. These programs must be expanded beyond the simple "counting" function that currently prevails, into the areas of needs assessment, policy analysis, evaluation of institutional mission and impact, and forecasting.

Although national and regional trends in environmental changes are important to understanding the broad context of current changes, almost all colleges and universities should conduct locally oriented studies. We believe that, except among the few nationally-oriented and prestigious institutions, too much emphasis has been placed on *national* trends and not enough attention paid to the quite different local conditions that are often much more significant to a local campus. There must be more care in contrasting local trends with national trends in order to make informed judgments about shifts in the client pool, shifts in public attitude and support, and shifts in demand for educational services and products.

Regional forecasting and policy analysis centers should be established, either through institutional consortia or by means of specially funded state or federal centers. These centers would be for the express purpose of providing information directly to campus administrators and other key decision makers—as opposed to serving as regional "research and development" centers, as has been customary in the past.

Colleges and universities should initiate comprehensive self-studies, thereby taking "unprovoked" positive action to examine and, as needed, modify institutional missions and purposes. Over the last decade many self-studies have been conducted, but it is our impression, at least, that at this critical period, when careful planning is a *must*, the number of careful self-studies have declined and the amount of "crisis" oriented decisions have increased.

Providing for Adequate Personnel Management. We believe that college and university presidents will become increasingly involved in the management of comprehensive union contracts and other kinds of formal employment agreements—whether the campus is unionized, or not. We have noted that not all colleges will unionize. Nevertheless, we predict that all top administrators will become directly involved in administering comprehensive employment agreements of some type within the next few years. To some extent, of course, this has already begun to happen. Affirmative action and "reduction in force" policies, independent of faculty unionization, have made it necessary for most administrators to implement and monitor employment practices. With increased federal and state emphasis upon various legal aspects of personnel policies, and with continued reductions in resources, both academic senates and unions will press for more formalized, more detailed, more comprehensive employment agreements. Such agreements, of course, are negotiated into institutional policy and are included within the general management responsibilities of campus administrators.

Personnel administration, therefore, will increasingly tax administrative time and other institutional resources. Many institutions will employ personnel specialists—members of the "technocratic cadre" cited earlier. Other institutions, however, will lack the resources needed to employ specialists. For these institutions, the implications are clear:

Top level administrators should assess—as objectively as possible—their expertise in personnel management issues, maximizing their existing expertise in light of new management demands, and supplementing their training where they are underprepared.

A special note is necessary here. In the past, administrators have come from the ranks of the faculty. We believe this is the appropriate recruiting ground for top administrators—including presidents—especially for administering academic areas. The problem, however, is that faculty selected for administrative posts have had little formal training in administration, budget management, or personnel procedures. Still, we do *not* believe colleges and universities should be turned over to technocrats, or that "trained managers" should replace the professor-turned-administrator. We *do* feel, however, that in this day of pressure, real skills are demanded; more skills than are picked up by chance in committees and senate work. Consequently we seriously urge that:

Long-range institutional plans provide for administrative development programs—in-service training, management workshops, and postgraduate (postdoctoral) course work from regional centers for graduate instruction.

Another issue should be mentioned. It is our judgment that graduate training programs in higher educational administration—such as those offered at UCLA, Berkeley, Stanford, and Michigan—overemphasize doctoral and predoctoral preparation to the exclusion of well-designed, timely, and convenient postdoctoral training opportunities. Thus, along with the above recommendations for practicing college administrators, we recommend that:

Regional graduate schools of education form planning consortia with regional academic administrators to develop advanced professional training programs in the areas of administration for which college and university administrators are becoming increasingly accountable and vulnerable.

Conflict Management. Presidents and other top administrative officers, we predict, will become increasingly involved in managing conflict among competing interest groups. We remarked that this kind of conflict is likely to increase as resources become scarce and battles for priorities rage. Top level administrators will be required to serve as a "court of last resort" in settling disputes among the various schools, divisions, departments, interest groups, entrepreneurs, superstars, research institutes, special program directors, and students. There is no way to resolve this dilemma, because conflicts *are* going to increase, no matter what methods people use to reduce them. Nevertheless, there is one useful suggestion:

College administrators, with their institutional research officers and academic advisory bodies, should develop short-range and long-range plans for the allocation of resources. Such plans would, at least to some extent, place conflicts in a broader perspective and mitigate the ad hoc character of decisions that are made in the heat of conflict. With careful planning, resources could more often go to priorities which are revenue-generating and quality-enhancing. Careful plans could sometimes act as a yardstick for measuring the merits of competing needs and interests.

As any student of organization theory knows, the resolution of such conflict will be handled whenever possible by creating new sets of "standard operating procedures." These include formularized budgets, formularized personnel assignments and distributions, formularized facility allocations, and formularized workloads and professional activities. Yet, issues and conflicts not easily resolved through standard procedures will present themselves at the highest levels of college and university administration. It is our recommendation, therefore, that:

However helpful standard operating procedures are in resolving conflicts over resources, administrators should guard against complete formularization. There *must* be some degree of resource flexibility to meet unexpected needs of politically necessary compromises in the process of negotiations and conflict resolution.

Financial Management and Educational Quality. We fear that the management of fiscal policies may take precedence over the management of programmatic and instructional policies in the decade to come. Throughout American higher education, the name of the game is survival—financial survival. Years ago, industry learned that when a business is getting close to bankruptcy it should rapidly expand its products and its markets—not cut expenditures to the point that the business can no longer produce goods. Education has never had occasion to learn that valuable lesson, and we may not learn it until it is nearly too late to save the "business." Obviously, higher education must devote attention to methods of saving money by increasing the effective utilization of resources. However, over-concern with fiscal policy to the exclusion of programmatic and instructional policies can only lead to disaster. Public and legislative pressure, coupled with a lack of public support and the inexperience of most college administrators to deal with "market fluctuations," could result in a preoccupation with fiscal management and a severe decline in educational quality—primarily as a result of forced neglect. Should this be allowed to go too far, loss of quality and, subsequently, of public trust might well result in fiscal as well as educational bankruptcy.

In spite of these generalized predictions, we still believe that not all institutions will be affected the same way by changes in academic management. Colleges and universities with the greatest resources—human and financial—will be in a position to adapt to these changes by employing specialists, by launching new development and public relations drives, and by preserving most aspects of distinctiveness. In this way, we believe, the rich will get richer and the poor will be hard pressed even to survive. There is, therefore, great need in the field of higher education to develop management systems, financial programs, and institutional development models geared specifically to the needs of the small, low-to-moderate resource institution. Management information systems which researchers have been developing over most of the past decade are not always appropriate to the needs and the institutional support systems of small colleges. We believe that preserving diversity in American higher education is a common problem and should be a common goal. The place to begin is with the development of college management systems that are appropriate to the more impoverished institutions. Specifically, we recommend that:

Special management information systems be developed and tested in the working environments of small colleges with limited financial and human resources. These smaller institutions have relatively limited information needs as compared to the large universities where most current systems are being used.

Existing management information systems should be carefully adapted to meet the needs and resource capabilities of the small college, perhaps by means of subprograms. Predictive systems—those which are based upon long-range forecasts in enrollment and resource requirements—are probably the most difficult and the most expensive systems to adapt to the small college. In most cases, the costs associated with such adaptions would not be justified by the benefits. However, information storage and retrieval systems are quite easily adapted to fit the needs and resource capabilities of the small college. Such systems are quite useful in colleges where manual data retrieval systems are too time consuming to allow the institution to conduct various kinds of longitudinal and comparative studies. Of course, these systems are even more economical when several institutions are able to form cooperative consortia. This practice should be encouraged in order to bring the cost of such systems within reach of the small college and in order to provide incentives for system developers to commit funds to such a market.

Any smaller college considering the adoption of a management information system should include provision for a management training program for all key personnel who will be involved in the design and utilization of the system. This is a recommendation based upon several national studies in which we are currently engaged at UCLA and at the Higher Education Research Institute. These studies show that one of the primary reasons for the failure of management information systems in small colleges is the lack of special training for those who are responsible for its use.

The Governance of Tomorrow's Colleges. To researchers

like ourselves who have devoted much of our academic careers to the study of college and university governance, it is particularly distressing that the concept of academic "governance" is being rapidly replaced by that of academic "management." The term *governance* connotes the holding of an institution in trust, guiding the academic community toward cooperative and mutual pursuits associated with institutional mission, goals, and purposes. The term governance draws out mental images of cooperative policy formulation processes, shared decision processes, and collegial deliberations among peers.

Unfortunately, in the current atmosphere of financial crisis, the "governance" approach smacks too much of slow, deliberate, and even obsolete practices, with too much control by committees, senates, and stuffy academic departments. We believe this process was—and is—necessary, but many people are rushing to "improve" and "streamline" the "obsolete" aspects of shared governance, and to institute more "businesslike management." Efficiency has become the byword.

Unfortunately the decision-making procedure asociated with academic "management" does not always fit well with our image of academic processes. In spite of our zealous comments about the need for improved management practices, we should be the first to caution college and university administrators against the thoughtless abandonment of the principles, practices, and, yes, even the romanticism, of shared authority associated with the rich American tradition of academic governance. In the face of the financial crisis, the rise of unionism, and the bureaucratization of huge state systems, we still believe there are academic values associated with "governance" that are important: shared authority, student and faculty participation, decisions influenced by professional and educational judgments, not just financial ones.

The threats to academic governance are many, and they are not easily thwarted. Perhaps foremost among these is the loss of local campus autonomy to multicampus system offices, state system offices and state legislatures. As we have noted so frequently throughout the book, higher education seems to be entering a period of public management—calling for increased formularization, systemwide uniformity, and highly centralized authority structures. Under these circumstances, not only has formal authority risen to a highly centralized level at state and multicampus system offices, but governance patterns have shifted at the local campus level as well.

For example, changes have begun to occur in the role definitions of trustees, administrators, faculties, and students in relationship to policy-formation and decision-making processes. Trustees, pressed with public and legislative pressures for increased accountability and campus efficiency, have begun to involve themselves in many of the routine administrative tasks formerly delegated to campus administrators. In fact, on many campuses in the public sector, trustees are opening campus offices, employing support staff, and functioning as part-time administrators over fiscal and personnel issues. In the decade ahead, this pattern will probably become increasingly prevalent and trustees and administrators will, together, constitute "management teams" whose purpose is to share jointly in the routine management of the academic organization. For these reasons:

Intensive training programs, workshops, and in-service experiences for trustees must provide them with background information and orientation to the unique characteristics of academic institutions, their purposes, their role in society, and their distinctiveness as professional organizations; and intensive planning sessions must be developed for trustees and academic administrators. One purpose of these would be to ensure that distinctions are drawn between the critical task of policy formulation and policy implementation. This distinction can enhance the effectiveness of the academic management system while preserving the integrity of the academic governance process.

Along with the apparent merging of certain aspects of trusteeship and administration has come an increased separation and polarization among the faculty, administration, and student populations on many campuses. We discussed earlier the growing adversarial relationship between central administration and unionized faculties. We have also observed that student power and influence is being eroded by unionization and many other factors. Here, we also argue that the separation of power by administrators, trustees, and faculties into adversarial groups further erodes student influence.

Students seem to have less and less participation and input into areas of academic policies and decisions. Thus, we strongly recommend that:

Provision must be made for the inclusion of formalized and systematic student input into the planning, devolopment, and evaluation of programs and services of the college. Students must help judge the quality of the educational experience and the quality of the outcomes.

A Concluding Comment. Patterns of academic governance, we have argued, take various shapes and forms on different kinds of campuses. We concluded from our study that diversity in governance patterns still prevails. Yet, we recognize that there are numerous and influential forces operating upon local campuses throughout the nation, and that these influences could, ultimately, undermine our strong heritage of shared authority in academic governance. In so doing, these same influences could conceivably reduce the diversity that we have reported here. It may be that the forces shaping higher education will lead to a uniform, bureaucratized, centralized system. But let us conclude on a more cheerful note. These trends are just as unpredictable and just as changeable as the ones that brought us to this point. And with some level-headed thought, and some real attention to our academic history and its rich heritage, we may yet see a resurgence of management, governance, and leadership that takes educational issues as its focal point.

Special Study:
Historical Developments,
1636-1970

๑๑๑๑๑๑๑๑๑๑๑๑๑๑๑๑๑๑๑๑๑๑

In most of the previous chapters, we have used survey data and case studies from the 1970s to take a cross-sectional snapshot of academic government and management today. In Chapter Nine, we projected some current trends into the future, speculating on how things will develop. This special section will seek to put the basic conceptual themes of these earlier chapters in historical perspective. Logically, this section might have come first, but we felt most readers would want to look at the contemporary situation first, so we have saved this history for last.

Governance patterns have their roots deep in the history of higher education. The past determines much of the present, and changes in patterns of academic governance are systematically linked to changes in the organizational structure of higher education. That is, the nature of decision processes, the distribution of power within institutions, and systems of suprainstitutional management have all evolved from major changes in the environment of academic institutions, the character of the academic profession, and the size and increasingly complex structure of institutions of higher education. By tracing these environmental and structural changes historically, we not only give depth, background, and insight into our data about contemporary governance and management, we can also better predict future governance and management trends.

For example, we have shown in Chapter Three that at least eight types of academic institutions currently exist. These types have developed out of the unique historical and social contexts of a developing nation, and new types will undoubtedly evolve in the future as the environment, nature, and structure of higher education change. Thus Harvard, now a private multiversity, originated as a small quasi-public liberal arts college. It and its early competitors had no need for complex governance systems: as small institutions, they were dominated by their presidents and their boards of trustees. But as changes throughout the years gave rise to several distinct types of colleges and universities, they gradually created the need for new kinds of governance structures. Following a pattern familiar to sociologists, the relatively simple system of liberal arts colleges gradually has differentiated as it has grown, enlarged its task, and generated increased resources. And in this increasingly diverse system of institutions, an increasingly complex multitiered governance system has emerged.

Just as the older types of institutions have not died out during this process of institutional diversification, so older decision-making systems have not been abandoned; they continue side by side with new ones. For example, along with strong presidential dominance in early times, faculty collegial activity gradually gained prominence; and more recently multicampus and state system influences have been added. All these basic patterns are intermixed in today's governance structure. At any given time, a single institution may have a dominant pattern of management and governance, but as different circumstances arise in its environment, in the professional responsibilities of its staff, and in its structure, this pattern is likely to be transformed. For instance, many institutions once dominated by strong presidential power have now developed collegial patterns of operation; but in times of financial crisis, these collegial patterns may be superseded by strong presidents. Thus, any given institution may see-saw back and forth between alternative styles of management as personalities change, the financial situation varies, or the environment makes new demands.

Beyond these short-term fluctuations affecting individual institutions, however, long-term patterns across whole groups of institutions persist and can be charted historically. That is, the overall trend of governance patterns are highly predictable despite changes that affect any single institution at any given time.

This section about these long-term patterns is not intended to be a general historical analysis of American higher education. Others, such as Brubacher and Rudy (1958), have already provided that in far greater breadth and detail than we can. However, we offer a frame of reference and an historical perspective for understanding the organizational and governmental complexities of the present and predicting those of the future. We do so by dividing the history of American higher education into six periods: (1) from the founding of Harvard in 1636 to the Dartmouth College Case in 1819; (2) from 1819 to the Morrill Land-Grant Act in 1862; (3) from 1862 to the founding of the American Association of University Professors in 1919; (4) from 1919 to the end of World War II in 1945; (5) from 1945 to the beginning of the Free Speech Movement at Berkeley in 1964; and (6) from 1964 into the 1970s. For each period, we will be asking the same three questions: (1) What were the *organizational characteristics* of colleges during the era, as influenced by environmental relations, professional task, and size? (2) Which of the eight *types of institutions* existed during the era? And (3) what were the dominant *governance patterns* during the era?

Period I: 1636–1819

It is easy to see why we begin our history of organizational characteristics, institutional types, and governance patterns in American higher education with the founding of Harvard—our oldest institution of higher learning—in 1636. But why use 1819 and the Dartmouth College Case as the milestone ending the first era, rather than, for example, the American revolution—a favorite dividing line drawn by other higher education historians? One hundred and eighty-three years is admittedly a long period to cover in a few short pages, encompassing both colonial and post-colonial periods. Yet the basic organizational and governance patterns existing in 1819 were not very different from those of 1636. Colleges had grown somewhat, their faculties had expanded, and their support had increased, but their basic structure and operations were similar throughout the period. To be sure, changes in organization that blossomed after 1819 had begun to grow before that date, just as governance patterns did not change overnight as a result of the decision in the case of *Dartmouth College* vs. *Woodward*. But the Dartmouth College case was of monumental importance to higher education, and American colleges and universities were changed forever after it. Thus 1819 is both an important and convenient date for sharpening our focus on major changes, and we will use it realizing that it is but a benchmark in an evolutionary unfolding.

Organizational Characteristics. Harvard was founded to preserve in the new world the continuity of old world tradition and learning. Within that general purpose was the very pragmatic and utilitarian need to provide for an educated clergy. "After God had carried us safe to New England," stated an 1643 pamphlet, *New England's First Fruits,* "and we had builded our houses, provided necessities for our livelihood, readied convenient places for God's worship, and settled the Civil Government; one of the next things we longed for and looked after was to advance learning and perpetuate it to posterity dreading to leave an illiterate ministry to the churches when our present ministers shall lie in the dust" (Knapp, 1967, p. 916).

This need for an educated clergy was the single most compelling reason for the establishment of colleges during the early colonial period. And since the colonies were religiously diverse, colleges were established in different regions to satisfy the doctrines of particular denominations— Harvard for Puritans, Yale for Congregationalists, the College of Rhode Island (Brown) for Baptists, Queens College (Rutgers) for the Dutch Reform Church, Princeton for the Presbyterians, William and Mary for the Anglican Episcopalians, and so forth. Yet these were more than theological seminaries. There was a concern for liberal education as well behind their establishment: their curricula were more oriented to liberal arts than theology, and by the time of the Revolution about four fifths of all their graduates were preparing for vocations other than the ministry (Hofstadter, 1964).

Only a small percentage of the population attended these colleges. Even by the Revolution, only one boy in fifty (and no girls) was entering college. In 1710, Harvard had only 123 students, and Yale 36 (Brubacher and Rudy, 1958). Yet any boy with the desire, resources, and ability to meet the minimal admissions standards could attend. In the early days of Harvard, these standards amounted very simply to a knowledge of Latin and Greek: "When any schollar is able to read Tully or such like classicall Latine Authour extemporare, and make an speake true Latin verse and prose Suo (ut aiunt) Marte, and decline perfectly the paradigmes of Nounes and verbes in the Greeke tonge, then may hee bee admitted into Colledge, nor shall any claim admission before qualification" (Brubacher and Rudy, 1958, p. 24).

The professional task of the colleges was a relatively simple one: to teach these students through the hearing of recitations. Research was neither recognized as an institutional responsibility nor undertaken by many instructors. In this and other ways, these early colleges were more akin to what we call secondary schools than to today's colleges and universities. For example, it would not have been correct during this period to maintain that "the faculty are the college": the tutors, fellows, or other faculty members were generally recent graduates who stayed on to teach only until a clerical position could be obtained. They were not only transient, they were not professional academics. Although there was a gradual move toward their specialization in the classroom, they did not consider themselves to be "historians," "chemists," or even "mathematicians." It would be much more accurate to say of these early institutions that "the president is the college." Initially, he was the only full-time faculty member; he was expected to be able to teach every subject offered by the college and he performed all administrative and maintenance functions himself.

In short, the term *organizational complexity,* which can certainly be used to describe a multiversity of these current decades, is out of place in describing the early colleges. There were no registrars, deans, assistant deans, vice-presidents for public relations, or even librarians. Other than the president, there were no administrators or officials at all, in the classic bureaucratic sense. Rather than bureaucracies, these schools might best be described as "establishments" and establishments dominated by the patriarchal figure of the president.

Types of Institutions. In terms of our present eight major types of institutions, these first colleges could all probably best be categorized as Private Liberal Arts Colleges. None of the original nine colonial colleges were public institutions in our current sense of the term, although all but three—Princeton, Brown, and Rutgers— received state funds, and with these subventions came board members appointed by colonial or state government. Among these colleges, a trend soon developed toward relying less and less on government support, and after the Revolutionary War state institutions began to make their appearance, primarily in the south and west—the University of Georgia (1785), the University of North Carolina (1789), the University of Tennessee (1794), and the institution that was later to become the University of South Carolina (1801).

A general split developed immediately after the Revolution between the liberal gentry and the sectarian clergy. The liberals, representing Jeffersonian ideals, tended to support schools that were publicly funded, while the clergy fostered the growth of the private denominational schools. But the public/private dichotomy was not clearly drawn until 1819 with the Dartmouth College case, and until then most of the colleges obtained a blend of public and private support that does not permit them to be fitted neatly into either category.

Governance Patterns. Formal control in the early colleges rested with the boards, variously called overseers, trustees, or governing boards. They had the responsibility to raise funds and the power to appoint presidents. And although the general pattern was to allow the presidents to run the colleges, there were numerous exceptions. In the beginning, the composition of these boards was predominantly clerical, but in all institutions there soon set in a gradual but steady shift toward lay control. At Harvard, the threshold from clerical to secular control was passed in 1727 "when primary influence on the Harvard governing board passed to wealthy Boston men of affairs" (Brubacher and Rudy, 1958, p. 10). And the pattern established at Harvard was followed by the other early colleges.

Understanding the role that lay government has played in American higher education is critical to understanding the current governance relationships in colleges and universities. "Nowhere outside the United States and Canada are modern universities governed by boards of laymen," Hofstadter, (1964, p. 120) has written. The significance of this fact is that the lay board, and not the faculty, is empowered by law to set institutional policy and to hire and fire staff. Hofstadter identifies three important ways in which the American situation gave rise to this arrangement. First, the American Protestants were cut off from the European tradition of academic guild—faculty self-government—and with many years of experience in lay government for their churches, did not find it difficult to extend the practice to the colleges. Second, "while the European universities evolved out of long-established communities of scholarship and teaching, the first American colleges were created, in a sense, as artifacts by communities that had to strain every limited resource to support them" (p. 123). These fragile institutions had to be nursed along carefully to prevent their demise, and the lay boards that created them exercised great control, and they were not willing to give it up even after the institution became stronger. Third and finally, "while in Europe a body of men belonging to what could be called a teaching profession existed before the emergence of the universities, the colleges in America were created first, and only afterwards did a considerable body of teachers emerge" (p. 123). As mentioned earlier, the teachers of the colonial colleges were, with the exception of the president, transitory clerics. They were not a professionalized body and had little interest in, or stake in, strong faculty input into the decision-making processes. All of this was to change with time, but these first governance relationships set the pattern for the future.

The lay boards, then, had both the responsibility for the institutions and the power to make and enforce decisions. However, some very practical problems were created by this absence of a strong faculty and existence of a strong lay board. The lay board was not present on the campus and therefore could not attend to the day-to-day problem solving that was necessary. Even though the colleges of the time were not complex organizations, there were still many housekeeping functions to be performed—keeping the books, hiring and supervising the staff, obtaining the supplies, and dealing with curricular problems. "Thus between the trustees, who had the legal capacity but not the time or energy to govern, and the teachers, who were considered too young and too transient to govern, there was created a power vacuum. This vacuum the presidents quickly began to fill."

The role of the president, and of governance relationships in those early colleges is eloquently summarized by Hofstadter:

> The early college president played a multiple role. As a cleric and learned man he taught. As a member of the governing board he participated in major decisions. As a leading citizen of his community he promoted his institution. As a faculty member he led the teaching staff. As a preacher he prayed and sermonized for the students. Since he was subject in most cases to dismissal by governing boards, he was the subordinate of the trustees, and yet as the man most familiar with college affairs he was also the leader of the governing board. In relation to his tiny teaching staff he was a leader or a boss, depending upon his situation and temperament. Unlike the European rector, he was not elected by the teachers nor in any formal way accountable to them. Teachers came and went as a matter of course. The president remained until he died or resigned or, in rare cases, was ousted by his board. The tutors, being temporarily servants, had little reason to resist or hamper his authority. The trustees, although they appointed and could replace him, could

not displace him. In legal theory they were the college, but in the eyes of the community, and often in his own eyes, the president was the college. Upon his reputation and his promotional energies its place in the community chiefly depended. He became at once its dynamic center of authority, its symbol, and its spokesman. He occupied and in a sense created an office which has no equivalent in academic systems outside the United States. The prestige and pride that elsewhere were vested in the faculties came to center in him—and there, with some modification, they have remained to this day [1964, p. 210].

In sum, what we had in the pre-1819 colleges were institutions very much attuned to their environment—playing a role explicitly assigned them by the society, with formal control lodged in governing boards and presidents, and with support not clearly distinguishable between the public and private sectors except in a few clearly public schools. The professional task was but one, teaching, and it was a generalized task much less complex than today, performed by nonprofessionals. All in all, these schools can in no way be described as complex organizations comparable to today's.

Period II: 1819–1862

1819 marks the year the Supreme Court handed down the decision in the case of *Dartmouth College* vs. *Woodward,* and in 1862 Congress passed the Morrill Land-Grant Act. The 43 years between these benchmark events marked a period of reconnaissance and trial and error in American higher education. The number of colleges increased, and the curriculum changed—shifting considerably from its earlier preoccupation with things classical and theological. Students sought to prepare not only for the ministry or law or medicine but for commerce and the new profession of engineering; and where traditional curricula proved too limited, new types of institutions sprang up to meet specialized needs.

Organizational Characteristics. In examining the environmental factors at work during this period, one must pay special attention to the Dartmouth case, an event of truly monumental import. Dartmouth College had been founded by a royal charter granted in 1769. Like all colleges of the period, control was vested in the hands of the president through the board of trustees. However, the presidency of Dartmouth had resided in a father and son dynasty that operated relatively independent of the board. Toward the end of the presidency of the son, John Wheelock, there began a controversy as to whether control would continue to reside in the president or whether the board would take a more active role. The issue took on political overtones, with the Democrats supporting the president and the Federalists backing the trustees. In 1816, the Democrats gained control of the New Hampshire legislature and passed a law nullifying the original charter and making Dartmouth a state university. The trustees and their Federalists friends fought the law to the United States Supreme Court, which ruled that a charter of the type originally granted Dartmouth could not be violated by a state government. Thus control at Dartmouth reverted to the original board.

The issue in the Dartmouth case had turned on the question of whether an institution established by governmental charter was or was not a public institution. The Court held that the state could not interfere with these corporations; it thus ensured, among other things, the existence of a mixed academic economy in the United States. Specifically, for higher education, the decision clearly drew the distinction between state and private colleges, and perhaps represents the beginning of the wariness of many private colleges toward accepting state or federal money.

The decision paved the way for the great proliferation of private colleges that followed. Denominational colleges particularly were established throughout the country. For those who took the position of Thomas Jefferson, that higher education should be managed by the public in the public trust, the decision also gave an impetus to the founding of state-supported institutions, and a number were established south of New England. However, "the decision . . . long postponed the movement for state universities in New England" (Brubacher and Rudy, 1958, p. 36).

Diversity is certainly one hallmark of American higher education, and that diversity was given impetus by the large number of institutions founded between 1819 and 1862. By 1862 there were

182 permanent colleges in the nation. But that figure does not tell the whole story. Tewksbury reports that of 516 colleges founded in 16 states before 1862, only 104 survived into the twentieth century (1932, p. 28). Naturally enough, as one moved farther from the centers of population into the West and South, the failure rate became more pronounced. In New York, 36 colleges were established and 15 survived; in North Carolina the figures were 26 and 7; in Missouri, 85 and 8; and in Texas, 40 and 2. For the most part these colleges were denominational in nature and established to provide places where "safe" new ideas could be learned. Though the great bulk of these institutions were Protestant, by 1860, 14 permanent Catholic schools had been founded (Brubacher and Rudy, 1958).

Even though the schools were denominational and founded primarily for sectarian reasons, many of them soon learned to temper theology with practicality. Ben-David has noted that "The most important condition of the system (of American higher education) has been that, composed of independent units, the institutions have had to compete with each other for community support, students and faculty" (1972, p. 63). And thus, this competition, especially for students, led the successful institutions to soften their religious emphasis and grant other denominations minor representation on their boards. Those institutions that failed did so primarily because they could not attract enough students, and they often could not attract students because of strict denominational stances.

An environmental factor that must not be overlooked is the growth of literacy among the general population. "This multiplication and diversification of colleges, seen in perspective, was but part of a larger movement for diffusion of knowledge to the people. American democracy in the nineteenth century was also building popular academies, establishing common schools and public high schools, developing a 'penny press,' enlarging its public libraries, and flocking to local lyceums and Chautauquas." (Brubacher and Rudy, 1958, p. 59). Certainly there would have been no need to expand the colleges had there been no parallel expansion of the public school system.

Financial support of colleges in this period generally derived from the same sources as during the earlier colonial days. The colonial colleges had received a relatively large proportion of their private gifts from England prior to the Revolution. That source had dried up considerably after 1776, but there still were private American benefactors who supported colleges. Furthermore, even after the Dartmouth case a number of private schools continued to receive public subventions. Massachusetts was still supporting Amherst in 1848, and even Dartmouth itself requested state support after the Supreme Court decision. A relatively large percentage of the costs were derived from tuition charges even though students often paid their fees with goods of different sorts—grain, animals, and other commodities. Then, even as now, educational independence was a function of financial independence, and those schools that were relatively better off and not dependent for survival upon single sources of income were the most educationally independent. Most schools had no endowment and survived precariously at best.

The political climate of the times could best be described as "in flux." The period saw presidents like Monroe, Adams, and Jackson, but also Harrison, Polk, and Buchanan. It was the period when slavery and states' rights were first debated then fought over. It was a period of great growth and expansion. The population tripled from less than 10 million in 1819 to more than 32 million in 1862. It was a time of westward and southern expansion; the number of states admitted to the Union rose from 21 to 34.

In the realm of ideas, it was Jacksonian democracy that most influenced higher education. Jackson's espousal of egalitarianism made free public education at the grammar school level available to greater numbers of people. But that same egalitarianism fostered a suspicion and disdain for higher learning. Indeed, in his first message to Congress, Jackson stated his confidence in the capacity of the average man (a man not possessed of a college degree) for politics: "The duties of all public officers are . . . so plain and simple that men of intelligence may readily qualify themselves for their performance. . . . In a country where offices are created, solely for the benefit of the people, no one man has any more intrinsic right to official station than another" (Mason, 1956, p. 430). That attitude spread, and respect for excellence and expertise diminished in all fields. For awhile, there was a resurgence of the apprentice method of learning skills as well as law and medicine. However, there were many who still looked to and respected higher education, and Jackson was president for only eight years.

During this time of expansion and political flux, the nature of the professional task performed by the faculty also changed. Research did not replace teaching as the major function, but faculty became more specialized even as curricular offerings rapidly expanded. The interest in science, both theoretical and practical, increased. Of the colonial colleges, Hofstadter could say "the first professor of mathematics and natural philosophy was the first professor of a secular subject. Often he was also the first professor whose personal background was secular" (p. 196). But all that was changing. The vehicle for this change was the elective system, whereby students were given some choice in the courses they took: "the central educational battle of nineteenth-century America was fought over the elective system. This is the question which aroused the greatest amount of controversy in the academic world, inflamed passions as no other educational issue was able to do, and most clearly reflected the impact of modern technology upon the traditional college" (Brubacher and Rudy, 1958, p. 96).

Thomas Jefferson was an early advocate of the elective principle, and his ideas were partially embodied in the University of Virginia, which was established in 1825. George Tichnor, a close friend of Jefferson's, sought to establish a variation on the elective theme at Harvard whose faculty by that year "organized into distinct departments of study" (Brubacher and Rudy, 1958, p. 98).

Not only were faculty beginning to specialize in teaching the more traditional disciplines—Latin, Greek, mathematics, natural science, philosophy, psychology, morals, and religion—but there was also an increased interest in what was called technical education. A number of institutions were established to specialize in technical training, the first being Rensselaer Polytechnic Institute in 1824. Rensselaer and a number of other new schools established curricula in husbandry, "manufactures," civil engineering, architecture, mining, and other applied fields. The older established schools soon followed suit, and both Yale and Harvard had "applied" schools or departments by 1847. The educational requirement to teach remained, in most places, a bachelor's degree with perhaps additional training in some field, usually theology. The doctorate was not yet on the rise in this country. The point not to be missed, though, is that the faculty were becoming ever more specialized in their teaching, and the colleges were taking on a wider array of subjects to teach. The combination of specialization plus broader curriculum increased the move toward departmentalization and hence greater complexity.

During the period 1819 to 1862, the departmental structure continued to develop, courses proliferated, and enrollments and budgets increased. But it was not until after the Civil War that the president received any substantial assistance to deal with the administrative complexities of this growth. In terms of organization, colleges and universities were still primarily fiefdoms of strong presidents who willed their way over the increasingly professionalized faculty. Some colleges, of course, remained quite small, and for them the organizational patterns were more similar to the Harvard of 1700 than that of 1862.

Types of Institutions. Most institutions of this period were of the same type as those before 1819, but because of the Dartmouth College case, the private colleges were more distinctly private and the public colleges more clearly public. Technical institutions like Rensselaer do not fit nicely into any present category, but in many respects they were the nineteenth century equivalent of the twentieth century public community college, offering technical programs for terminating students. Institutions in the educational vanguard of the period were evolving toward new types of institutions, but the process has not been completed by 1862.

Governance Patterns. In 1862 presidents still exercised great control over their institutions. But change was occurring in governance patterns in some places—generally in the larger and more established colleges. Among these changes was a shift of certain kinds of decision making from the presidents to the faculty and greater caution in how presidents exercised their power. Hofstadter points out that while the early faculties had been composed of rather young and transient teachers, the same could not be said of faculties after 1819. In the better institutions they were mature men, respected for their knowledge, who could not be directed in the traditional cavalier fashion. The presidents themselves came to be drawn on occasion from the faculty rather than from the ministry, and as former faculty members they identified more closely with concerns voiced by the teachers. So, as noted by Hofstadter, "from being the spokesman of the board to the faculty, the president tended to become more the intermediary between the board and the faculty, obliged to find a substantial measure of harmony in both bodies in order best to carry out his work" (1964, p. 233).

Though faculty at Harvard were gradually exerting more influence, it was at Yale that the role of faculty in decision making was most advanced. President Jeremiah Day (1817–1846) assumed his office having spent a number of years as a professor. He made it his habit to consult with the *assembled* faculty on matters of important policy. Though this was his personal way of doing things, a precedent was established "that even the corporation should not take action without the recommendation or assent of the instructors" (Hofstadter, 1964, p. 35). Additionally, the principle was established in the better Eastern colleges that no new faculty should be appointed without the consent of his future colleagues.

It remained, however, for the faculty of a later day to broaden their sphere of influence and formalize their voice. By 1862 this process had begun in a few Eastern schools and would eventually spread both west and south.

Period III: 1862–1915

This period begins with the passing of the Morrill Land-Grant Act in 1862, and ends with the formation of the American Association of University Professors in 1915. It began in the middle of one war and ended in the middle of another. It spanned decades of vast economic growth and industrial expansion, during a time when millions of immigrants came from Europe and thousands of American scholars went there. It saw great financial empires built, and huge fortunes in railroads, oil, and steel won and lost, with men like Carnegie, Stanford, Rockefeller, and Mellon giving millions to colleges and universities. In short, it was a period when events great and small brought profound changes in the nation, and in its higher education apparatus.

Organizational Characteristics. The federal government had shown an interest in higher education as early as 1802, when the Military Academy at West Point was established, and when Congress gave two parcels of land to endow a state university in the new state of Ohio—a practice continued for every state entering the Union with the exception of Maine, Texas, and West Virginia. But this practice of granting land for the support of higher education received its greatest impetus in 1862 with the passage of the Morrill Land-Grant Act, "An Act donating Public Lands to the several States and Territories which may provide Colleges for the Benefit of Agriculture and the Mechanic Arts." The act provided that each state would establish at least one college where "the leading object shall be, without excluding other scientific and classical studies . . . to teach such branches of learning as are related to agriculture and the mechanic arts . . . in order to promote the liberal and practical education of the industrial classes."

It was clearly the intent of Congress that the colleges should be vocational. Practical congressmen, especially in a time of war, believed that liberal arts did not adequately meet the needs of a rapidly expanding technological society. While the framers of the law would probably be quite pleased with the results of their legislation, there might be some question that the University of California, University of Georgia, Massachusetts Institute of Technology, Cornell, University of Illinois and other stars among the land-grant institutions became the kinds of colleges the congressmen had envisioned.

There are a number of reasons why the land-grant colleges, and other colleges as well, developed in the way they did. Veysey points out that college growth since the Jacksonian period had been minimal, while the general population had expanded greatly. During the 1870s the nation's population grew by 23 percent while enrollment in the "oldest leading colleges" rose by only 3.5 percent. The percentage of college graduates in Congress was declining, and business and commerce welcomed men of ability regardless of whether they possessed a college diploma (Veysey, 1965, p. 4). Business was the business of America after the Civil War, and T. H. Safford, a professor at Williams, remarked that "the varied attractions of city life restrain intellectual tendencies in the minds of many boys, and the variety of careers which they see opening before their older schoolmates leads to a strong tendency to follow business rather than classical courses" (Safford quoted in Veysey, 1965, p. 5).

This led to problems within academia. Static enrollments made expansion very difficult, and professors remained impecunious. In a time when men of ability were making their fortunes in the world of affairs, professors found themselves among the lowest paid and least prestigious of the professions.

But during this nadir in its domestic prestige and influence, American academics became engaged in a foreign affair. American scholars returning from the great universities of Germany encouraged by both word and deed many others to follow in their footsteps, and more than 9,000 Americans studied in Germany in the nineteenth century. The overwhelming majority of these went there after 1862.

It was this German influence more than any other single factor that gave American higher education a new impetus and changed its character forever. The conception of the university as a research institution is primarily a German idea, and the roots of the modern American university can be traced to the founding of Berlin University in 1809. At Berlin, "the emphasis was on philosophy and science, on research and graduate instruction, on the freedom of professors and students (*Leberfreiheit* and *Lernfreiheit*). The department was created, and the institute" (Kerr, 1963, p. 11). Scholars returning from Germany brought with them new notions about the importance of research, research methodology, the lecture and seminar format for teaching, departments, institutes, academic ranking, and academic freedom. None of these ideas were introduced without change in their new environment, but introduced they were.

Earlier attempts to transplant the German experience had been unsuccessful. Tichnor failed at Harvard in 1825; Wayland was unsuccessful at Brown in the 1850s; and Tappan could not even institute a system of electives at Michigan in the late 1850s. Although Yale granted the first American doctorate in 1861, the opening of Johns Hopkins in 1876 announced the genesis of the university in this country. Other institutions were soon shaped or reshaped in the same mold—Harvard, Cornell, Michigan, Minnesota, Stanford, California, and Yale, to name a few.

The way to understanding the university phenomenon lies in

understanding the importance assigned to the doctor of philosophy degree. The doctorate became necessary for obtaining a position on the graduate faculty. Specialists must teach specialists, and scholars quickly learned that prestige lay at the top—teaching graduate students. But there were limited positions available on graduate faculties. Some with doctorates began teaching undergraduates, and soon doctorate holders permeated the entire faculty. It was not long before universities and even colleges were judged qualitatively on the percentage of doctorates on the faculty. The doctorate became the hallmark of the academic professional.

Metzger is quick to point out that "America took from German sources only that which fitted her needs, only that which was in harmony with her history. In a certain sense, the German academic influence, powerful as it was, reinforced rather than initiated native American tendencies toward change" (1961, p. 93). The battle, then, over Darwinism which preceded the great scholarly exodus to Germany prepared the ground for many of the ideas that were later to come. During the controversy over evolution, empiricism was embraced by many scientists, and the German-trained empiricists found themselves welcome in many universities.

The Morrill Land-Grant Act envisioned vocational schools, but some of the institutions it funded became German-model research universities. To Metzger, "the significant point . . . is not that the land-grant colleges and graduate schools coexisted, for each served its own area of need; the significant things is that they coexisted in the same institution" (1961, p. 106). As research organizations, these schools emphasized the applied sciences, and as teaching organizations they included not only the traditional curriculum but also added courses in the "applied" subjects.

As the state universities grew in prestige and influence, two new concepts became associated with them. The first was the all-purpose curriculum embodied in Cornell University—the idea that higher education was to be available in almost all subject matter areas. The second concept was that of service to the community— best exemplified in the University of Wisconsin. Both of these new "purposes" of higher education tended to increase support within legislatures as well as encourage their expansion.

Financial support for higher education institutions fluctuated somewhat during this period, although there was an overall pattern of increasing expenditures both in the private and public sectors. The land-grant act gave impetus to the state schools, and by the turn of the century the wealthier states were providing more than a million dollars a year to their state universities (Brubacher and Rudy, 1958).

Private benefactors also greatly enriched higher education during this time. Universities today bear the names of these benefactors—Stanford, Vanderbilt, Carnegie-Mellon, Johns Hopkins, Cornell. Others, such as Rockefeller, Clark, Lawrence, Sage, and Ford, also donated millions to the support of higher education. The diversity of higher education today, in fact, is due in great part to the gifts made by these men during the nineteenth century.

With higher education expanding both in enrollments and in numbers of schools, the job market for professors expanded as well during this period. Expanding enrollments were directly related to high school enrollment, and while in 1870 there were 72,158 students enrolled in 1,026 high schools, by the turn of the century there were 519,251 students enrolled in 6,005 high schools (Brubacher and Rudy, 1958). All of this growth, expansion, and diversification greatly expanded the professional job market. Also expanding this job market was an increasing number of course offerings.

The combination of factors including land-grant support, German research influence, and expansion of curriculum enrollment all worked together to make many universities truly complex organizations. Relatively large budgets made them even more complex by the addition of departments, schools and institutions. By 1910 there were already a number of universities with enrollments of over 5,000 students (Veysey, 1965). The university of the late nineteenth and early twentieth century was becoming recognizable as a university as we know it today.

Types of Institutions. The institutional types mentioned before—Liberal Arts Colleges and Public Colleges—continued to exist between 1862 and 1915. But a number of other institutions evolved into both Public Comprehensive universities and a type that closely resembled what we call Elite Liberal Arts Colleges. Additionally, some new comprehensive universities were founded. The multiversity as we know it today did not yet exist, but the seeds had been planted.

Private Junior Colleges also made their appearance during this period. It is interesting that junior colleges were a direct outgrowth of the German influence, and that two of their earliest proponents, David Starr Jordan and William R. Harper, are actually most remembered for their influence on the much larger research universities. Junior colleges were seen by both Jordan and Harper as feeder institutions for their universities—assuming the role of the gymnasium of Germany. The first junior colleges certainly were not the open-admissions institutions of today that teach everything from Chaucer to changing tires.

By 1915, existing institutional types were the Private Liberal Arts, Public Colleges, Public Comprehensive, and Private Junior Colleges. These institutions were themselves in the process of change, and many would soon evolve into different types of colleges and universities.

Governance Patterns. Veysey notes that "by 1910 the structure of the American university had assumed its stable twentieth-century form" (1965, p. 338). Within that structure there existed many of the governance relationships with which we are now familiar. And even though the present structure existed as early as 1910, there have been a number of subtle and less subtle shifts in the locus of decision making within institutions.

One of the more important changes in higher education in the period 1862–1915 was in the administration of the expanding and increasingly complex universities. We have already discussed the growing number of departments, schools, institutes and students— as a result of which "the complexity of the university made the former college seem a boy's school in contrast" (Veysey, 1965, p. 2). Gone were the days when the president alone could perform all of the many administrative functions. Though the pattern varied among institutions, the addition of administrators generally included a librarian, a registrar, deans (academic and then student personnel), business officers, directors of public relations, and vice presidents. The secretaries and staff needed to support the administrative functions expanded even more rapidly. Typists, clerks, bookkeepers, maintenance personnel, and groundskeepers all proliferated in expanding institutions.

The basic function of the president changed also. Different abilities were required to manage a complex of 5,000 students than were necessary when the institutions were much smaller. Timothy Dwight accepted the presidency of Yale in 1892 only with the stipulation that he not be required to teach. And President Hadly of Yale marked the change in the role of presidents by noting that "when he visited old President Porter he like as not found him reading Kant, but when he called on president Dwight he was more likely to find him examining a balance sheet" (Phelps, quoted in Brubacher and Rudy, 1958, p. 351).

The period from 1862 to 1915 saw the emergence of parallel hierarchies within the institutions—administrative and academic. The administrative functions were created to relieve the presidents and faculty of the burdens of necessary detail so that they could concentrate their efforts on things academic. The academic hierarchy was the decision-making structure that existed within the departments and schools and at the institutional level to deal with the matters which most concerned faculty—curriculum, academic standards, and the hiring of new faculty. Then, however, as now, there were no clear distinctions between academic policies and the administration of those policies.

Brubacher and Rudy point out that, as institutions grew, there generally were faculty committees which dealt in a detailed fashion with many affairs besides curriculum matters—discipline, athletics, and the like. However, with increasing size and complexity, these committee assignments required greater amounts of time. Gradually, the pattern emerged of administrators proposing policies and presenting them to the faculty for ratification. Faculty were free to teach and conduct their research, but they also lost considerable control over decision-making processes.

Even before 1776 a trend away from clerical control of boards of trustees had begun. The trend grew during the nineteenth century. Instead, boards both public and private were composed of businessmen and men of affairs. Many of these trustees did not see any significant difference between a large corporation and a large university, and consequently there often were attempts to treat colleges and universities as businesses.

Boards interjected their opinions about specific course offerings, academic requirements, faculty promotions, and, most importantly, faculty firings. The faculty, who had passively let academic decision making slip from themselves and from a president who had been first among equals to a president who was dominant, then saw much of that decision-making authority assumed by boards of trustees. Faculty members were abruptly stirred from their doldrums by a series of faculty dismissals made by boards and sometimes even presidents. These dismissals were especially significant because in most instances the faculty were fired for advocating theories or positions which offended certain trustees. Metzger details the incidents—Henry C. Adams at Cornell for a prolabor speech; George Steel, president of Lawrence College, for leanings toward free trade and greenbacks; Richard Ely at Wisconsin for heretical social and economic writings; Docent Hourwich at the University of Chicago for participation in a Populist Convention; Edward A. Ross at Stanford for his opinions on silver and coolie immigration.

All of these incidents were important, but the Ross case had a special effect. In 1900 the American Economic Association launched an investigation of the case. "With this decision, the first professional inquiry into an academic freedom case was conceived and brought into being—the predecessor, if not directly the parent, of the proceedings of Committee A of the American Association of University Professors (AAUP)" (Metzger, 1961, p. 168). Even though the association was unsuccessful in its efforts to get the facts in the Ross case, the point had been emphasized that peers were the most competent to judge the professional behavior of professors.

Period IV: 1915–1945

Period IV begins early in World War I and finishes at the end of World War II. The period encompasses thirty years that might be characterized as manic-depressive. The "roaring twenties" reflected the ebullience of a postwar period. It was the time of the speak-easy, the flapper, the charleston, and raccoon coats at college football games. For most, that ended in 1929. The thirties were a bleak time in which the future offered little hope. The ideas and institutions—capitalism, free enterprise, Wall Street, business—upon which so many had placed their hopes had seemingly failed just when expectations were highest.

In higher education it was a period of maturation, and the modern era of colleges and universities was upon us. There were many changes, some of which were quite significant, including the continued enlargement of institutional size and professional responsibilities. But in terms of higher education over a three hundred year span, the period 1915–1945 appears to be one of consolidation and "settling in."

Organizational Characteristics. It is difficult to draw direct relationships between women's suffrage, prohibition, and higher education. Yet there can be no doubt that the nineteenth amendment has had a tremendous effect upon the nation, and that Prohibition may well have been the primary influence of the twenties. Enrollments in higher education increased both during the high-spirited twenties and the depression-ridden thirties—though for quite different reasons. In the 1919–20 academic year there were approximately 600,000 college and university students. Ten years later that figure had almost doubled, to 1,100,000. By September of 1939 the number had risen still further, to 1,500,000. This overall increase was far greater than that of the population at large. In 1919, 8.1 percent of the college-age population were enrolled; by 1939 this percentage had increased to 15.3 (Devane, 1965).

The twenties, and to a lesser extent the thirties, were the period of the "Gentleman's C." Students were enrolled to have a good time and to get a degree, and "getting a degree" was significantly different from studying for an education. The popular image of the student of the twenties was essentially all too correct in most places—hip flask, raccoon coat, escorting a blond with short hair to a postgame fraternity party. Equally correct was the image of the student of the thirties—waiting tables and burning the midnight oil to stay in school. While the students of the twenties had attended college purely as a matter of choice, those of the thirties often did so out of economic necessity. Jobs were difficult to obtain, and a great number concluded that if survival required struggle then they might just as well struggle in college.

Since the influx of the German-trained doctorates in the late nineteenth century, American educators had been torn between the English notion of educating the "whole man" and the German concern only for the intellect. The position one took had serious implications both for the curriculum and for the way the institution handled students. Neither position totally held the field, as American colleges and universities adopted various aspects of both approaches. But during the post–World War I period many institutions exhibited a renewed interest in the student at times other than when he was in the classroom or laboratory.

This concern was manifested in the construction of dormitories, in the rise of the student personnel movement, and in the development and adoption of the idea of *in loco parentis*. The established Eastern schools had always housed their students, either in college-run dormitories, eating clubs, or fraternities. The newer schools of the Midwest and West had generally provided fewer such arrangements. In addition to university residences, the "concern for the whole student" brought forth the whole array of student personnel professionals—deans of men, deans of women, counselors, and dormitory directors. Logical extensions of the new concern were also university health centers (also staffed with psychiatrists), placement offices, and financial aid offices.

The new concern with the whole man also brought a reexamination of the elective system. Though it was probably superior to the older curriculum, which totally specified one's course of study, there were also some acknowledged defects. "Too often the curriculum was utterly without pattern and comprised a great number of short and sometimes superficial courses" (Devane, 1965, p. 63). The freedom for a student to explore the subjects that interested him was also an opportunity to dabble in courses that he knew were easy, or that perhaps had little coherence. A new balance was needed.

Primarily during the twenties and thirties the curriculum evolved into the system of "majors" we know today. By deciding on a "major," a student concentrated on one body of knowledge in a systematic fashion. He generally worked from the general to the more specific. The new system also encouraged breadth by requiring a certain number of courses outside one's area of major specialization. The new system of majors proved popular among students and faculty and was quickly adopted by almost all colleges and universities.

Another significant change on the campuses after World War I was the rise of spectator athletics—especially football. The volunteer amateur coach gave way to the professional, and colleges were often known and judged (then as now) more by the quality of their football teams than by the reputation of the faculty. College "sport" became more a business as "ringers" often played for more than one school and the filling of the stadium on weekends evolved into an economic necessity.

In terms of the factors we have considered for the earlier periods—political climate, academic marketplace, financial dependency, types of formal control, and curriculum—the period between the two wars was similar to that which existed in 1915. Certainly the colleges and universities suffered during the depression as did all other areas of the society. But with the exception of the changes already noted, the period was primarily one in which the basic system matured. The changes brought about by the war were realized more after 1945 than before, and will be considered in the next section.

Types of Institutions. The major development in the evolution of institutional types was the appearance during this period of the public junior college. Though in the 1920s and 1930s these institutions were known as junior colleges, they might well be called Community Colleges—they certainly had the same characteristics. In 1915 there were fewer than 50 such colleges. By 1941 there were approximately 450 (Devane, 1965). Although many of these institutions began as vocational schools, many ultimately became liberal arts-oriented transfer institutions due to the curricular choice of students and the prestige aspirations of the faculty.

It was also during this period that one could begin to identify Elite Liberal Arts Colleges. For the most part, these institutions were not new. But with increasing enrollments they could afford to be more selective in their choices of students. Better students often enrolled in these schools because the schools were "old and known" and hence had reputations and prestige. These schools could very often attract quality faculty for related reasons. There is a symbiotic relationship between good faculty and students—both seem to attract and nourish one another. The tests provided by the College Entrance Examination Board allowed these "elite" colleges to separate the wheat from the chaff.

Other types of institutions also continued to grow, evolve, and settle in. By the end of World War II, all of the institutional types had emerged except the Private and Public Multiversities.

Governance Patterns. It was after World War I that students first became involved in academic governance. Perhaps we should say they became involved in *student* government, for their involvement in substantive policies did not come until later. Students were generally content with influencing some athletic policies, student honor codes, dormitory regulations, and social events. But *student government* had been established, and became the precursor of more serious student involvement in later years.

Boards of trustees continued to be composed of more businessmen and fewer churchmen. Where in 1860 clergymen made up 30 percent of the membership of boards, by 1930 they comprised less than 7 percent (Devane, 1965).

Relationships between the faculty, the president, and the boards did not change appreciably during the period. Institutions grew, new administrators were hired, and faculty gained influence in some places and lost it in others. The structure, though, had been set as early as 1910, and the changes between the two wars occurred within that structure.

Period V: 1945–1964

This period between the end of World War II and the Free Speech Movement at Berkeley encompasses the Korean War, McCarthyism, Sputnik, the freedom riders, and sit-ins. It was also the time when college enrollments expanded tremendously, when federal money exerted a significant impact, when "a college education for all who can benefit" became a national goal, and when the first United States advisors were sent to Viet Nam.

As we approach the present in this historical overview,

subtle relationships become more important. A detailed analysis is required even though most readers are quite familiar with the postwar history of American higher education. We will attempt to relate all of the pertinent sophisticated patterns of relationships without burdening the reader with a story he has already heard. Our emphasis will be upon how the events of the forties, fifties, and early sixties influenced governance patterns.

Organizational Characteristics. The two most important developments in higher education after the war were the tremendous increases in student enrollment and the new federal involvement. The two are not unrelated. Federal money poured into the institutions through the G.I. Bill and support for research, scholarships, and building programs.

The influx of students into colleges and universities after the war was unprecedented. Congress, fearing a very high unemployment level and desiring to reward those who had made sacrifices in the national interest, passed the G.I. Bill. Approximately 5 million ex-servicemen received tuition costs and living allowances through this program. The addition of 5 million mature, goal-oriented students taxed the institutions in the extreme. Overflow classes and housing composed of barracks and trailers were but the outward manifestations of the changes. The G.I. Bill money plus support for contract research reduced, if not eliminated, previous suspicions about federal "intervention" in higher education. Elimination of this suspicion eventually led to fierce competition for the previously tainted money.

This influx of ex-soldiers had other effects, as well. They soon voiced the 1946 equivalent of a call for relevance. Having been delayed by the war from starting their careers, they were now in no mood to tolerate courses containing no real intellectual or practical value. Another difference was the difficulty of applying a policy of *in loco parentis* to students who had landed at Normandy or Guadalcanal.

The increases in enrollment did not end when all the eligible veterans had completed their education. There were 1,364,815 students enrolled in 1939; 2,078,095 in 1946; 2,468,596 in 1954; 3,610,007 in 1960; and 4,600,000 in 1964 (American Council on Education, 1964). Although both undergraduate and graduate enrollments increased, graduate enrollment proportionally increased more rapidly.

These increases were the result both of individual desires for more education and of a series of national policy statements which encouraged higher levels of attendance. In 1947 President Truman's Commission on Higher Education suggested that at least half and possibly more of the population could benefit from higher education. The 1952 report of the Commission for Financing Higher Education was less encouraging, but still maintained that the one-third most able students could benefit from education beyond high school. By 1964 the Educational Policies Committee had shifted the emphasis considerably and asked "whom can the society . . . exclude?" (in Mayhew, 1970, p. 63). The increase in the number of students had been staggering, and in 1964 the expectations were that it would increase even more.

In addition to providing great numbers of students afterwards, World War II in a sense provided a proving ground for American higher education. Out of the laboratories of the universities came the Norden bombsight, radar, the proximity fuse, analysis of bombing effectiveness, advice on effective propaganda, and of course the atomic bomb. The nation, or at least the federal government, had also learned that college and university faculties could be of assistance in addressing the many problems facing the nation after the war. The national government influence was so pervasive in some institutions that Clark Kerr referred to them as Federal Grant Universities, and from them sprang the multiversities. Ben-David notes that the infusion of federal research funds started during the war and then continued afterwards in reaction to the Soviet Union's testing of a thermonuclear bomb, its launching of Sputnik and other developments. As Ben-David notes: "Federal expenditure on research and development, which was $0.07 billion in 1940 rose to $1.59 billion in 1945, then dropped to $0.92 in 1946 and to $0.85 in 1948. Then it started climbing again to $4.46 billion in 1956 and to $14.87 billion in 1965" (1972, p. 106).

The increased financial support of higher education was not limited to the federal government. Endowments of private colleges continued to climb, and in every state the pattern was an increased appropriation each year for the support of postsecondary education. Between 1940 and 1960 college and university endowments rose from $1.8 billion to $4.6 billion. During the same period, state support increased from $154 million a year to over $1.3 billion, and by 1964 state aid had further increased to more than $2.1 billion per year. Between 1940 and 1964 local support, primarily for junior colleges, had increased from $24 million to $240 million. The financial situation of all of higher education during this period could only be described as "rosy."

The academic marketplace was also rosy during this period. Colleges and universities were in their heyday of expansion, and with expansion came many academic job opportunities. Discussing the tremendous demand for faculty talent in the late fifties and early sixties, Caplow and McGee noted that "although the increase of demand for scholarly services poses a problem for society at large, it presents the academic profession with an opportunity to increase its share of social rewards" (1958, p. 4). Faculty enjoyed a professional mobility they had seldom experienced, and this mobility also brought a new sense of independence.

Formal control during this period was beginning to change, especially in the public institutions. Junior colleges expanded greatly, and local control in public higher education became much more extensive than before. In many states the board of control for junior colleges was the same board that established policies for grades one through twelve. However, the most important changes in formal control were at the state levels. Multicampus state universities very often had a "central" administration, thereby reducing local control on individual campuses. Even more important than these developments was the idea of statewide coordination of all state-supported institutions.

The California Master Plan, adopted in 1959, served as the model for statewide planning and coordination. The three major segments of higher education in California—the University of California system, the state college system, and the network of junior colleges—would each have its own governing board. And in the words of the state governor Edmund Brown, "Beyond all this there was a need to minimize duplication and waste created by competition among the three segments of higher education. To accomplish this the planners created the Coordinating Council for Higher Education" (in Wilson, 1966, p. 106). It was the creation of the Coordinating Council that was especially important. For although the policy and budget powers of the Council were weak in California, other states adopted variations of the California model and created councils that were considerably stronger, and which gradually acquired greater and greater powers that formerly had resided on the individual campuses. It was not until after 1964, however, that the coordinating boards began to exert a significant effect upon the autonomy of the institution.

With the exception of the McCarthy years, the political climate of this period was very favorable to an expanding higher education establishment. We have already mentioned the various national policy statements supportive of increasing educational opportunity. And the financial support of higher education—federal, state, local, and private—was indicative of a general support of the endeavor. The McCarthy years, the effect of which was detailed in Lazarsfeld's and Thielens' *The Academic Mind,* cast a pall of gloom and repression over many campuses, but the era was relatively short and its long-range effects were few.

A political and social upheaval which had a major impact upon higher education was the black struggle for equal rights. Hopes were raised in 1954 with the *Brown* vs. *Board of Education* decision, and the movement resulted in sit-ins, marches, the Freedom Riders, a Governor "barring the schoolroom door," mass arrests, and even murders. The movement was important not only for the achievements made by blacks, but because it set the philosophical tone of the questioning of authority, vividly demonstrated in the later Free Speech Movement at Berkeley. The philosophical and sociological linkages are quite complex and have been dealt with in detail elsewhere (Dogan, 1969; Cohen and Hall, 1966). An admittedly superficial explanation would be that many hundreds of liberal students had joined the sit-ins, eat-ins, and Freedom Riders in protest against laws they felt to be immoral, unjust, or even illegal. Civil disobedience thus became a respectable and effective way to deal with injustice. And if civil disobedience could work in Alabama, perceived injustices on the campuses could also be righted by organized group disobedience. The fruits of such an outlook would be harvested after 1964, but the beginnings can be traced to the late fifties and early sixties.

The major change in the curriculum during the period was in the emphasis placed upon graduate programs. After the war, the total number of both graduates and undergraduates had increased considerably, but the change in their proportions had not been great. In 1940, 7.1 percent of the students were graduates; in 1964 that figure was 10.5 percent (Ben-David, 1972, p. 51). The enrollment figures do not tell the entire story, however. We mentioned earlier that the doctorate culture reigned supreme on most American campuses by the turn of the century. After World War II, the phenomenon increased. Prestige lay in publishing, obtaining grants, and teaching graduate students. Consequently, undergraduates on many campuses were subjected to relative neglect while professors pursued their research and taught their graduate students.

Another curriculum matter of some importance, especially during the fifties, was the General Education Movement. The curriculum in American colleges and universities had been through a number of changes. Beginning as a totally prescribed regime of courses, the first major shift had been to a totally elective curriculum. Between the world wars, the idea of a "major" emphasis coupled with electives was introduced. But many believed that even with the major/elective pattern, a certain essence was missing from the education of undergraduates. That essence was in integration of the whole, and the general education movement was a search for interdisciplinary courses, comprehensiveness, and an overview to provide that integration. The Report of the Harvard Committee, *General Education in a Free Society,* was probably the most influential document in providing a rationale for general education. It expressed the goals of higher education as being broad and general— thinking effectively, communicating thought, making relevant judgments, and discriminating among values.

A number of institutions did attempt general education courses. But their proponents were generally disheartened by the results. General education required an interdisciplinary or cross-disciplinary approach, and the power of departments was such that few faculty would attempt interdisciplinary courses when their evaluations and promotions were usually based on work done *within the discipline*. Although a number of smaller liberal arts schools were able to establish and maintain general education programs, the movement was short-lived in most places.

The nature of the professional tasks performed by most faculty in most colleges and universities remained teaching. However, for faculty in the more prestigious institutions—both universities and colleges—the emphasis was upon research, and on teaching graduate students rather than undergraduates. Specialization was the watchword, and generally the greater the specialization the more one was perceived as "professional." And specialization, research, and publication gave one visability and reputation. With reputation came consultation and an even greater opportunity to publish. The faculty star system had been born. The stars, and even lesser lights, received federal grants, consulted, researched, taught small numbers of very qualified graduate students, and became academic entrepreneurs. These cosmopolitans were men of national status whose evaluators and peers resided outside of the particular campus where they held rank.

But it must be emphasized that the academic stars and cosmopolitans were relatively few in number. The great bulk of the professorate in the greatest number of schools remained "locals," men whose reputations generally did not go far beyond the grounds of the campus. They taught classes, perhaps published a few articles—though very seldom in the national journals—and were evaluated by their discipline peers on their own campuses. But though they were few in number, we still see how the star system influenced governance procedures both on the campuses where they resided and even nationally.

Finally, we must consider organizational complexity. Certainly during the forties, fifties, and sixties there were institutions with various degrees of complexity. There were small denominational colleges and large, church-supported universities. There were liberal arts colleges, large and small, junior colleges, and state colleges of all sizes. And there were multiversities.

Clark Kerr coined the term "multiversity" in his 1963 Codhin Lectures at Harvard. He described the multiversity as "a whole series of communities and activities held together by a common name, a common governing, and related purposes" (Kerr, 1963, p. 1). What he saw in the multiversity was a very complex undertaking. He described the University of California, a prime example of the multiversity, in the following way:

> The University of California last year had operating expenditures from all sources of nearly half a billion dollars, with almost another 100 million for construction; a total employment of over 40,000 people, more than IBM and in a far greater variety of endeavors; operations in over a hundred locations, counting campuses, experiment stations, agricultural and urban extension centers, and projects abroad involving more than fifty countries; nearly 10,000 courses in its catalogues; some form of contact with nearly every industry, nearly every level of government, nearly every person in its region. Vast amounts of expensive equipment were serviced and maintained. Over 4,000 babies were born in its hospitals. It is the world's largest purveyor of white mice. It will soon have the world's largest primate colony. It will soon also have 100,000 students—30,000 of them at the graduate level; yet much less than one third of its expenditures are directly related to teaching [1963, p. 7.]

Though not all Multiversities were of the size and complexity of the University of California, there were very many that reflected a similar variety of tasks.

Types of Institutions. By 1964, the full modern range of organizational complexity—from very small, exclusively teaching institutions to large Multiversities—had been established. A number of institutions moved from one category to another, especially in the public sector, and a number of Public Colleges that had primarily been teachers colleges moved into the Public Comprehensive category. Every multiversity, both public and private became more complex after the war.

Community Colleges continued their expansion but increased in numbers only from 591 at the end of the war to 644 by 1964. Enrollment in Community Colleges during this same period on the other hand, increased from some 250,000 to well over a million. Community Colleges existed primarily in the wealthier states to provide those in urban areas with an opportunity for higher education (Harris, 1972).

So by 1964 the total range of institutions was in existence. Individually, however, they continued in organizational flux, and in any given year a number of institutions might move from one organizational type to another.

Governance Patterns. The basic governance patterns established before the war continued to exist afterwards. But within these basic patterns there were certain subtle shifts of power; and one new element, statewide coordination, was added.

The parallel hierarchies—administrative and academic—continued, with the administrative hierarchy growing in size, the academic hierarchy gaining more power. With increasing size and complexity, the number of administrators and administrative support personnel grew tremendously. Certainly an institution as complex as that described by Kerr would need a virtual army of administrative and staff personnel. But these administrators generally dealt with decisions relating to the resources of the institution and left to the faculty those decisions that dealt with the core technology—the specialized teaching and research of the faculty. Most of the key decisions which affected faculty were made at the departmental level, and the departments gained in their control over these decisions.

The reasons for the faculty gains in power are relatively easy to understand—they are closely related to the academic marketplace and the star system. Faculty had for years demanded authority over a number of areas: the curriculum; hiring, evaluating, promoting, and firing of faculty; establishing entrance and graduation requirements; controlling what they would teach and when; and selecting key administrators. With the academic marketplace wide open, faculty had many of their demands met by threatening to leave. The departure of an academic star could have dire consequences for a department, or even an entire university. If the star had research funds, they were *his,* not the institution's. A departing faculty member would often take not only his grant money, but also students and sometimes other faculty members. With the possibility of such an outcome, it is not much of an exaggeration to say that what the faculty wanted, the faculty generally got.

It is true that most of the grant money went to physical

scientists in the large and prestigious institutions. But the gains by
the physical scientists were also the gains of other faculty in the same
institution, and of some faculty in other places. As go Harvard, the
University of California, Oberlin, Dartmouth, and certain others,
there also attempts to go most of American higher education. Professors everywhere seek independence and autonomy as well as to
set the goals and influence the structure of the organization. Professors generally attempt to emulate the success of other professors.

But these areas over which the faculty sought control are
not areas of decision making which the central administrators of
colleges and universities have entirely abandoned. In 1961, Burton
Clark saw as a continuing thing the shifting of power from sources
external to the university toward the core departments (in Wilson,
1961, p. 87). But he saw that shifting of power as causing a number
of problems between faculty and administrators, and each side had
cogent arguments:

> Going into battle, the faculties march under the
> banner of self-government and academic freedom, empha-
> sizing equality of relations among colleagues and de-
> emphasizing administrative hierarchy. The administrators
> move forward under a cluster of banners: let's bring
> order out of chaos, or at least reduce chaos to mere con-
> fusion; let's increase efficiency, utilize our scarce re-
> sources—men and money—effectively; let's give the
> organization as a whole a sense of direction, with
> knowledgeable hands on the helm; let's insure that we
> handle external forces—the legislative or our constit-
> uencies—in ways that will insure the survival and
> security of the whole enterprise [1961, p. 88].

While faculties were gaining power, and even though Clark
in 1961 still saw power shifting from external sources toward internal sources, there was a countervailing process underway—
statewide coordination. The events of the early sixties had prompted
Lyman Glenny to say that "at the state level the new watchwords
are cooperation and coordination, with institutional independence
only within certain new parameters" (in Wilson, 1966, p. 87). Although public institutions in only ten states still retained their classic

autonomy in 1965, state coordinating agencies were not yet really flexing their muscles. But the organization for flexing existed, and events after 1964 would see increasing encroachment by these coordinating agencies upon the independence of the campuses.

Period VI: 1964–Present

The sixties may well best be remembered for the Viet Nam War, social war in the cities, and student "unrest" on campuses. Many maintain that all are closely related. The American buildup in Viet Nam, begun in the early sixties, reached significant warfare proportions in the summer of 1965. That war unseated a United States president, made a shambles of the domestic economy, cost thousands of dead and wounded, divided the nation, and contributed to violence and an armed-camp psychology on campuses. Student unrest—some would say rebellion—began at Berkeley in 1964 over "free speech." By 1968, student disturbances were designed, in the words of a student, "to call attention to the unconscionable violence in Viet Nam, the police state in Harlem, and the intolerable oppression by the United States in Latin America" (Hook, 1969, p. 77).

All of these events had an effect, directly and indirectly, on higher education. The student actions—marches, sit-ins, trashings—had a tremendous effect in themselves. But there were also repercussions which greatly affected academic governance patterns.

Organizational Characteristics. On most campuses, 1964 began as 1963 had ended, with high hopes and great expectations. Federal, state, and private support were high, the job market excellent, the political climate favorable, and enrollments were still increasing. At first the events at Berkeley did not seem terribly important. However, as the sixties progressed, student unrest took far more serious forms. There were campus strikes, closings, demonstrations, bombings, burnings, trashings, and beatings at Stanford, Harvard, Columbia, San Jose State, Duke, Cornell, and countless other institutions.

Interestingly enough, most of the demonstrations had little to do with the central purposes of the institution which most affected students—teaching and the curriculum. There were a few major demonstrations about black studies programs. But at Columbia students demonstrated over a gymnasium, the Institute for Defense Analysis, and a prohibition against demonstrations in university buildings. At Duke, altercations arose over a desire for official statements of mourning for Martin Luther King. Stanford students wanted to end defense-related research and to sever ties with Reserve Officer Training Corps (ROTC) programs. And at Berkeley, the worst days of demonstrations were over a plot of ground that street people wanted preserved as a "People's Park."

That is not to say, however, that students did not have complaints. Impersonalization, professors in absentia, a perceived disregard for undergraduate education, and irrelevance of courses were taken by some as the root causes of student unrest. However, a poll of students at Berkeley, an institution where students complained loudly and received much national attention, revealed that the majority of students were quite satisfied with their education. In any event, regardless of the ultimate causes of the unrest, it was widespread, and even those campuses that did not have demonstrations were affected.

Colleges and universities are affected by what happens in the political arena, and calls by politicians for law and order referred both to the streets and to the campus. In California, Ronald Reagan was elected governor on a pledge that he would, among other things, straigthen out the "mess" at Berkeley. As one step, Clark Kerr was removed as president of the university. And in 1970, Mayhew warned that "If campus disorders do not end, the political establishment will assume control of colleges and universities, and higher education will lose its freedom, which is the acme of its past achievements" (1970, p. 3).

Legislators, aware that their constituents were watching disorders, riots, or disrespectful students each night on television, looked critically at campus requests for funds. If the fruits of higher education were the burning or trashing of the campuses, then perhaps the money could be better used elsewhere. The statistics on support for higher education make it difficult to substantiate a cutback in funds for the universities during this period, for expenditures increased each year. However, we do not have to question what the figures might have been had the troubles not existed on campuses.

The period 1967–1970 was especially bad for student demonstrations, and Weld notes that "Capital outlays . . . increased by more than 17 percent per annum compounded from 1955 to 1967, although the rate of growth dropped to less than 2 percent per annum *between 1968 and 1970*" (emphasis added; Weld, 1972, p. 424). Speeches in legislatures and before television cameras and reports in the newspapers certainly indicated that legislators were not inclined to favorably support higher education.

But disenchantment with higher education was not the only reason to scrutinize support for these institutions. The Viet Nam War brought increasing economic problems at home. Inflation soared, and the call for additional services by government, especially in the welfare sector, sent the costs of government ever higher. Did higher education have a greater priority than feeding and housing the poor, curing the sick, or even providing "quality education" for students from kindergarten through twelfth grade. The scores of ghetto children on tests of reading and mathematics concerned every knowledgeable citizen even after allowances were made for cultural biases.

Support for private schools was also affected. Private giving fluctuated in part as a function of peace and tranquillity on the campus. Recently, the trustee of one prestigious west coast university warned corporations that they should not support campuses that harbor faculty and students hostile to corporate interests. (*Journal of Higher Education,* Nov. 12, 1973, p. 1). And that warning came after many individuals had already withheld money when they thought it would not be used in their own best interests.

The enrollments slowed. Institutions did not grow as fast as predicted, and by 1972 there actually were decreases in enrollment in some institutions. There were a number of reasons for these decreases—disenchantment with higher education by many youth; a job market that forced college graduates to drive taxis or work in jobs for which they were "overeducated"; the ending of the draft (it having always been suspected that many young men were in college to avoid the draft). In 1973, the proportion of eighteen- and nineteen-year-old males in college dropped to the 1962 level of 37.6 percent from a high in 1969 of 44 percent (*Chronicle of Higher Education,* 1973). Furthermore, new colleges, especially junior colleges, had been constructed, and consequently there were more chairs for fewer students. And the near future does not promise a reversal of this trend. Population projections indicate that the number of persons in the 18–21 age range will peak in 1980, then decrease dramatically at least until 1990. Legislators are understandably hesitant to fund new buildings that may stand partially empty in ten years or less.

Among those attending colleges and universities in the 1970's were the "new students." Patricia Cross defined them as follows:

> America's newest college students are not necessarily black or brown or red; most of them are the white sons and daughters of blue-collar workers. The young people who did not attend college in the 1950s and '60s, but who will enter college in increasing numbers in the 1970s and '80s are distinguished not by their color so much as by their past experience with failure in the American school system. The greatest single barrier to college admission in the 1960s was lack of demonstrated academic ability—as that ability is nurtured and measured in the schools. College entrance has become commonplace for students demonstrating above-average academic performance: toward the end of the 1960s nearly three-quarters of those ranking in the upper academic half among high school graduates were entering college—even if they ranked in the lowest quarter on socioeconomic measures. As the country continues the move toward increased college access, it is lower-half students who constitute the available reservoir of the new students to higher education: poor students *academically* and—more often than not—poor students *financially* [1971, p. 14].

Two thirds of the new students are first generation college students; two out of three are from blue collar backgrounds; over half are Caucasian, about a fourth are Black, and about 15 percent are other minorities (Cross, 1971).

The academic marketplace was in a shambles, if indeed there was much of one at all by 1972. Graduate students attending conferences told stories of 600 candidates scrambling for the 23 available positions. Letters of regret to unsuccessful job seekers began with such sentences as: "Over 300 people responded to our announcement for the position of." There was truly an academic depression caused by the dual forces of a stabilizing enrollment and an overabundance of doctorates seeking faculty positions. Though all disciplines were affected, those especially hard hit were foreign languages, English, political science, sociology, physics, and education. The already bad job market for physical scientists was compounded by the recession and lack of expansion in the business sector.

Throughout this traumatic period, there was little change in the nature of professional tasks or in the curriculum. Federal money had become more scarce, but the star professors in the star universities continued to be supported. Black studies were added in some institutions, and here was new-found interest in studying ecology and the environment. There was much talk, but little action, about interdisciplinary programs and courses. There were some fine examples of courses that utilized multidiscipline approaches to particular problem areas, but these were generally the efforts of individuals in widely separated institutions. Some schools of education, and a few experimental institutions introduced competency-based or performance-based curricula. The idea was to specify competencies in advance, devise means for the students to achieve them, assess the achievement, and give students credit only if they achieved the competency. The competency-based idea was hazy even in the minds of some of its most articulate advocates, and today the merits of competency programs are still being debated.

There was a great deal of experimentation with grading. Some institutions allowed a credit/no credit option; others stopped recording Ds and Fs; some adopted written evaluations in place of grades; and some of the experimental schools reported competencies achieved rather than grades. But these changes generally were peripherally related to the curriculum—means rather than ends.

The same organizational complexity which existed earlier continued through the sixties and into the seventies. If anything, institutions became more complex. Even the largest of them continued to grow through the sixties, and with more students came additional faculty and more research money. But in terms of implications for governance, the growth and additional complexity was not significant.

Types of Institutions. As we mentioned earlier, by 1964 all of our institutional types were in existence. But within the types of institutions there were significant changes.

Florida, Illinois, Texas, and some other states introduced the capstone universities—the upper division/graduate institutions. These were designed to articulate closely with the junior college of the states and provide the final two years of college plus graduate work in some cases. Most of these institutions claimed to serve the needs of the nontraditional student—older than twenty-two, employed, married, often minority, usually from a blue collar background, and vocationally oriented. These new institutions generally referred to themselves as innovative or nontraditional and attempted experiments to facilitate learning—emphasis on technology, new calendar arrangements, organization along lines other than departments, different grading options, and various other approaches that were experimental but also advocated by various of the Carnegie Reports and the Newman *Report on Higher Education.*

Elsewhere, a number of factors combined to adversely affect private institutions, especially the institutions we have called Private Liberal Arts Colleges. Generally, their endowments were never large, and their major source of funds was student tuition. With costs spiraling for everything from faculty salaries to fertilizer for the lawns, these schools were forced to increase tuition. But with every increase in tuition, the recruitment of students became more difficult—public institutions almost always charged lower tuition—and the enrollments in private colleges began to drop off dramatically. The closing of a private school was not an uncommon event in the early seventies, and those that remained open often sought students the same way Trans World Airlines seeks passengers—by large scale advertising and marketing techniques.

The Elite Liberal Arts Colleges were affected to some extent by the cost squeeze, but generally not as much as the nonelite schools. The prestige schools usually had a larger endowment and drew students from a wealthier pool. Admission to these schools was also competitive, and the major fear of admissions officers was that the quality, not quantity, of students might be affected.

Still, it is fair to say that all of the institutional types continued to exist even though some were quite severely shaken by the academic depression. Enrollment patterns were changing and most private schools were especially hard hit. Diversity remained, however, and freshmen contemplating college could choose from among some 2,500 different institutions, each claiming to offer a unique educational experience.

Governance Patterns. The first nine chapters of this book are concerned with contemporary patterns of governance, management, and leadership. The trends we have noted for the future, discussed at length in Chapter Nine, grew out of the environmental and structural changes of the postwar era.

This book closes as it opened, taking a sociological perspective. The management and governance of higher education is in many ways a reflection of the patterns that form the social context. And the on-going changes that are reshaping higher education today are social forces that are in many ways out of our control, beyond the power of those of us inside the institution to change. Nevertheless, we still have some limited control over the form and pattern of institutional governance and management, and it is our obligation to work continually to make these institutions responsive to the best professional traditions, accountable to the legitimate demands of the environment, and sensitive to the needs of students.

References

ALLISON, G. T. *Essence of Decision: Explaining the Cuban Missile Crisis.* Boston: Little, Brown, 1971.

American Council on Education. *Fact Book.* Washington, D.C.: American Council on Education, 1964.

ANDRES, J. A. *Developing Trends in Content of Collective Bargaining Contracts in Higher Education.* Washington, D.C.: American Collective Bargaining Information Service, 1974.

ASTIN, A. W., and LEE, C. B. T. *The Invisible Colleges: A Profile of Small, Private Colleges with Limited Resources.* New York: McGraw-Hill, 1972.

ASTIN, H. S. "Where Are All the Talented Women?" In W. T. Furniss and P. A. Graham (Eds.), *Women In Higher Education.* Washington, D.C.: American Council on Education, 1974.

ASTIN, H. S., and BAYER, A. E. "Sex Differentials in the Academic Reward System." *Science,* May 23, 1975, pp. 796–802.

BALDRIDGE, J. V. *Power and Conflict in the University: Research in the Sociology of Complex Organizations.* New York: Wiley, 1971.

BALDRIDGE, J. V., and others. *An Overview of the Stanford Project on Academic Governance.* R & D Memorandum No. 128. Stanford, Calif.: Center for Research and Development in Teaching, Stanford University, October 1974a.

BALDRIDGE, J. V., and others. *Alternative Models of Governance in Higher Education.* R & D Memorandum No. 129. Stanford, Calif.: Center for Research and Development in Teaching, Stanford University, November 1974b.

BALDRIDGE, J. V., and others. *Diversity in Academic Governance Patterns.* R & D Memorandum No. 120. Stanford, Calif.: Center for Research and Development in Teaching, Stanford University, January 1975.

BAYER, A. E. *College and University Faculty: A Statistical Description.* Washington, D. C.: American Council on Education, 1970.

BEN-DAVID, J. *American Higher Education: Directions Old and New.* New York: McGraw-Hill, 1972.

BERNARD, J. *Academic Women.* University Park: Pennsylvania State University Press, 1964.

BIDWELL, C. E. "The School as a Formal Organization." In J. G. March (Ed.), *Handbook of Organizations.* Chicago: Rand McNally, 1968.

BLAU, P. *The Organization of Academic Work.* New York: Wiley, 1973.

BLAUNER, R. *Alienation and Freedom: The Faculty Worker and His Industry.* Chicago: University of Chicago Press, 1964.

BOLAND, W. R. "Size, Organization, and Environmental Mediation." In J. V. Baldridge (Ed.), *Academic Governance.* Berkeley, Calif.: McCutchan, 1971.

BORDUA, O. J., and REISS, A. J. "Command, Control and Charisma: Reflections on Policy Bureaucracy." *American Journal of Sociology,* 1966, *72,* 68–76.

BOWLES, F., and DE COSTA, F. A. *Between Two Worlds: A Profile of Negro Higher Education.* New York: McGraw-Hill, 1971.

BROWN, E. G. "Public Higher Education in California." In L. Wilson, *Emerging Patterns in Higher Education.* Washington, D.C.: American Council on Education, 1966.

BROWN, H. S., and MAYHEW, L. B. *American Higher Education.* New York: Center for Applied Research in Education, 1965.

BRUBACHER, J. S., and RUDY, W. *Higher Education in Transition.* New York: Harper & Row, 1958.

BRYCE, J. *Modern Bureaucracies.* New York: Macmillan, 1921.

CAPLOW, T., and MCGEE, R. J. *The Academic Marketplace.* Garden City, N.Y.: Doubleday, 1958.

CARLSON, R. O. "Environmental Constraints and Organizational Consequences: The Public School and its Clients." In D. E. Griffiths (Ed.), *Behavioral Science and Educational Administration.* Chicago: National Society for the Study of Education, 1964.

Carnegie Commission on Higher Education. *A Classification of Institutions of Higher Education.* New York: McGraw-Hill, 1973a.

Carnegie Commission on Higher Education. *Governance of Higher Education.* New York: McGraw-Hill, 1973b.

Carnegie Commission on Higher Education. *Opportunities for Women in Higher Education.* New York: McGraw-Hill, 1973c.

CHANNING, R., STEINER, S., and TIMMERMAN, S. "Collective Bargaining and Its Impact on Board-Presidential Relationships." In M. Brick (Ed.), *Collective Negotiations in Higher Education.* Washington, D.C.: ERIC Clearinghouse for Higher Education, 1973.

Chronicle of Higher Education, November 12, 1973.

CLARK, B. R. *The Open Door College.* New York: McGraw-Hill, 1960.

CLARK, B. R. "The Role of Faculty in College Administration." In L. Wilson and others (Eds.), *Studies of College Faculty.* Boulder, Colo.: Western Interstate Commission for Higher Education, 1961.

CLARK, B. R. *The Distinctive Colleges: Antioch, Reed and Swarthmore.* Chicago: Aldine Press, 1970.

CLARK, B. R. "Faculty Organization and Authority." In J. V. Baldridge, (Ed.), *Academic Governance.* Berkeley, Calif.: McCutchan, 1971.

COHEN, M., and HALL, D. *The New Student Left.* Boston: Beacon Press, 1966.

COHEN, M. D., and MARCH, J. G. *Leadership and Ambiguity: The American College President.* New York: McGraw-Hill, 1974.

CORSON, J. J. *Governance of Colleges and Universities.* New York: McGraw-Hill, 1960.

CROMAN, C. "Women and Unions." In E. Reuben and L. Hoffman (Eds.), *Unladylike and Unprofessional: Academic Women and Academic Unions.* New York: Modern Language Association Commission on the Status of Women, 1975.

CROSS, K. P. "New Students of the 70's." *The Research Reporter,* 1971, *4.* Berkeley: Center for Research and Development, University of California, Berkeley.

DAHL, R. *Who Governs?* New Haven, Conn: Yale University Press, 1961.

DEVANE, W. C. *Higher Education in Twentieth-Century America.* Cambridge, Mass.: Harvard University Press, 1965.

DOGAN, D. L. *Campus Apocalypse.* New York: Seabury, 1969.

DORNBUSCH, S. M., and SCOTT, W. R. *Evaluation and the Exercise of Authority: A Theory of Control Applied to Diverse Organizations.* San Francisco: Jossey-Bass, 1975.

DUNHAM, E. A. *Colleges of the Forgotten Americans: A Profile of State Colleges and Regional Universities.* New York: McGraw-Hill, 1969.

Educational Policies Commission. *Universal Opportunity for Education Beyond the High School.* Washington, D.C.: 1964.

FEIN, R., and WEBSTER, G. I. *Financing Medical Education: An Analysis of Alternative Policies and Mechanisms.* New York: McGraw-Hill, 1971.

FELDMAN, S. *Escape From the Doll's House.* New York: McGraw-Hill, 1974.

GALES, K. E. "Berkeley Student Opinion, April 1965." In C. Muscatine, *Education at Berkeley: Report on the Select*

Committee on Education. Berkeley: University of California Press, 1968.

GAMSON, W. A. *Power and Discontent.* Homewood, Ill.: Dorsey Press, 1968.

Harvard Committee. *General Education in a Free Society.* Cambridge, Mass.: Harvard University Press, 1945.

GLENNY, L. A. "State Systems and Plans for Higher Education." In L. Wilson, *Emerging Patterns in Higher Education.* Washington, D.C.: American Council on Education, 1966.

GOODMAN, P. *The Community of Scholars.* New York: Random House, 1962.

GOULDNER, A. "Cosmopolitans and Locals: Toward an Analysis of Latent Social Roles." *Administrative Science Quarterly,* 1957–1958, pp. 281–306, 408–444.

GREELEY, A. M. *From Backwater to Mainstream: A Profile of Catholic Higher Education.* New York: McGraw-Hill, 1969.

GROSS, E., and GRAMBSH, P. V. *University Goals and Academic Power.* Washington, D.C.: American Council on Education, 1968.

GROSS, E., and GRAMBSH, P. V. *Changes in University Organization, 1964–1971: A Report Prepared for the Carnegie Commission on Higher Education.* New York: McGraw-Hill, 1974.

GUION, R. M. "Industrial Morale (A Symposium): The Problem of Technology." *Personnel Psychology,* 1958, *(2).*

HARRIS, S. H. *A Statistical Portrait of Higher Education.* New York: McGraw-Hill, 1972.

HEDGEPETH, R. C. *An Exploratory Analysis of the Consequences of Collective Bargaining in Higher Education: The Role of the Faculty.* Washington, D.C.: ERIC Clearinghouse on Higher Education, 1974.

HENDERSON, A. D. *The Innovative Spirit.* San Francisco: Jossey-Bass, 1970.

HODGKINSON, H. L. *The Campus Senate: Experiment in Democracy.* Berkeley: Center for Research and Development in Higher Education, University of California, Berkeley, 1974.

HOFSTADTER, R. *Academic Freedom in the Age of the College.* New York: Columbia University Press, 1964.

HOOK, S. *Academic Freedom and Academic Anarchy.* New York: Dell, 1969.

JENCKS, C., and RIESMAN, D. *The Academic Revolution.* Garden City, N.Y.: Doubleday, 1968.

KEMERER, F. R., and BALDRIDGE, J. V. *Unions on Campus: A National Study of the Consequences of Faculty Bargaining.* San Francisco: Jossey-Bass, 1975.

KERR, C. *The Uses of the University.* New York: Harper & Row, 1963.

KNAPP, R. "Changing Functions of the College Professor." In N. Sanford (Ed.), *The American College.* New York: Wiley, 1967.

KREPS, J. *Sex in the Marketplace.* Baltimore, Md.: Johns Hopkins University Press, 1971.

LADD, E. C., and LIPSETT, S. M. "What Professors Think: A Series of Articles." *The Chronicle of Higher Education,* January 15, 1975 to May 24, 1976.

LAZARSFELD, P. F., and THIELENS, W., JR. *The Academic Mind.* New York: Free Press, 1958.

LIKERT, R., and WILLITS, J. M. *Morale and Agency Management. Vol. I: Morale—the Mainspring of Management.* Hartford, Conn.: Life Insurance Rates Research Bureau, 1940.

MASON, A. T. *Free Government in the Making.* New York: Oxford University Press, 1956.

MAYHEW, L. B. *Arrogance on Campus.* San Francisco: Jossey-Bass, 1970.

MAYHEW, L. B. *Colleges Today and Tomorrow.* San Francisco: Jossey-Bass, 1969.

METZGER, W. P. *Academic Freedom in the Age of the University.* New York: Columbia University Press, 1961.

MICHELS, R. *Political Parties: A Sociological Study of the Oligarchical Tendencies of Modern Bureaucracy.* (E. Paul and C. Paul., trans.) New York: Free Press, 1959. (Originally published 1915.)

MILLETT, J. *The Academic Community.* New York: McGraw-Hill, 1962.

MORISON, S. E., and COMMAGER, H. S. *The Growth of the American Republic.* New York: Oxford University Press, 1960.

NEWMAN, F. *Report on Higher Education.* Washington, D.C.: U.S. Department of Health, Education and Welfare, 1971.

OLTMAN, R. "Administrative Patterns and Careers in Academic Settings," Boulder, Colo.: Western Interstate Commission on Higher Education, 1970.

Organization of Economic Cooperation and Development. "Reviews of National Science Policy: The United States." In J. Ben-David (Ed.), *American Higher Education: Directions Old and New.* New York: McGraw-Hill, 1972.

PACE, C. R. *Education and Evangelism: A Profile of Protestant Colleges.* New York: McGraw-Hill, 1972.

PACE, C. R. *The Demise of Diversity?: A Comparative Profile of Eight Types of Institutions.* New York: McGraw-Hill, 1974.

PARSONS, T. "Introduction." In M. Weber, *The Theory of Social and Economic Organization.* New York: Free Press, 1947.

PARSONS, T., and PLATT, G. *The American University,* New York: Free Press, 1972.

PHELPS, W. L. "Autobiography with Letters." In J. S. Brubacher and W. Rudy (Eds.), *Higher Education in Transition.* New York: Harper & Row, 1958.

ROBINSON, M. L. *Curriculum of the Women's College.* Washington, D.C.: U.S. Government Printing Office, 1971.

ROETHLISBERGER, F. J., and DICKSON, W. J. *Management and the Worker.* Cambridge, Mass.: Harvard University Press, 1939.

ROSE, A. "Voluntary Associations Under Conditions of Competition and Conflict." *Social Forces,* 1955, *34,* 159–163.

RUSSELL, M. (Ed.). *The College Blue Book.* (13th ed.) Vol. 1. New York: CCM Information, 1970.

SALWAY, S. "Salaries in Academic Employment," University of Michigan, 1971. Mimeographed paper.

SCHWARTZ, H. "Women Faculty and the Union at Oakland University." In E. Reuben and L. Hoffman (Eds.), *Unladylike and Unprofessional: Academic Women and Academic Unions.* New York: Modern Language Association Commission on the Status of Women, 1975.

SCOTT, W. R., DORNBUSCH, S. M., BUSCHING, B. C., and LAING, J. D.

"Organizational Evaluation and Authority." *Administrative Science Quarterly*, 1964, *8*, 1–22.

STEWART, C. "The Place of Higher Education in a Changing Society." In N. Sanford (Ed.), *The American College*. New York: Wiley, 1967.

STROUP, H. *Bureaucracy in Higher Education*. New York: Free Press, 1966.

TEWKSBURY, D. G. *The Founding of American Colleges and Universities Before the Civil War*. New York: Teachers College, Columbia University, 1932.

VEYSEY, L. R. *The Emergence of the American University*. Chicago: University of Chicago Press, 1965.

VROOM, V. H. *Work & Motivation*. New York: Wiley, 1964.

WEICK, K. E. "Educational Organizations as Loosely Coupled Systems." *Administrative Science Quarterly*, 1976, *21*, 1–19.

WELD, E. A., JR. "Expenditures for Public Institutions of Higher Education, 1969–70," *Journal of Higher Education*, 1972, *43* (6).

WILSON, L. *The Academic Man*. New York: Oxford University Press, 1942.

WILSON, L. *Emerging Patterns in Higher Education*. Washington, D.C.: American Council on Education, 1966.

Index